THE MIGHTY TRANSFORMER
THE HOLY SPIRIT ADVOCATES FOR SOCIAL JUSTICE

THE MIGHTY
TRANSFORMER
THE HOLY SPIRIT ADVOCATES
FOR SOCIAL JUSTICE

EDITED BY

ANTIPAS L. HARRIS

G/I\E\L\D
academic
press

GIELD Academic Press
Irving, TX 75039

The Mighty Transformer
The Holy Spirit Advocates for Social Justice

ISBN: 978-0-578-57928-3 (paperback)

Library of Congress Cataloging-in-Publication Data.

*The Mighty Transformer: The Holy Spirit Advocates For Social Justice
(PUB661-16) ISBN: 978-0-578-57928-3
Work is categorized as Book, Poetry, Written Work*

G/I\E/L\D
academic
press
www.gield.org

Cover Design by Evelina Johnson Buendia at LinaImaging

TABLE OF CONTENTS

TRUTH TO POWER

PROPHETIC CONSCIOUSNESS

CARING FOR PEOPLE, FIGHTING FOR JUSTICE

INTRODUCTION

Antipas L. Harris

> Here is my servant whom I have chosen, the one I love, in whom I delight; I will put my Spirit on him, and he will proclaim justice to the nations (Mt. 12.18 NIV).

> The evil do not understand justice, but those who seek the LORD understand it completely (Prov. 28.5 NRSV).

> But as for you, return to your God, hold fast to love and justice, and wait continually for your God (Hosea 12.6 NRSV).

This volume is limited in scope. There is far more to consider in critical reflection on the current state of affairs. I only hope that the following chapters shed light on the ways in which the Holy Spirit works among God's people to convict a world of structural and systemic sins with ramifications of social stratification that privilege some and oppress others with regard to race, ethnicity, gender, and social status. I hope they inspire divine imagination for future Spirit-filled leaders to envision and advocate for a world in which all of God's children experience equal human affirmation.

The Holy Spirit

The Holy Spirit is God's presence in the world. Before God speaks in Gen. 1.3, the Spirit (breath or essence) of God was active to bring order amid disorder. The Spirit (breath or essence) of God also moved after the first global destruction referenced in the story of Noah in Genesis 8. The Holy Spirit as cosmic transformation is endowed upon God's people in the New Testament. Believers in Acts 2 become agents of the Holy Spirit's advocacy to bring about God's vision for the world.

Introduction

In Jesus' last discourse with his disciples in John 16, He promises His disciples when He ascends to the Father, He would send the Holy Spirit as advocate to advance God's mission of righteousness and justice: "the Advocate will not come to you; but if I go, I will send him to you. And when he comes, he will prove the world wrong about sin and righteousness and judgment" (κρίσεως – also properly translated as "justice") (Jn 16.7b-8). The NRSV and NIV translate the Greek word ἐλέγξει as "will prove wrong." However, it may be translated as "convict." Convicting the world of sin has at least two implications: 1) showing or pointing out where the sin is, and 2) arresting society's consciousness about sin. The ultimate goal is divine purgation that is only available through the saving grace of our Lord.

Evangelicals have commonly focused on personal sin. While personal obedience to God is important, limiting sin to the personal has blinded many Christians to the paramount structural and systemic immorality. As a result, at times and in some places, Christian history wears the marks of human brutality, oppression, injustice and even violence – sponsored with self-righteousness, myopic views of sin, and in the name of God. Moreover, the following chapters express an alternative view, insights on Spirit-filled Christian movements, ministries, and churches whose theology and practice of ministry have not bifurcated personal sins from structural and societal sins. Other chapters attend to the need for greater prophetic agency in light of the wreckage structural sin causes. I hope that the clear message that weaves throughout of the chapters is that the Holy Spirit is calling God's people to rise to the call of God to continue Christ's work of both spiritual and social liberation.

Structural Sin

The holistic view of sin is present in Scripture. For example, Paul's gospel addresses both personal and structural sins. This book is concerned with structural sins that privilege some and oppress others. Galatians 3.28 states, "There is no longer Jew or Greek, there is no longer slave or free, there is no longer male and female; for all of you are one in Christ Jesus." Paul's gospel, moreover, echoes the Old Testament theme of righteousness and justice. So, to take Paul seriously, one must not limit the gospel to personal salvation. The Gospel also dismantles systemic and structural oppression that has far too long privileged some people over others. Paul teaches that in Christ humanity rediscovers equal human status – that which God intended from the beginning. While this remains the Christian vision of Paul's gospel, structural sin persists, and insists on socially stratified systems. And, far too long those who claim the name of Christ have uncritically participated in them. Many are oblivious to social sins and others develop theologies to redefine human diversity as sameness to avoid dealing with the deeper structural problems. As Stephen Mattson aptly puts it, "They see verses such as Galatians 3.28 that states, "*There is neither Jew nor Gentile, neither slave nor free, nor is there male and female, for you are all one in Christ Jesus*" (NIV) to mean that nothing else matters beyond our faith in Christ."[1] Mattson, furthermore, points out,

> Paul is validating all of the cultural issues associated with Jews, Gentiles, slaves, the free, men, and women rather than disregarding them. He's stating that Jesus is relevant to these differences, and is working throughout their lives by understanding and recognizing the unique pros and cons they're dealing with – the privileges, disadvantages, stereotypes, assumptions, treatment, rights, social value, and expectations they face on a daily basis.[2]

Moreover, in the words of Martin Luther King, Jr, in his famous "I Have A Dream" Speech, "there is a fierce urgency of now"! The Holy Spirit beckons God's people to deep social conscientiousness or social discernment (if you will).

A conscientious analysis reveals that normalized structural sins lift some people at the expense of inflicting social pain on others. Paul's social gospel dismantles social stratifications that assign levels of dignity to human persons based on gender, race, ethnicity, disabilities, and social location. A righteously indignant Paul starkly exclaims to those who preach a gospel of social functionality in the

---

[1] Stephen Mattson, "Social Justice is A Christian Tradition – Not A Liberal Agenda," *Sojourners* (August 11, 2015). No page numbers. Online: https://so jo.net/articles/social-justice-christian-tradition-not-liberal-agenda?fbclid=IwAR3kWKDUE6nN5LZGxSPM-N3_gbntN9LeJq1U3juXjDXwFvAWHcfgCyHwpZg (Accessed, September 1, 2019).

[2] Mattson, "Social Justice is A Christian Tradition – Not A Liberal Agenda," np.

face of structurally and systemically oppressive dysfunction, "[E]ven if we or an angel from heaven should proclaim to you a gospel contrary to what we proclaimed to you, let that one be accursed"! (Galatians 1.8 NIV)

Moreover, this short volume may be considered a clarion call to Spirit-filled believers. We must cry aloud and cut to the chase on social injustice; injustice is sin. Leaving aside part of Paul's gospel proclamation so desperately needed in our world, also dismisses an opportunity to lead in social transformation. Spirit-filled Christians must not adhere to party political categories that label the socially conscientious believers as liberals. To borrow another insight from Mattson, "Participating in social justice is a Christian tradition inspired by Jesus, not liberal causes, populist agendas, media platforms, lawmakers, or mainstream fads. It's a deeply spiritual practice."[3] As people of the Spirit, Pentecostals and Charismatics are uniquely positioned to continue the work of Christ in liberating the oppressed.

Overview of Chapters

The chapters that follow are organized in the following manner. Chapter One entitled "The Social Concern of Early American Pentecostals" by Cecil M. Robeck, Jr serves as an anchor essay for the diverse perspectives that follow. It questions the Spirit-filled Christian movement of the Century (Pentecostalism) for its irregular participation in social justice advocacy. He admits that within Pentecostalism African Americans have led the charge on social justice advocacy. However, for unclear reasons, maybe social location, Caucasian Pentecostals have demurred participation in social advocacy and even at times rejected the notion that social justice as a legitimate Christian concern. This explains why at the Pentecostalism Interest Group Meeting in Chicago at the 2008 Annual Meeting for the American Academy of Religion, James Cone insisted on the question: "What are Pentecostals going to do about White Supremacy?" In this anchor chapter, Robeck beckons for all Spirit-filled

---

[3] Mattson, "Social Justice is A Christian Tradition – Not A Liberal Agenda," np.

Christians to question unjust social constructs with a clear understanding that God cares about people and rejects social oppressive structures.

The rest of the chapters are organized into five sections: "Economic Empowerment," "Racial/Ethnic Conciliation," "Truth to Power," "Prophetic Consciousness," and "Caring for People, Fighting for Justice." There are two chapters in each of the sections.

The first section on "Economic Empowerment" comprises of chapters by David D. Daniels, III, and John Mark Robeck. Daniels' chapter entitled "Against Poverty: The Holy Spirit and Pentecostal Economic Ministries" is groundbreaking. Theologically, he concludes that based on evidence in the history of black Spirit-empowered ministry, the Holy Spirit promotes economic justice through surreptitious, assertive, interventionist, disruptive, subversive, reformative, redemptive, and transformative economic empowerment.

Along the same wavelength, John Mark Robeck's chapter on "The Prosperity Gospel and the Option for the Poor" addresses Spirit-empowered economic empowerment as expressed in the so-called "Prosperity Gospel Movements." Robeck points out that while North American Pentecostalism developed within the context of an individualistic, capitalistic society, it has a long religious history that bridges spirituality and concern about social problems with a goal of a better life for the Spirit-filled people. This message has particularly resonated among marginalized people such as blacks in America, in Latin America, and around the world, particularly in developing countries.

The second section on "Racial/Ethnic Conciliation" comprises of chapters by Tommy Cásarez and Rodolfo Galvan Estrada. Cásarez's "Confronting White Nationalism: Making Space for Identities, History and Cultural Memory Through a Framework of Christ-Centered Love" is provocative. It takes on a white nationalist argument that true unity in diversity has to do with diverse people assimilating to the ideas of white nationalists. The North America originated with such fallacious ideas. However, with the influx of diverse people groups in contemporary North America, white nationalist ideas are challenged. While Cásarez is critical of pervasive whiteness, he affirms white people just as he seeks affirmation of other people, particularly black people and Latinx people groups. Theologically,

Cásarez notes that in Christ all people under the banner of one God, creator of all people with equal need for love, compassion, peace and fulfillment. The Holy Spirit is the great equalizer, continuing the work of Christ to both affirm diverse ways of thinking and diverse gifts to advance a unity in diversity that is not subjugated to any triumphalist view.

Furthermore, Estrada's "Do Brown Immigrant Lives Matter? The Spirit in John and Social Justice" is a clarion call for Bible believing Christians in the United States to reconsider the ramifications of bootstrapping religious ideology with party politics. With particular concern about American poor treatment of mostly Latin Americans at the borders who are seeking political asylum from the hostility of their birth-nations. A country that boasts to be the greatest nation on earth treats those who Estrada affectionately calls "brown people" as if they do not matter. Yet, his greater concern is that evangelical Christians have become so politically blindsided by special interests that they fail to see the marginalized as part of the family of God. Estrada's chapter notes that the Holy Spirit in the Gospel of John locates all of God's children in one family by the Spirit.

Chris E.W. Green begins the third section on "Truth to Power" with an insightful chapter entitled "The Spirit of the Lord is Freedom: The God of the Gospel and the Abolition of Mastery." Green denounces racism with its roots in corrupt interpretations of Christ. He cites 18th-Century Cotton Mather, a Presbyterian minister who theologically reasoned black oppression, preaching that that black people could have white souls if they were washed "White in the blood of the Lamb." Moreover, racism was not merely a product of corrupted social structures but the prevailing Christian theology of early American civilization. Green explains that normalized racism has pervaded American society and Christian theology. While many are immune to it, racism is an unnatural reality. The Holy Spirit empowers believers to resist claims to racist powers. As people who share in the divine nature, people led by the Spirit and at one with Christ, believers have the power and the authority – which is to say, the responsibility – to alter reality.

Daniel Morrison concludes this section with a fresh read of John's message to the church of Ephesus in Revelation in light of contemporary abuse of power. The title of Morrison's chapter is "Hearing What the Holy Spirit Says Today: Prophetic Proclamation against

Abuse of Power." Morrison posits that the while legal debates currently abound within the church regarding the relationship between ethnic minorities and the local government, congregations must hear the cries of the oppressed and reclaim their prophetic voices within the public sphere. Christian partiality nods to the perpetuation of power struggles.

Furthermore, Dara Coleby Delgado begins section four on "Prophetic Consciousness," setting the record straight that Black Holiness Pentecostals have a long history of social advocacy and community engagement. Delgado builds her case by highlighting the life and ministry of Bishop Ida Bell Robinson, founder of the Mt. Sinai Holy Church of America (1925-1946).[4] Delgado explores the issues of class, race, and gender in relation to holiness. She explains that the distinct practices of early Black Holiness Pentecostals proved critical to living a sanctified, or clean, life and also determined the ways local churches addressed and worked to remedy problems around poverty (both social and economic) in their communities.

Furthermore, Babatunde Adedibu adds a chapter in this section from his own African context. The title of his work is "A Call for the awakening of the Prophetic Voice of African Neo-Pentecostals." Adedibu argues that act of kindness as social ministry do not constitute the full scope of social justice ministry. Reflecting on the African New-Pentecostal churches, Adedibu explains that these churches tend to be heavily involved in acts of kindness – providing basic social, economic and educational infrastructures to their citizens. However, he argues that the nexus between salvation and social justice is weak. Similar to Morrison in section three, Adedibu points to the urgent need for Spirit-filled, prophetic ministries to speak up against injustice. Adedibu is gravely concerned about African structural injustices, marginalization, corruption, and nepotism.

---

[4] Bishop TD Jakes' famous biblical preaching "Woman thou art loosed" continues a Spirit-filled prophetic tradition that Bishop Robinson's ministry started in the early 1920s. Bishop Robinson had a vision in which she heard the Spirit say, "Come out on Mount Sinai," so that "I will use you to loose the women." This goes to show that leaders from within the Pentecostal movement have a long history of women's empowerment and prophetic consciousness to lift the downtrodden and empower God's people for success.

Introduction

The final section on "Caring for People, Fighting for Justice" features two essays, the first by Adeline Jean and the second by Michal Meulenberg. Jean brings an important ecumenical twist to the overall volume with her research of a Haitian Catholic congregation in Miami. The title of the chapter is "Notre Dame D'Haiti Catholic Church Mission: The Holy Spirit and Justice at this 'Living Room of the Haitian Community'" Jean discovers that clergy associated with Notre Dame engage in and promote a pneumatological ecclesial praxis. This has positively impacted their congregants and transformed their marginal positions as non-English-speaking immigrants living in a foreign English-speaking country to that of spiritually empowered Haitian-Americans. This congregation exhibits a Spirit-filled theology of hospitality. Such hospitality is transcendent and transforms the congregants to embodied agents of justice.

Secondly, Michal Meulenberg powerfully closes this anthology of essays with her passionate polemic against unjust systems to which the church often assimilates and thus fails to be the Church God intends. The chapter is entitled "'When the Truth Does Not Set Free': False Accusations, Wrongful Convictions, and the Church." Meulenberg brings her journalistic background to bear on critical theological reflection in regard to wrongful convictions and tending to the needs of the falsely accused. American justice history is paved with wrongful convictions. It is no denying that that the justice system is not always just. Wealth, prestige, and power wield a strong arm to shield some from justice while it beats down the vulnerable. Meulenberg sheds light on the facts, which are evidence of injustice that lands far too many young people in prisons. Ironically, others who are guilty of crimes go free. Importantly, she highlights the role of the Holy Spirit in awakening the Christian conscience to such injustice of false accusations, wrongful convictions, and incarceration. And she concludes with a hope that Christians would submit to the formational work of the Spirit of Truth with compassion for those who are psychologically traumatized and socially ostracized in systems that are often unyielding to the cause of justice.

Acknowledgments

I wish to thank each of the contributors for their tireless efforts to help make this volume a success. Their keen insight, spiritual depth, and commitment to Jesus Christ coupled with robust scholarship is nothing short of amazing!

Also, I wish to thank Bryan T. Froehle, my PhD dissertation chair and the director of the PhD program at St. Thomas University in Miami Gardens, Florida, for pushing me to apply critical social theory to enhance my scholarly agenda. This volume is part of a life-long effort to advance scholarship and theological education that is attuned to situations in everyday life, raising critical questions for deeper understanding of the power and work of the Holy Spirit in the world.

Last but not least, thank you, the reader for taking the time to read the pages ahead. I am a doctor for Church; therefore, I research and write to advance the mission of God in and through the Church. I pray that the pages ahead challenge as well as inspire you to participate with the Holy Spirit to advance God's mission of righteousness and justice for all of God's children!

CHAPTER ONE

THE SOCIAL CONCERN OF EARLY AMERICAN PENTECOSTALS*

Cecil M. Robeck, Jr*

Interest and Participation in Matters of Social Concern

The most beautiful thing about the Pentecostals was their ability to pour themselves into the power of the Holy Spirit. They could blend like nobody's business into the words of the Holy Scriptures and do their best to uphold their conception of Christianity. It was a miracle how they could shut out the hot and cold running cockroaches and king-size rats and all the added horrors of decaying rotten tenement houses and garbage-littered streets, with drugs running through the veins of our ghetto kids. It was a miracle that they could endure the indignities poured upon our Barrios. I knew that every one of them didn't get weaker. They got stronger. Their prayers didn't get shorter. They got longer. Those who looked for God to come closer were blessed with *El Bautismo*

* This chapter was originally published in Jan A.B. Jongeneel, A.O. (ed.), *Pentecost, Mission and Ecumenism: Essays on Intercultural Theology* (Studies in the Intercultural History of Christianity 75; Frankfurt am Main: Peter Lang, 1992), pp. 97-106. It appears here in an updated and edited form.

* Cecil M. Robeck, Jr (PhD, Fuller Theological Seminary) is an ordained Assemblies of God minister who serves the church as Senior Professor of Church History and Ecumenicism. He also serves as Special Assistant to the President for Ecumenical Relations at Fuller Theological Seminary in Pasadena, California.

del Espirito Santo, and they spoke a language that I could not understand. Tia had said it was the tongue of the angels, and only a few could interpret it.[1]

Pentecostals frequently receive criticism for showing a lack of interest and participation in matters of social concern and justice.[2] On the surface, this criticism has some merit. Pentecostals seem to be especially concerned with matters of the soul rather than matters related to the body.[3] However, as Miroslav Volf has pointed out, appearances may be deceiving, for Pentecostals have traditionally taken a positive approach to the "materiality of salvation."[4] The body has been important even if the soul had been given priority.

To be sure, Pentecostals have frequently chosen not to participate in matters of social justice as they are often defined today. They have placed considerable energy into the so-called "compassionate ministries,"[5] but overall, few Pentecostals in the U.S. have become involved in the struggles that seek to identify and overcome evil in social structures and institutions. Many African American

---

[1] Piri Thomas, *Savior, Savior, Hold My Hand* (Garden City, NY: Doubleday & Company, Inc., 1972), pp. 19-20.

[2] J. Deotis Roberts, *Black Theology in Dialogue* (Philadelphia, PA: The Westminster Press, 1987), p. 59, says, "It is notoriously short on social conscience and social justice. Corporate sins are seldom recognized, and there is little concern for social transformation." Similarly, Richard J. Mouw, *The God Who Commands* (Notre Dame, IN: University of Notre Dame Press, 1990), p. 189, notes, "Unfortunately little has been done within either the older Pentecostal or newer charismatic movements by way of exploring the implications of a strong emphasis on the Holy Spirit for ethical theory."

[3] This idea is clearly expressed in "Sidetracked," *Mountain Movers* 31.3 (March 1989), p. 3; Norm Correll, "Out to Change the World," *Mountain Movers* 31.4 (April 1989), pp. 10-11; and "Dead Faith," *Mountain Movers* 31.6 (June 1989), p. 3. For a more balanced approach see J. Philip Hogan, "Because Jesus Did," *Mountain Movers* 31.6 (June 1989), pp. 10-11.

[4] Miroslav Volf, "Materiality of Salvation: An Investigation in the Soteriologies of Liberation and Pentecostal Theologies," *Journal of Ecumenical Studies* 26.3 (1989), pp. 447-67.

[5] One celebrated example, which extends from the earliest days of the movement, is the work of Lillian Trasher among Egypt's orphans. See Beth Prim Howell, *Lady on a Donkey*, (New York, NY: E.P. Dalton & Company, 1960), and *Letters from Lillian* (Springfield, MO: Assemblies of God Division of Foreign Missions, 1983).

Pentecostals have participated actively in the Civil Rights movement and other social justice efforts for decades.[6] Civil Rights aside, however, this generalization can be made. There is at least one very significant factor that *may* cast light on why some Pentecostals have refrained from social justice advocacy. That factor is related to their social location. While this factor does not provide adequate justification for the continued rejection of involvement in matters of social justice, it has clearly been a major factor in the past.

In the early days of the Twentieth Century when Pentecostals were beginning to develop an identity of their own, they were commonly representative of the lower classes and the dispossessed.[7] They often found themselves to be effectively blocked from places of power: cultural, educational, political, financial, and ecclesiastical. They were often oppressed people, former slaves or the children of former slaves, poor whites, and linguistically limited Hispanic American immigrants.

Early Pentecostals were ridiculed or harassed in the public and were often the brunt of private jokes.[8] The oppression they experienced on numerous fronts helped to direct them toward the needs of others who were marginalized like themselves, the poor, the alcoholic, the prostitute, and the drug addict. They turned their attention to evangelistic preaching and compassion for the poor and disenfranchised, often ignoring the structures and institutions which they felt powerless to transform. They functioned like

---

[6] One example is that of Bishop Ithiel Clemmons of the Church of God in Christ, who played a significant role in helping map the strategy of Dr. Martin Luther King, Jr, in New York during the early 1960s. See C.M. Robeck, Jr, "Ithiel Conrad Clemmons," in Stanley M. Burgess and Gary B. McGee (eds.), *Dictionary of Pentecostal and Charismatic Movements* (Grand Rapids, MI: Zondervan Publishing House, 1988), p. 222.

[7] See, for instance, Robert Mapes Anderson, *Vision of the Disinherited: The Making of American Pentecostalism* (Oxford: Oxford University Press, 1979).

[8] Headlines were particularly cruel. Cf. "Religious Fanaticism Creates Wild Scenes," [subtitled "Holy Kickers Carry on Mad Orgies"] *Los Angeles Record* (July 14, 1906), p. 1; "Howling Ground Is Offered to the Household," *Pasadena Evening Star* (July 18, 1906), p. 12; "Jumpers to Kill Children" [Subtitled: "Holy Rollers Plan a Slaughter of Innocents"], *Los Angeles Herald* (July 20, 1906), pp. 1-2; "Big Crowd Routs the Holy Rollers," *Whittier Daily News* (November 2, 1906), p. 1.

extended families or therapeutic encounter groups in their brush arbors and store fronts. They emphasized personal salvation, transformed lifestyles, developing relationships, and hope for the future.[9]

Frank Bartleman's Criticism of War and Capitalism

Wow, I thought to myself. If ever there were an escape, this has got to be it. Is God gonna make it up to us in heaven?

Caramba, I smiled, maybe it ain't an escape, maybe like a somber Pentecostal guy had once told me. Maybe, like he had said, they aren't interested in material wealth. God's Kingdom will provide enough for all in the sweet bye and bye. God's work and God's will be done. But ... "How about starting here on earth, brother, with the nitty-gritty reality?" I had asked this Pentecostal guy. He had looked at me funny and had said, "God's Kingdom is not of this earth." "But we are," I had insisted. He just shook his head and walked away.[10]

At the popular level, the idea that God's Kingdom was not part of the present world reality was widespread. Frank Bartleman, an early participant–observer of the Pentecostal Movement, was one of those who drew a clear distinction between the Kingdom of God and the kingdoms of this world. He argued as late as 1934 that "Our government is in heaven, not of this world."[11] Jesus had noted that His kingdom was not of this world (Jn 18.36), and Bartleman observed, "as He [was], so are we in the world."[12]

---

[9] See especially Anderson, *Vision of the Disinherited*, pp. 195-222.

[10] Thomas, *Savior, Savior*, p. 20.

[11] F. Bartleman, "The Great Divide," *Maran-atha* 9.3 (1934), p. 6.

[12] Frank Bartleman, "Not of This World," *Word and Work* [circa 1915), p. 226. In an undated tract (circa 1916) on "Christian Citizenship," Bartleman opined,

As Christians, we are "born again," this time into the Kingdom of God. We are citizens of the country we are born into. The Christian is a "man without a country" as far as earthly citizenship is concerned. He renounces his earthly citizenship in this world when converted as surely as one renounces his citizenship in the U.S. should he swear allegiance to a foreign country. "Who hath delivered us from the power of darkness, and hath translated us into the Kingdom of His dear Son," Col. 1.13. Our "citizenship" is in heaven. Heaven is our country. We are to

Unlike Frank Sandford, John Alexander Dowie, to some extent Dr Finis Yoakum, and even Charles Fox Parham, Bartleman held no utopian dream of a church-run or church-based society.[13] Bartleman was too pessimistic for that. He constantly appealed to history, concluding that whenever the Church became enmeshed in the concerns of the State, the life and message of the Church were compromised.[14] For this reason, he believed firmly in two aspects of the doctrine of separation between Church and State. First, the State has no right meddling in the affairs of the Church. The Church must be free from State domination. Second, the Church has no right to

---

"render unto Caesar the things that are Caesar's." But our lives and souls belong to God. He gave them. We must "render unto God (not Caesar) the things that are God's." Caesar disputes this ownership with God.

A Christian has no more to do with the politics of the world than an American has with the politics of Europe. The church can only take part in politics when she is worldly. The early Christians were persecuted because they were Christians. They were not accorded a place in the world. They were not citizens here. And the world recognized the fact. They were different. This treatment kept the church clean. Only "new creatures" could hear the test and live under such persecution and hatred. "Because ye are not of the world, therefore the world hateth you." – John 15.19.

[13] Bartleman clearly sought to dissociate himself from Dowie and Sandford whom he classed among spiritual charlatans in "All Things in Common," *Confidence* 6.4 (April 1913), p. 79. On Frank Sandford see Shirley Nelson, *Fair Clear and Terrible: The Story of Shiloh Maine* (Latham, NY: British American Publishing, 1989); on Dowie see Gordon Lindsay, *John Alexander Dowie: A Life Story of Trials, Tragedies, and Triumphs* (Dallas, TX: Christ for the Nations, reprint, 1986); and Grant Wacker, "Marching to Zion: Religion in a Modern Utopian Community," *Church History* 54 (1985), pp. 496-511; on Yoakum see Jennifer A. Stock, "Finis E. Yoakum, MD, Servant of the Disinherited of Los Angeles: 1895-1920" (paper presented at the Society for Pentecostal Studies in Dallas, Texas, November 1990), and Robert H. Vine, *California's Utopias* (San Marino, CA: The Huntington Library 1953), pp. 153-54; and on Parham see James R. Goff, Jr, *Fields White Unto Harvest: Charles F. Parham and the Missionary Origins of Pentecostalism* (Fayetteville, AR: The University of Arkansas Press, 1988.

[14] F. Bartleman, "Last Day Conditions," *The Bridegroom's Messenger* 180 (March 1, 1916), p. 4; Bartleman, "The Great Divide," p. 7.

participate in the affairs of State.[15] Bartleman did believe, however, that Christians had not only a right, but also an obligation to criticize the affairs of State on moral and ethical grounds. Indeed, his own continuous criticism, even harassment of public policies throughout the world suggests that he may be the most outspoken social critic the Pentecostal Movement has produced to date.

Most of Bartleman's social commentary is limited to the tracts and articles he authored. Few of these nearly 600 articles are extant today, but a survey of what does exist indicates that the outbreak of hostilities in Europe in 1914 changed him. By 1915, his writings were full of social analysis and criticism. One of his earliest such articles was published in March 1915 under the title, "The Situation in Europe."[16] Bartleman argued that the war was merely an act of God's judgment. He warned his readers to be objective and maintain neutrality lest they find themselves in rebellion against God's sovereign purpose. God had dealt patiently with the nations for years. Now, observed Bartleman, "The Lord has simply changed the tone of His voice. He is now speaking from the cannon's mouth." The targets of God's judgment were clear. "Russian despotism, German militarism, and English imperialism together spell 'devilism,'" he charged.[17]

Throughout the war, Bartleman kept readers of *The Bridegroom's Messenger* (Atlanta, GA), the Assemblies of God's *Weekly Evangel* (Springfield, MO), and the New England Pentecostal paper, *Word and Work* (Framingham, MA) regularly appraised of the moral and ethical issues, which he judged as lying behind the war. Foremost among them were illegitimate quests for power, greed, and the ever-present danger of hypocrisy.

Bartleman was particularly piqued by the lack of discernment among Pentecostals regarding the real reasons that stood behind the war. An ardent pacifist himself, he tolerated German Pentecostal participation in the war on the ground, that they had no exception clause in their conscription law. The churches in Germany did not have the same light on the subject as the British and Americans, he argued, and they justified their engagement in the war by viewing it

---

[15] Bartleman, "The Great Divide," p. 6; Bartleman, "The Great Divide," p. 7.

[16] F. Bartleman, "The Situation in Europe," *The Bridegroom's Messenger* 168 (March 1, 1915), p. 1.

[17] Bartleman, "The Situation in Europe," p. 1.

as an effort to evangelize among their own troops. Still, Bartleman hoped they would choose not to serve, and they would die as martyrs [traitors] for the sake of their faith.[18]

Bartleman was far less tolerant toward American Pentecostals. He resented their calls to enter the war following the sinking of the *Lusitania*. "We send shiploads of ammunition to Europe, and cover the cargo with American citizens, and then want to go to war if they got blowed [sic] up," he complained.[19] To respond in this fashion was, at best, hypocritical, but Bartleman dug more deeply than that. The reason that ammunition was being sent to Europe was not the justness of the cause so much as it was capitalist profit. "A handful of rulers, capitalists, and ammunition makers are exploiting the whole human race for gain," he contended.[20]

Concern with greed and profit as underlying motivations for American involvement in the war led Bartleman to criticize what went under the guise of patriotism. "The fact is" he declared, "American patriotism, except for the 'almighty dollar', is just about as cracked on the whole as our revered liberty bell. We sell to the highest bidder, even if he be an enemy. This sin is going to undo us."[21] So taken was he by this, that he even suggested that Americans should "pluck out the stars from our flag and instate dollar marks in their place."[22]

Because of his concern that American capitalists and investors kept the war alive, Bartleman criticized capitalism and American economic policy more broadly. The war was, after all, a "commercial

---

[18] F. Bartleman, "Through the War Zone," *The Bridegroom's Messenger* 171 (June 1, 1915), p. 3.

[19] F. Bartleman, "The War – Separation," *The Bridegroom's Messenger* 190 (January 1, 1917), p. 4; Cf. F. Bartleman, "The Present Day Conditions," *Weekly Evangel* (June 5, 1915), p. 3. The passenger ship, *Lusitania,* was carrying both passengers and munitions, when a German submarine sank it on May 7, 1915. Both American and British governments denied this claim at the time, but a search of the wreckage have shown their denials to be false.

[20] Bartleman, "The War – Separation," p. 4.

[21] Bartleman, "The War – Separation," p. 4.

[22] F. Bartleman, "The European War," *Weekly Evangel* (July 10, 1915), p. 3.

struggle ... for final supremacy."[23] By 1930, Bartleman was more adamant than ever about what he perceived to be the evils of capitalism. "The Capitalistic system is all unscriptural," he charged.[24]

Capitalistic practices were a favorite target of Bartleman's criticisms. He believed in the idea that all things should be held in common in much the same way they had been in Acts 2.44 and 4.32. Capitalists were responsible for producing inequitable salary structures,[25] artificially inflated markets affecting food prices,[26] immoral policies, which destroyed surplus food, and inequitable land distribution policies, which in the case of the United States, he asserted, had been stolen from its rightful stewards in the first place, Native Americans.[27] Ultimately, this led Bartleman to conclude that while Soviet communism was wrong to be wedded to atheism, the spirit of communism was right, for it was consistent with New Testament practice.[28]

It may be that Bartleman's frustration with his own social location, and his lifestyle lived at the poverty level, contributed to such ideas, for he clearly supported the poor over against the rich. "The Soviets have given the land to the people in Russia, for the common good," he wrote. "They have equalized rights and possessions. The system of selfish land ownership is broken. What a blessing if we all could have some land to till here in America. But, 'none but the wealthy.'"[29] One cannot help but detect a tinge of wistfulness in this lionized description of Soviet reality.

Such class distinctions, he argued, were not limited to the United States, but were prevalent in England as well. "God is done with [the] class system in England," he maintained. People were starving to

---

[23] F. Bartleman, "In the Last Days," *Word and Work* (September 23, 1916).

[24] F. Bartleman, "Last Days Facts," *Maran-atha* 6 (March-April 1930), p. 8.

[25] F. Bartleman, "Christian Preparedness," *Word and Work* (*circa* 1916), p. 114.

[26] F. Bartleman, "The World War," *Word and Work* (August 22, 1916), p. 196; "In the Last Days," p. 394.

[27] Bartleman, "Last Day Facts," p. 9. Bartleman argued that judgment was coming to America because God was no respecter of persons. Besides, "We stole the U.S. from the Indians anyway."

[28] Bartleman, "Last Day Facts," p. 9.

[29] Bartleman, "Last Day Facts," p. 9.

death while the wealthy kept vast hunting preserves which, if planted with potatoes, could feed the starving poor.[30]

Much more could be said of Bartleman's social criticism, but one item of injustice he seems to have left unaddressed was the issue of racism within the American context.

William J. Seymour's Criticism of Racism

William J. Seymour, the soft-spoken, African American pastor of the Apostolic Faith Mission on Azusa Street, uniquely addressed the issue of racism. Seymour was not nearly as vocal on social issues as Bartleman was. Bartleman was widely read, widely travelled, and made ready use of the press. Seymour was a pastor who instructed those who attended his church, but who, more than anything, modeled with his life the lessons he hoped to convey to those who heard him.

Elder Seymour arrived in Los Angeles, California on February 22, 1906. He came at the invitation of a group of what he called "the colored people of the city,"[31] who had asked him to serve as their pastor. Almost from the start, he was locked out of the church to which he had been called. Undaunted, he met for several weeks in a home Bible study on North Bonnie Brae Street. While the group to whom he ministered was largely black, several white people moved with ease and regularity in and out of the group.[32]

When on April 9, 1906 people who attended Seymour Bible study began to speak in tongues, word spread rapidly, and a mission was organized. The Azusa Street Mission quickly became known in the

---

[30] F. Bartleman, "The European War," p. 3; "What Will the Harvest Be?" *Weekly Evangel* (August 7, 1915), p. 1.

[31] "The Same Old Way," *The Apostolic Faith* 1.1 (September 1906), p. 3; W.J. Seymour, *The Doctrines and Discipline of the Azusa Street Apostolic Faith Mission of Los Angeles, Cal.* (Los Angeles, CA: W.J. Seymour, 1915), p. 12.

[32] F. Bartleman, *How Pentecost Came to Los Angeles* (Los Angeles, CA: F. Bartleman, 1925), pp. 43, 64. This work is reprinted in *Witness to Pentecost: The Life of Frank Bartleman* (New York: NY, Garland Publishing, 1985).

local press as "the old negro church."[33] Even the mission's leadership admitted to this description.[34] As the days went by, however, an increasing number of other nationalities and ethnic groups joined the African Americans at Azusa Street leading Bartleman to note that at Azusa, "the 'color line' was washed away in the blood."[35]

The Azusa Street Mission was established during a period of intense racial prejudice throughout the United States.[36] Because Los Angeles lay outside the South, Jim Crow laws, which enforced strict segregation elsewhere, were not generally in force there. To say this does not mean that racial prejudice did not exist in Los Angeles. It did, though it was aimed more pointedly at Mexican and Asian workers.[37] There were areas of the city in which African Americans were not welcome.[38] Some restaurant owners attempted to

[33] "Religious Fanaticism Creates Wild Scenes," *Los Angeles Record* (July 14, 1906), p. 1.

[34] "Bible Pentecost," *The Apostolic Faith* 1.3 (November 1906), p. 1. Early descriptions place attendance as high as 700 with mostly black participants. Cf. "Weird Babel of Tongues," *Los Angeles Daily Times* (April 18, 1906), 2.1; "Rolling and Diving Fanatics 'Confess'," *Los Angeles Daily Times* (June 23, 1906), 1.7.

[35] Bartleman, *How Pentecostal Came to Los Angeles*, p. 54.

[36] Douglas J. Nelson, "For Such a Time as This" (PhD Thesis; University of Birmingham, 1981), has amply demonstrated this fact, and Iain MacRobert, *Black Roots and White Racism of Early Pentecostalism in the U.S.A.* (New York, NY: St. Martin's Press, 1988).

[37] On Mexicans, see William Deverell, *Whitewashed Adobe: The Rise of Los Angeles and the Remaking of the Mexican Past* (Berkeley, CA: University of California Press, 2004), pp. 11-48. On Asians see, Sucheng Chan, *This Bitter-Sweet Soil: The Chinese in California Agriculture, 1860-1910* (Berkeley, CA; University of California Press, 1986); Lisa See, *On Gold Mountain: The One-Hundred-Year Odyssey of My Chinese-American Family* (New York: Vintage Books, 1995); Brian Masaru Hayashi. *"For the Sake of Our Japanese Brethren": Assimilation, Nationalism, and Protestantism among the Japanese of Los Angeles, 1895-1942* (Stanford, CA: Stanford University Press, 1995).

[38] "Edendale Indignant over Negro Neighbors," *Los Angeles Express* (October 2, 1907), p. 2.11; "Police Aid Negroes to Occupy House," *Los Angeles Herald* (October 8, 1907), p. 6.

discriminate based on color, only to be rebuffed by city leaders.[39] There were churches, which were organized along racial lines,[40] but there were also churches that had held racially integrated services for years. Among them were churches associated with the Holiness Church of Southern California and Arizona.[41]

Seymour invited participation of both whites and blacks in the Azusa Street Mission from the outset. Not only were whites present from the earliest services, but in 1907 when the mission was incorporated, whites were listed among the trustees, as church secretary, business manager, and later, as camp meeting organizer.[42] What caught the attention of the press, however, was Seymour's unorthodox willingness for blacks and whites to mingle so freely at the altar, including a good deal of physical contact, with hugging and kissing across racial lines. Many newspaper reports made mention of this phenomenon in Seymour's meetings. Indeed, it appears to have been the fact found to be most offensive by outsiders.[43]

The freedom with which the races mingled under Seymour's leadership was apparently difficult even for some of those who were open to other aspects of his message. Gaston B. Cashwell, an evangelist from North Carolina, noted that when he arrived at the mission "a new crucifixion began in my life and I had to die to many

---

[39] "Negroes Turned Down," *Pasadena Evening Star* (August 21, 1906), p. 1; "Puts Ban on Anti-Negro Signs," *Los Angeles Herald* (May 7, 1907), p. 12; "Negroes Thank Mayor Harper," *Los Angeles Herald* (May 12, 1907), p. 2.5.

[40] G.R. Bryant, "Religious Life of Los Angeles Negroes," *Los Angeles Daily Times* (February 12, 1909), p. 3.7.

[41] On this, see Josephine M. Washburn, *History and Reminiscences of the Holiness Church Work in Southern California and Arizona* (South Pasadena, CA: Record Press, 1912; ret, New York, NY: Garland Publishing, 1985).

[42] Cecil M. Robeck, Jr, "Azusa Street Mission," in Stanley M. Burgess and Gary B. McGee (eds.), *Dictionary of Pentecostal and Charismatic Movements* (Grand Rapids, MI: Zondervan Publishing House, 1988), p. 34.

[43] "Religious Fanaticism Creates Wild Scenes," p. 1; "Women with Men Embrace," *Los Angeles Daily Times* (September 3, 1906), p. 11; "How Holy Roller Gets Religion," *Los Angeles Herald* (September 10, 1906), p. 7; "Negro Bluk Kissed," *Indianapolis Star* (June 3, 1907), p. 3; "Bluk Feet, Little and Big, Scrubbed," *Indianapolis Star* (June 16, 1907), p. 10.

things."[44] Carl Brumback and Vinson Synan both note that this "crucifixion" had to do with Cashwell's willingness to be prayed over and
touched by a black brother.[45] Still, the Mission celebrated the fact
that "No instrument that God can use is rejected on account of color
or dress or lack of education."[46]

In spite of Seymour's commitment to the total integration of the
races in all facets of life at the Mission, there were those who disa-
greed with his policies. Charles Parham's attacks upon Seymour
were relentless. He labelled Azusa Street "a cross between the Negro
and Holy Roller form of worship," and made repeated racial slurs
against the Mission.[47] Bartleman hints at more widespread racial
dissatisfaction, which was manifest when "most of the white saints"
left Azusa Street when Elmer K. Fisher established the Upper Room
Mission nearby. Surely, some did, but many who left did so for other
reasons. [48]

In 1915, Seymour reflected on the situation at some length. He
expressed his sorrow at the divisions and problems, which had
spring up along racial lines. He continued to maintain and affirm a
deep love for white Pentecostals, articulating his teaching that
Christ is all and for all. "He is neither black nor white man, nor

---

[44] G.B. Cashwell, "Came 3000 Miles for His Pentecost," *The Apostolic Faith* 1.4 (December 1906), p. 3.

[45] Carl Brumback, *Suddenly ... From Heaven: A History of the Assemblies of God* (Springfield, MO: Gospel Publishing House, 1961), p. 84; Vinson Synan, *The Holiness-Pentecostal Movement in the United States* (Grand Rapids, MI: Eerdmans, 1971), p. 123.

[46] "Bible Pentecost," *The Apostolic Faith* 1.3 (November 1906), p. 1.

[47] Untitled comments, *New Year's Greeting* [Baxter Springs, KS] (January 1912), p. 6. This parallels the comments of a Los Angeles pastor in "New
Religions Come, Then Go," *Los Angeles Herald* (September 24, 1906), p. 7.

[48] Bartleman, *How Pentecost Came to Los Angeles*, p. 84. It is difficult
to assess the precision of Bartleman's comment here. Los Angeles was an
extremely cosmopolitan city, with multiple ethnic neighborhoods in which
the many new immigrants lived. My research suggests that people left to
form their own churches – Russian, Armenian, Spanish, Danish, Swedish,
etc. – primarily in order to worship in their native tongue. The Upper Room
Mission was a split from First New Testament Church, not from Azusa
Street. The fact that Fisher and Seymour signed ordination papers together
after the Upper Room Mission came into existence suggests a good relationship between these men.

Chinaman, nor Hindoo [East Indian], nor Japanese, but God," Seymour argued.[49] Nevertheless, he declared the interracial character of the Azusa Street experiment to be at an end for the sake of peace among the churches.[50] It may be that the fully integrated character of the Azusa Street Mission in an otherwise segregationist society was a prophetic distinctive of the movement, which was lost due to overriding jealousy and bigotry on the part of many.

Other Early Prophetic Figures: Ambrose J. Tomlinson, Finis E. Yoakum, etc.

Deeply entrenched moral biases, value preferences, and social prejudices, sometimes expressed systemically in structured forms of sexism, classism, or racism, are ushered into eschatological judgment in the Spirit's charismatic restructuring of the church. All the dividing walls of the old social order are forever undermined in the *koinonia* that the Spirit creates. In replicating the kingdom ministry of Jesus through the *charismata*, the Holy Spirit creates *koinonia* that witnesses to the inclusive scope and the egalitarian nature of God's reign.[51]

Bartleman and Seymour are but two early Pentecostal pioneers who were moved by specific issues of social justice: war, economic oppression, and racism to name but three. Robert Mapes Anderson has astutely observed that, "Pentecostalism was a movement born of radical social discontent, which, however, expanded its revolutionary impulses in veiled, ineffectual, displaced attacks that amounted to withdrawal from the social struggle and passive acquiescence to a world they hated and wished to escape."[52] It is clear that Bartleman and Seymour represented some of early Pentecostalism's social discontent. Each in his own way, Bartleman through well-crafted words, and Seymour through the model of his life, hoped to affect some level of social change. They were not alone.

---

[49] Seymour, *Doctrine and Discipline*, p. 13.

[50] Seymour, *Doctrine and Discipline*, p. 13.

[51] Murray W. Dempster, "Evangelism, Social Concern, and the Kingdom of God," in Murray W. Dempster, Byron D. Klaus, and Douglas Peterson (eds.), *Called and Empowered: Global Mission in Pentecostal Perspective* (Peabody, MA: Hendrickson Publishers, 1991), p. 29.

[52] Anderson, *Vision of the Disinherited*, p. 222.

Considerable work needs to be undertaken by historians and theologians of the movement to recover and restore to contemporary Pentecostalism some of its earlier prophetic edge. Ambrose J. Tomlinson, for instance, was greatly concerned with Appalachian poverty, with the lack of food and clothing for children and the unavailability of basic educational opportunities for you and old alike. For several years, he raised money, bought land, taught school, and fed scores of poverty-stricken children in the rural mountains of North Carolina, Georgia, and Tennessee.[53]

Finis E. Yoakum, MD, established a medical practice in Southern California after a dramatic healing in his own life in 1895. As time passed, he invested his entire personal savings and donations, which he solicited to meet the needs of the chronically ill (especially those with tuberculosis and cancer), the poor and destitute, the alcoholic, prostitute, and other social outcasts. Often controversial, his Pisgah Home Movement grew to encompass a ministry in 1911, which provided 9,000 clean beds and fed 18,000 meals each month to the needy. He established a "free" Pisgah store as a distribution center for donated clothing, canned goods, and fresh fruits and vegetables, Pisgah Ark, a halfway house for women with addictive behavior, Pisgah Gardens, which fed the needy and acted as a rehabilitation center for the chronically ill, a small orphanage, and Pisgah Grande, a 3225 acre utopian–like community.[54] Some of the work continues to the present.

The names of others such as Aimee Semple McPherson, George and Carrie (Judd) Montgomery, Lillian Trasher and Bishop Charles H. Mason could be added to the list of early Pentecostals with ministries of social justice of one sort or another. Unfortunately, as these prophetic figures passed from the scene, their social ministries often went with them, or they were continued on a much smaller scale.

The Social location of Pentecostals in the United States has increased dramatically, especially since World War II. The relationship of the Kingdom of God to the present reality has become less partitioned in the thinking of many. It is time, once again, to question the construct of the contemporary social order in light of newer

---

[53] A.J. Tomlinson, "A Brief History of Mission Work in the Mountains of North Carolina, George and Tennessee," *Samson's Foxes* (Culberson, NC: A.J. Tomlinson, no date), unpaginated.

[54] See above, note 13.

Pentecostal understandings of the Kingdom of God. The social concern expressed by several early American Pentecostals may yet help to inform and direct future Pentecostal thinking in constructive and powerful ways.

Bibliography

Anderson, Robert Mapes, *Vision of the Disinherited: The Making of American Pentecostalism* (Oxford, England: Oxford University Press, 1979).

Bartleman, Frank, *How Pentecost Came to Los Angeles* (Los Angeles, CA: F. Bartleman, 1925).

Brian Masaru Hayashi, *"For the Sake of Our Japanese Brethren": Assimilation, Nationalism, and Protestantism among the Japanese of Los Angeles, 1895-1942* (Stanford, CA: Stanford University Press, 1995).

Brumback, Carl, *Suddenly ... From Heaven: A History of the Assemblies of God* (Springfield, MO: Gospel Publishing House, 1961).

Bryant, G.R., "Religious Life of Los Angeles Negroes," *Los Angeles Daily Times*. February 12, 1909.

Burgess, Stanley M., and Gary B. McGee (eds.), *Dictionary of Pentecostal and Charismatic Movements* (Grand Rapids, MI: Zondervan Publishing House, 1988).

Cashwell, G.B., "Came 3000 Miles for His Pentecost," *The Apostolic Faith* 1.4. December 1906.

Chan, Sucheng, *This Bitter-Sweet Soil: The Chinese in California Agriculture, 1860-1910* (Berkeley, CA; University of California Press, 1986).

Dempster, Murray W., Byron D. Klaus, and Douglas Peterson (eds.), *Called and Empowered: Global Mission in Pentecostal Perspective* (Peabody, MA: Hendrickson Publishers, 1991).

Deverell, William, *Whitewashed Adobe: The Rise of Los Angeles and the Remaking of the Mexican Past* (Berkeley, CA: University of California Press, 2004).

Goff, Jr, James R., *Fields White Unto Harvest: Charles F. Parham and the Missionary Origins of Pentecostalism* (Fayetteville, AR: The University of Arkansas Press, 1988).

Howell, Beth Prim, *Lady on a Donkey* (New York, NY: E.P. Dalton & Company, 1960).

Lindsay, Gordon, *John Alexander Dowie: A Life Story of Trials, Tragedies, and Triumphs* (Dallas, TX: Christ for the Nations, reprint. 1986).

Nelson, Doublas J., "For Such a Time as This" (PhD Thesis; University of Birmingham, 1981).

Nelson, Shirley, *Fair Clear and Terrible: The Story of Shiloh Maine* (Latham, NY: British American Publishing, 1989).

MacRobert, Iain, *Black Roots and White Racism of Early Pentecostalism in the U.S.A.* (New York, NY: St. Martin's Press, 1988).

Mouw, Richard J., *The God Who Commands* (Notre Dame, IN: University of Notre Dame Press, 1990).

Roberts, J. Deotis, *Black Theology in Dialogue* (Philadelphia, PA: The Westminster Press, 1987).

Robeck, Jr, Cecil M., "Azusa Street Mission," in *Stanley M. Burgess and Gary B. McGee* (eds.), *Dictionary of Pentecostal and Charismatic Movements* (Grand Rapids, MI: Zondervan Publishing House, 1988).

See, Lisa, *On Gold Mountain: The One-Hundred-Year Odyssey of My Chinese-American Family* (New York: Vintage Books, 1995).

Seymour, W.J., *The Doctrines and Discipline of the Azusa Street Apostolic Faith Mission of Los Angeles, Cal.* (Los Angeles, CA: W.J. Seymour, 1915).

Stock, Jennifer A., "Finis E. Yoakum, MD, Servant of the Disinherited of Los Angeles: 1895-1920" (paper presented at the Society for Pentecostal Studies in Dallas, Texas, November 1990).

Synan, Vinson, *The Holiness-Pentecostal Movement in the United States* (Grand Rapids, MI: Eerdmans, 1971).

Thomas, Piri, *Savior, Savior, Hold My Hand* (Garden City, NY: Doubleday & Company, Inc., 1972).

Tomlinson, A.J., "A Brief History of Mission Work in the Mountains of North Carolina, George and Tennessee," in *Samson's Foxes* (Culberson, NC: A.J. Tomlinson, no date).

Vine, Robert H., *California's Utopias* (San Marino, CA: The Huntington Library 1953).

Volf, Mirsolav, "Materiality of Salvation: An Investigation in the Soteriologies of Liberation and Pentecostal Theologies," *Journal of Ecumenical Studies* 26.3 (1989), pp. 447-67.

Wacker, Grant, "Marching to Zion: Religion in a Modern Utopian Community," *Church History* 54 (1985), pp. 496-511.

Washburn, Josephine M., *History and Reminiscences of the Holiness Church Work in Southern California and Arizona* (South Pasadena, CA: Record Press, 1912).

ECONOMIC EMPOWERMENT

CHAPTER TWO

AGAINST POVERTY: THE HOLY SPIRIT AND PENTECOSTAL ECONOMIC MINISTRIES

David D. Daniels, III*

Pentecostal economic ministries intersect the economy by preparing people to enter in it as Spirit-empowered economic agents. They also recognize the Pentecostal movement's role in the economy with the Spirit-graced economic cultures as life-bearing sites which the movement houses. While there are sectors within Pentecostalism that have been coopted by certain economic systems, Pentecostal economic ministries can be interpreted as being constituted by a set of Christian economic practices and ethics that are more committed to the gospel than any particular economic system or ideology. The presence of the Holy Spirit within these Pentecostal communities challenges the economic forces that produce an economy controlled by one percent of the population in which the majority hardly benefits from the economy, being marginal to or excluded from the economy itself. In this way, through the presence of the Holy Spirit, many of these Pentecostal economic ministries confront poverty by working for economic justice.

The Pentecostal economic ministries in this chapter will focus on two types of economic ministries. First, there are Spirit-filled ministries that empower the poor, the working class, and middle class to enter the formal economy constituted by the major banks,

* David D. Daniels, III (PhD, Union Theological Seminary, New York) serves as one of the Bishops in the Church of God in Christ and Professor of Church History with expertise in history and historical theology at McCormick Theological Seminary in Chicago, Illinois.

corporations, technology firms, entertainment companies and other industries as well as subjected to federal economic policies, stock markets, and globalization. These economic ministries that focus on the formal economy range from those who sponsor job fairs, job training, and entrepreneurship schooling. While the second type of Pentecostal economic ministry also operates within the formal economy, it challenges the existing economic system. These ministries engage in civil disobedience, other forms of protest, and advocacy to reform or reinvent the economy.

Two sections organize this chapter besides the introduction and conclusion. The first section presents case studies of two types of Pentecostal economic ministry. The second section examines ways to explore theologies of the Holy Spirit and the economy in light of the case studies. In this chapter, I will argue that Pentecostal economic ministries exist which engage the economy by seeking to expand the participation of populations that have been excluded; the expansion of participation by the formerly excluded can be deemed an issue of economic justice. While some Pentecostal economic ministries accept the existing economic order, there are others which work to reform and transform the economy, orienting the economy toward economic justice. Related to the Pentecostal economic ministries is the theological challenge of framing the ways that the Holy Spirit might engage the economy as an economic actor since Pentecostals believe that the Holy Spirit can operate in all spheres of life.

Two Types of Pentecostal Economic Ministries

Pentecostal Economic Ministries Engaging the Economy

Two major Pentecostal economic ministries that work within the system of capitalism are found in the United States and Nigeria. These ministries are led by Dr. William "Bill" Winston of Living Word Christian Center in United States and Rev. Samuel Adeyemi of Daystar Christian Center in Nigeria. Both, while being prosperity gospel preachers, stress entrepreneurship within their reframing of the prosperity gospel.

When business education joins prosperity doctrine, a pragmatic form of prosperity gospel emerges. This pragmatic form of prosperity teaching, with its emphasis on entrepreneurship and other business skills, interjects a new divine-human agency equation, personal responsibility for learning business skills requisite for "realizing" prosperity, blending of business and biblical knowledge, and an educational apparatus to disseminate a prosperity doctrine-oriented business education. The pragmatic approach also shifts the economic behavior of prosperity gospel adherents from consumption to entrepreneurship. This pragmatic approach consequently interjects a new sector within the economic arena spawned by prosperity gospel ministries.

In addition to the classic type of "Prosperity Gospel" made popular by televangelists such as Kenneth Hagin, Benson Idahosa, and Paula White, there is what Ogungbile calls a "middle position" or what I call a pragmatic prosperity gospel. This prosperity gospel includes the teaching and learning of entrepreneurial skills to achieve the "more abundant life."

While "Bill" Winston is a well-known televangelist, less known is his founding of the Joseph Business School in 1998 with its vision being "To Eradicate Generational Poverty" and its mission being to use:[1]

> practical and biblical principles to empower adults to develop indispensable skills as successful entrepreneurs and business leaders thus equipping them to eradicate poverty in their lives and communities ... [and] to develop successful Christian entrepreneurs who will create income and employment opportunities for others, through the wealth and job creation that entrepreneurship and vocational training can provide. This, in turn, will assist in the rebuilding of the inner cities.

As a former executive with IBM, Bill Winston learned first-hand about the business world from his work experience. His pragmatic approach recognized a resonance between sound biblical principles and solid business principles. Rather than focus on teaching about prayer or positive confession alone, Winston established the school to train a new generation of Christian entrepreneurs. Through this new class of Christian entrepreneurs, wealth will be generated, and

---

[1] The Joseph Business School brochure 2014; tour to the Living Word Christian Center complex and the Joseph Business School on Sunday, January 11, 2015 as well as attendance at the Sunday worship service and the Joseph Business School Graduation.

jobs will be created. Additionally, the Joseph Business School would offer a program in vocational training in order for the school to be able to reach students from all educational backgrounds and interests. The faculty of the Business School consist of Spirit-filled Christians who are drawn from the ranks of business executives, entrepreneurs, and professionals that are graduates of elite business programs such as Harvard University's Graduate School of Business, University of Pennsylvania's Wharton School of Business, the University of Chicago's Booth Business School, and Northwestern University's Kellogg School of Business, internationally renowned research universities.[2]

Dr William "Bill" Winston grounds the vision of the Joseph Business School in Isa. 48.17 (KJV): "teacheth thee to profit." The use of the word profit in Isaiah connected with Dr Winston's previous profession of being a corporate executive prior to his entry into full-time ministry during the 1980s. As a word associated with the corporate world, it jumped out of the biblical text at him. According to Deloris Thomas, vice-president of Joseph Business School, Dr Winston received a prophecy that ministry wasn't just for the pulpit; there were to be marketplace ministers like Joseph and Daniel in the Bible; marketplace ministers were businesspeople who advanced the kingdom of God and its message in the marketplace. In response to the prophecy, Dr Winston began holding business workshops. He taught people "how to use their money to advance the kingdom, how to use their finances for the good of the kingdom." Workshop participants started asking Dr Winston to teach them not only about prosperity in an inspirational way but also teach them in practical terms about entrepreneurship, financial literacy, and other related topics.[3]

Dr Winston recruited Deloris Thomas and her husband to launch this new initiative. The Thomases were executives in different major corporations and graduates of MBA programs (U of Chicago and Harvard). They discovered Kathy Ashmore and an Ohio State University initiative: Program for Acquiring Competency for Entrepreneurship (PACE). The Joseph Business School would build

---

[2] See, www.jbs.edu/training_et_faculty.php.

[3] Phone Interview of Delores Thomas, vice-president, Joseph Business School on 7 January 2015 by David Daniels.

upon the Ohio State University program. Dr Winston wanted the Joseph Business School to target those who were excluded from the economy: high school dropouts, Welfare Moms, the underemployed. He wanted to reach those who were left-out of the economy, the disenfranchised. Dr Winston thought that by reaching this population with the gospel through the Joseph Business School these converts would be powerful testimonies of transformed lives. As living testimonies, they would attract others to the church. He wanted the Joseph Business School to focus on "people who could learn that they could achieve, that they were actually endowed with wisdom (Ex. 31). His goal was that JBS would teach them how to generate one million dollars in three years."[4]

The Joseph Business School is a business and entrepreneurship program that can be completed in nine months. The academic year consists of three terms. Students complete over 30 classes, attending class each term for about 11 Saturdays, comprising 161 contact hours; this is the equivalent to one semester of college classes. Within its nine months format, there are courses which clearly reflect the Christian orientation of the Joseph Business School such as "Christ and the Corporation," "Life as a Christian Entrepreneur," and "Prayer." Other courses would fit in any business school program: "Time Management." "Marketing," "Intro to eCommerce/eBusiness," "Business Management," "Financial Analysis," and "Business Plan Preparations." In the "Christ and the Corporation" course, the specifically Pentecostal focus is expressed in the course description which seeks to inculcate "the wisdom and understanding of being an anointed entrepreneur called and appointed by God" as well as introduce the student to "learn how to hear the voice of God." In the "Life as a Christian Entrepreneur" course, students will study biographies of "entrepreneurs who operate under the anointing and direction of God." Whereas in the "Prayer" course, students will "learn what, why, and how to pray for their businesses." Additionally, course subjects include the following: mission statement writing, feasibility study, pricing, sales and selling, human resources, accounting, financial literacy, and negotiation strategies. The major

---

[4] Phone Interview of Delores Thomas.

writing project for the program is drafting a comprehensive business plan.[5]

In addition to the campus program, the Joseph Business School sponsors an online program, making the curriculum available through the internet. According to Deloris Thomas, a high percentage of the graduates have become successful businesspeople. The Joseph Business School combines the teaching of "biblical principles to business management and entrepreneurship." The business curriculum was "developed by the Joseph Business School in conjunction with the Program for Acquiring Competence and Entrepreneurship, the Center on Education and Training for Employment, and Ohio State University (PACE-CETE/OSU)." The Joseph Business School campus program has received approval from the Illinois Board of Higher Education Division of Private Business and Vocational Schools and accreditation from the Accrediting Council of Continuing Education and Training (ACET), an accrediting agency recognized by the U.S. Department of Education.[6]

The Joseph Center, an affiliate of the Joseph Business School, was founded in 2005 and includes a Small Business Development Center (SBDC); it was "one of the first faith-based SBDC's in the United States." The SBDC receives matching funds from the U.S. Small Business Administration through a partnership between the federal office (Small Business Administration) and the Illinois Department of Commerce and Economic Opportunity; the federal funds are matched by funds raised by the Joseph Center. This program offers the following services: "professional business consulting, business training, workshops, and assistance in obtaining business loans." It offers "individualized, confidential business consultations at no cost" related to patent/new product development, business acquisition, business start-ups, and market analysis and strategies. Workshops cover topics such as intellectual property and government procurement.[7]

Additionally, the Joseph Center hosts an incubator for business start-ups by sponsoring continuing education workshops on "Starting a Business." In these workshops, the students learn about

---

[5] The Joseph Business School brochure 2014.
[6] Phone Interview of Deloris Thomas.
[7] Joseph Center brochure 2014.

patents, business certification, basic accounting, social media use, eCommerce, intellectual property, and business plan components, along with other topics. For a "nominal rental fee," the incubator office provides secretarial support and space for start-up businesses to operate administratively. It "offers a wide array of business support resources including fully-furnished, large and small office spaces, voicemail and mailbox service, furnished workstations and conference rooms fully equipped with internet services, presentation boards, LCD projectors, audio conferencing and more." The Joseph Center offers its business start-up clients "business coaching, as well as assistance." Deloris Thomas states that, at the center, students are introduced to equity or debt funding as well as potential financial partners from the government and the private sphere who are interested in minority- and women-run businesses.[8]

The Joseph Business School also sponsors a vocational program for high school graduates with certificates in information technology, health care services, food services, environmental services, and transportation services. These training programs are co-sponsored by companies or labor unions in order to make the graduates readily employable. The business school's various programs promote the pragmatic approach to teaching the prosperity doctrine with its dual emphasis on human and divine agency in operating within the economic arena.[9]

The Joseph Business School Global Network was formed to introduce this pragmatic approach to prosperity doctrine to Africa as well as other continents. Participates in the Global Network are affiliates of the school and not satellite programs. The Joseph Business School also has an online E-Learning program which is available to students outside of the United States. Through participation in the Global Network, congregations, schools, or colleges can have access to select academic offerings of the Joseph Business School: syllabi, online classes, and webinars.[10]

In 2014, there were 16 affiliates of the Joseph Business School on four continents, including three campuses in Africa. There are two

---

[8] Phone Interview of Deloris Thomas.

[9] Phone Interview of Dr. Eddie Kornegay, Dean of Continuing Education and Professional Development at the Joseph Business School on 22 August 2014 by David D. Daniels.

[10] Phone Interview of Deloris Thomas.

affiliates in South Africa, Durban and Johannesburg, and one affiliate in Uyo, Nigeria. The affiliates use the JBS curriculum, but they recruit and employ their own faculty. Each affiliate is based in a congregation. In Zambia, Swaziland, Ghana, and Zimbabwe, Joseph Business School has sponsored workshops to introduce participants to entrepreneurial training from a biblical perspective. Annual economic summits have been held in South Africa since about 2007.[11]

According to Dr Eddie Kornegay, a Pentecostal ethicist and the Dean of Continuing Education and Professional Development at the Joseph Business School,

> Dr Winston has a huge vision for education. He dedicates resources to it. He has a heart for the community and a concern for youth. He began with a vision for a Bible College. His heart is for those with little or no education. He envisions that JBS creates the model and replicates it throughout the city, the state, the nation, and the globe. He wants to create a hub-and-spoke system.[12]

For Kornegay, prosperity is understood in the context of the Holy Spirit bringing or producing prosperity. The Holy Spirit is seen as bringing the resources for the Christian to use. The task of the graduate of the Joseph Business School is to use these resources to manifest God's kingdom and reflect God's glory. This is a spiritual endeavor. Echoing the mission statement, Kornegay adds that prosperity doctrine "uses practical and biblical principles to empower adults" to be "successful entrepreneurs and business leaders."[13]

With over 450 alumni/ae, the Joseph Business School has interjected a new element into the teaching of the prosperity gospel in North America and in Africa: a focus on skill-building in addition to its message of faith. Some of the alumni of the Joseph Business School testify that they learned how "to use the anointing to reform or elevate one's skills, gifts, and education." They achieve a standard of living that exceed their social circle. They believed through what they learned to brought "from heaven the power of the principle to prosper the work above one's own strength."[14]

---

[11] Phone Interview of Deloris Thomas.
[12] Phone Interview of Eddie Kornegay.
[13] Phone Interview of Eddie Kornegay.
[14] Phone Interview of Eddie Kornegay.

Parallel to the layering for the prosperity gospel with entrepreneurial skill development and business education as developed by Bill Winston and the Joseph Business School is the ministry of Samuel Adeyemi of Daystar Christian Centre and of Success Power International. Danny McCain, in his study of Pentecostalism in Nigeria, recognizes a similar shift in Nigeria within the teaching of the prosperity gospel that resembles the pragmatic emphasis that I have been describing concerning Winston and the Joseph Business School.[15]

McCain quotes Paul Adefarasin to make this point: "In the old days, prosperity was postulated as a miracle of giving and receiving, and it didn't require much responsibility from the individuals. It was a 'bless me' cup." McCain explores similar developments in Daystar Christian Centre, a Lagos congregation pastored by Samuel Adeyemi, where Adeyemi has turned the first of his four Sunday services into a class on entrepreneurship. Additionally, Adeyemi's congregation sponsors Daystar Leadership Academy which offers classes in "financial management, project management, systems development, organizational growth, entrepreneurship, and building an excellence-oriented organization." McCain notes that other ministries in Nigeria have followed the shift.[16]

Located in Lagos, Nigeria, Adeyemi's ministry includes Daystar Leadership Academy which offers a business education program. Adeyemi was inspired by Sunday Adelaja, a Nigerian pastor of a megachurch in the Ukraine, and his History Makers Training. Adeyemi is able to transmit his ideas on radio and television through his broadcast, Success Power. He is the author of *Parable of Dollars*, *Success Is Who You Are*, *Multiply Your Success*, *We are the Government*, and other books.[17]

Adeyemi envisioned that through relevant biblical teaching the church could impact the government, the economy, and local

---

[15] Danny McCain, "The Metamorphosis of Nigerian Pentecostalism: From Signs and Wonders in the Church to Service and Influence in Society," in Donald E. Miller, Kimon H. Sargeant, and Richard Flory (eds.), *Spirit and Power: The Growth and Global Impact of Pentecostalism* (Oxford, UK: Oxford University Press, 2013), pp. 160-81.

[16] McCain, "The Metamorphosis," pp. 166-68.

[17] McCain, "The Metamorphosis," p. 177.

neighborhoods. Adeyemi saw the need for a shift in the preaching of the prosperity gospel. He said:

> Generally, I see that people in the society are getting tired of the so-called prosperity message for a few reasons. One, the idea that everybody will become millionaires after believing that for ten, fifteen, twenty years, some people are getting weary of that. Secondly ... the money [raised] is not even used to improve the infrastructures of the church so that the church members enjoy it, not to talk about not even being used to affect the society. So church members become suspect. So I think that people are getting tired of the over-emphasis on money. At the same time, I see now that there are some of us who want to come through again with the wholesome thing, that it's spiritual prosperity, mental development, and security development ... I think that the balance is now beginning to come in.[18]

Through Daystar Christian Centre, Adeyemi has led efforts that have renovated five public schools in 2001, built science labs and donated science equipment and other supplies to public schools, and donated medical equipment and pharmaceuticals to public hospitals. Danny McCain, professor at the University of Jos in Nigeria, characterizes this shift in the teaching of the prosperity gospel as a shift toward "more stress on human responsibility in acquiring prosperity" biblically. According to Adeyemi, "There is no substitute for hard work in the school of success." Adeyemi further contends: "For a long time, people in church thought that by praying and fasting alone, they could manipulate God into giving them a powerful breakthrough. It does not work that way ... Prayer and fasting are necessary, but they cannot take the place of skill."[19]

With the Daystar Leadership Academy, the courses taught include the following: financial management, entrepreneurship, time

---

[18] Interview of Rev. Samuel Adeyemi on 9 June 2011 by Danny McCain of the University of Jos; the interview is used with permission from Danny McCain which was granted by email on 25 December 2014.

[19] Danny McCain, "From Idahosa to Adeyemi: The Evolving Theology of the Prosperity Gospel in Nigeria" (paper presented at the 42nd Annual Meeting of the Society of Pentecostal Studies, Seattle, WA, on 22 March 2013), pp. 14, 19, 21; quotes from the paper are used with permission granted by Danny McCain on 25 December 2014.

and life management, problem solving, delegation strategies, and organizational growth. In addition, there is a course on the supernatural. On the faculty are instructors with accounting degrees as well as with Master of Business Administration (MBA) degrees. They earned degrees from universities in Nigeria, the Netherlands, and Great Britain.[20]

The pragmatic approach to the prosperity gospel with its shift from consumption to entrepreneurship has interjected new economic behavior on the religious landscape of Black America and Africa. Surveying these prosperity gospel ministries and their impact on the religious landscape in order to ascertain the extensiveness, density, and variety of the economic activity these have generated might be an initial way to chart their presence in the economy.

Educational institutions such as Joseph Business School and the Daystar Leadership Academy sponsored by prosperity gospel ministries reinforce currents in the wider Pentecostal and Charismatic movements in Africa and black America spurred by Business degree programs based at Pentecostal universities and business journals sponsored by these universities. The pragmatic innovation in the teaching of the prosperity gospel by megachurch and televangelists such as Bill Winston and Samuel Adeyemi illustrate the ways that African Americans and African Christians are contextualizing the prosperity gospel as well as impacting the economic sectors of their respective economies through their different pragmatic prosperity gospel of entrepreneurship.

Pentecostal Economic Ministry Confronting the Economy
While the Pentecostal economic ministries of Joseph Business School and Daystar seek to work within the economic system of capitalism, the economic ministry of Rev. Herbert Daughtry works to reform the economy in the short term and transform it in the long term. Daughtry, the presiding bishop of the House of the Lord Church, an African American Pentecostal denomination, in his clarion call at a 1981 national protest rally in Washington, D.C, exclaimed: "Let us struggle until the social order has been transformed into democratic and economic fairness."[21]

---

[20] www.dlaonline.org.
[21] Herbert Daughtry, *Seize the Future: Two Speeches by Rev. Herbert Daughtry* (Brooklyn, NY: National Black United Front, 1981), p. 24.

To reorient the economy toward economic fairness and justice, Daughtry famously led marches on Wall Street in New York City, the financial epicenter of the United States, in 1978. The march originated in downtown Brooklyn, crossed the Brooklyn Bridge over into Manhattan, and ended with a protest rally on Wall Street. With almost 1,000 marches, he captured the attention of the financial district and the city. In his speech at the beginning of the march, Daughtry surmised: "Somebody's making an awful lot of money from the way we live, and some of those who are making the most money is located where we are going now." He argued that the financial sector needs to be held accountable and reforms need to be made to the economy. Among the issues impacting the black neighborhoods the 1978 March on Wall Street that he addressed were poverty, unemployment, ghettos, and capitalism.[22][23] The year prior, in 1977, Daughtry was a key leader in the Coalition of Concerned Leaders and Citizens to Save Our Jobs. That year he led a "three-month boycott" against the businesses of Fulton Street, a major commercial section within a black community in Brooklyn. To end the boycott, the merchants and United Way agreed to "contribute to a scholarship and community fund." In response to a 1979 economic protest demonstration on Fulton Street, Daughtry negotiated with key merchants around securing "5,000 part-time summer jobs for minority youth."

By 2005, Daughtry had over twenty-five years of Pentecostal activism related to economic justice. With this social capital, he and other leaders in 2005 were instrumental in securing the first community benefits agreement in New York City: Brooklyn's Atlantic Yards Community Benefits Agreement. While elements of the agreement related to mixed-income housing awaits to be developed, over $300,000 dollars has been "awarded to sixty-eight Brooklyn-based community organizations" since 2005 through a community foundation headed by Daughtry. This foundation supports "not-for-profit organizations which actively foster economic self-sufficiency

[22] Quoted in Anna Quindlen, "Blacks Mourning the Death of Miller March to Wall Street in a Protest," *New York Times* (November 7, 1978), p. 49.
[23] Mark Liebermann, "Warn of New Fulton Street Boycott," *Daily News* (NY, NY), June 20, 1979, p. 576; Bob Kappstatter, "Busmen & Daughtry," *Daily News* (NY, NY), June 25, 1979, p. 341.

through workforce development and business skills training"[24] along with other projects.

In his 1979 publication, *Seize the Future*, Daughtry expressed his Pentecostal theology of economics. He stated that the "ultimate goal" was to "radically rearrange the present institutions of the American society." By specifically targeting the economy, he sought to end "exploitative capitalism" and "monopoly capitalism" which in tandem with institutional racism left many African Americans underemployed and unemployed. In 1979, he cited that "Black men are out of work to the tune of 40%, teenagers 70-80%.... [T]he meager gains of yesterday are stamped out ... [because] the American government allows itself to be the tool of monopoly capitalism." In 2011, Daughtry concluded that "[n]ot much has changed over the past 33 years. People – black people, in particular, are still confronted with unemployment" and poverty within an exploitative capitalistic economy tied to institutional racism.[25]

Pivotal to Daughtry's theology is that the economy was based on products from the earth, ranging from agriculture to fishing and fowl to minerals and other natural resources. Since the earth belonged to God in the words of the Psalmist, his theology identifies as a goal: making "the resources of God's earth available to all people equitably." Daughtry's theological perspective echoes Augustine. M. Douglas Meeks in following Richard McKeon argues that for Augustine "God is the lord and owner of the world. God's grants the right to use God's property to the righteous, providing they render fealty to God." This reflects Daughtry's perspective, too.[26]

To reallocate "the resources of God's earth," Daughtry identified a number of strategies initially to reform and ultimately to transform the economy: economic and social protest, boycott, economic

---

[24] Atlantic Yards/NETS/DBNA Community Foundation website. https:// www.thedbna.org/atlantic-yardsnetsdbna-community-foundation-grant.

[25] Daughtry, *Seize the Future*, p. 2; "33 Years Later: 1978 March on Wall Street Re-visited," Amsterdam News (NY, NY), November 2, 2011. http://amsterdamnews.com/news/2011/nov/07/33-years-later-1978-march-on-wall-street-re/.

[26] Daughtry, *Seize the Future*, p. 2; M. Douglas Meeks, *God the Economist: The Doctrine of God and Political Economy* (Minneapolis: Fortress Press, 1989), p. 209, endnote 56.

initiatives, and the control of key unions. Committed to incremental change, he joined other economic justice advocates in mobilizing people to participate in economic and social protest. Economic and social protest included economic boycotts, street marches, public rallies, and civil disobedience. He employed these forms of protest in order to secure better economic relationships and outcomes. He was clear that, while economic protest "can prevent government from functioning, businesses from operating and literally bottle up the city," it was often the only way to produce change in the economy.[27]

Daughtry also supported developing business cooperatives to model a collaborative versus competitive way to distribute and sell products. Cooperatives turn workers into entrepreneurs. They place black people on the producer side of the economic equation and not just on the consumer or labor side. While the wealth generated by cooperatives is communal, it is still wealth-generation emerging from the black community. Herein more dollars stay in the black community: sales and profits.[28]

Daughtry joined others in striving to "gain control" of "predominately black" unions with white leadership in New York City in order for these unions to work less toward the self-interest of union members and more towards economic justice; these unions could join in the lobbying of politicians for more just economic policies as well as negotiate with different industries and government employers to better economic opportunities for workers.[29]

Through these economic strategies and a vision of economic justice, Daughtry worked to destroy the alliance between "capitalism and racism." Racism and economics produced a form of American capitalism that disproportionately benefited whites and marginalized blacks through the racial segregation of the economy, actually excluding blacks from certain sectors such as the managerial and executive positions in major industries up until the 1970s or even later. According to Daughtry, the economy left unguided relegated African American and other populations to poverty.[30]

---

[27] Daughtry, *Seize the Future*, pp. 6-10.
[28] Daughtry, *Seize the Future*, p. 7.
[29] Daughtry, *Seize the Future*, p. 9.
[30] Daughtry, *Seize the Future*, p. 14.

In his reading of the Bible, Christians are called to reform and transform the economy toward economic justice. Rather than focusing on alleviating poverty, economic democracy addresses the structural causes of economic inequality and elements of economic justice. Daughtry advocated a restructuring of the economy to advance economic justice and promote flourishing economy.

In building upon Daughtry's critique of capitalism, the Holy Spirit might be nudging the economy away from ruthless economic competition embodied in the economic "survival of the fittest" or the survival of the cleverest with its winners and losers towards economic collaboration informed by the Pentecost community where they held "all things common" and shared with everyone according to "need" in Acts 2.44-45 (KJV) as "they continued steadfastly in the apostles" doctrine and fellowship, and in the breaking of bread, and in prayers as highlighted in Acts 2.42 (KJV).

Four Theological Approaches to the Economy

These two types of Pentecostal economic ministries fit within four theological approaches to the economy identified by M. Douglas Meeks, an American theologian. The first view contends that the free market possesses the capacity to nurture Christian values. According to this theological perspective, "Christianity is primarily a source of individual virtues" of trust, honesty, integrity, liberty, and reason. The free market creates a context for the Christian virtues to be cultivated. From this perspective, while Christian faith has nothing to offer concerning the "operation of the market," the free, self-interested use of private property produces an economy where most people benefit from these exchanges when the individual virtues thrive." The Holy Spirit fashions virtuous individuals to operate in the economy in beneficial ways. While Winston and Ademeyi would agree this perspective, they resonate as much or, possibly, more with the second option.[31]

---

[31] M. Douglas Meeks, "Economy and Christianity: Ethics and Christian Theology" and "Economy and Christianity: Economic Studies of Christianity," in Daniel Patte (ed.), *The Cambridge Dictionary of Christianity* (Cambridge: Cambridge University Press, 2010), pp. 346-347; note Meeks list three options and I add a fourth option from his discussion on page p. 347.

The second view uses economic theories to interpret the Bible and the Christian Faith. The principles of investment explain the "law of sowing and reaping;" the parable of the talents; private property; and the division of labor between occupations of workers (farmers, fishermen, and shepherds), merchants, priests, and rulers. From this theological perspective, Jesus' teachings clearly "exemplify market rules and the human inclination to accumulate." Economic principles resonate with the biblical tradition. The Holy Spirit, then, teaches Christians through Scripture how God has structured the economy actually to work. Winston and Ademeyi offer this theological perspective in their respective ministries.[32]

The third view, which Meeks labels the "mainstream approach," spotlights the strengths and limits to the free market economy. Limits must be set on the economy for ethical reasons and the common good. This view recognizes the need in the society for sources of "value creation" to arise from spheres in the society outside of the economy such as religion; economic frameworks must not be the only creators of values in the society. Religion fosters values which are priceless, ranging from compassion, care for the poor, empathy to hospitality. In resisting life being reduced to economics and totally explained by economics, the Holy Spirit nurtures sources of "value creation" beyond the economy. Daughtry's perspective resonates with this third view; yet, he seeks clear reforms and, ultimately, a new economy.[33]

In seeking to eradicate poverty and support sustainable development, the fourth view identifies the economic framework as insufficient in and of itself to realize the common good; alternative frameworks such as Christian ones must guide the economy. Some theologians would propose biblical "forms of economy" that operate according to biblical economic logic. For example, the Exodus story could be interpreted as God undermining Pharaoh's economy of scarcity and erecting an economy of abundance depicted as a "land of milk and honey." Also, the Pentecost community in Acts can be interpreted as the Christian displacement of the economy of

---

[32] Meeks, "Economy and Christianity: Economics," p. 347.
[33] Meeks, "Economy and Christianity: Ethics," p. 346-347.

personal possessions to an economy of "common possessions" marked by voluntary downward mobility, reciprocity, and generosity.[34]

From this theological perspective, economic justice based on the biblical economy rather than profit-motive should drive the economy. In the third and fourth options, "[g]rowth should not be based on infinite needs and acquisition leading to an ever-widening appropriation of nature for the sake of accumulation of wealth as power. Rather growth should be a deepening of human capacities for the service of human development within community" in Meeks's words.[35]

Additionally, in the fourth perspective alone, though, property can be framed in two ways as Aquinas stated: "own in common, use privately for the common good." Or as Aquinas preferred: "own privately, use in common." According to M. Douglas Meeks, Aquinas proposed a doctrine-regulated economy marked by fair pricing, just wages, a concept of approximate of consumption, and safe places for the exchange of goods and services. In this fourth option, the goal was to "hold all things in such a way that they may be common for all" which, according to Meeks, is what Aquinas desired.[36]

The Holy Spirit, therefore, according to the fourth view, operates in two manners. As in the Exodus narrative, the Holy Spirit is active and interventionist, undermines the economy of scarcity tied to Egypt and erecting the economy of abundance in the wilderness. In the Pentecost narrative, the Holy Spirit empowers the people joyfully to live in the economy of sharing. The fourth position captures the thrust of Daughtry's transformed economy. Unwilling to "sanctify" capitalism as economic system, he works to orient the economy toward economic justice.

Toward a Pentecostal Theology of the Holy Spirit and Economic Justice

Frederick Kakwata offers a direction to frame a Pentecostal theology of the Holy Spirit and economic justice. To him, the Holy Spirit's role

---

[34] Meeks, "Economy and Christianity: Ethics," p. 347.
[35] Meeks, *God the Economist*, p. 57.
[36] Meeks, *God the Economist*, p. 209, endnote 56.

is being transformative by enlightening, guiding, and empowering people and communities. By transforming lives and communities, including congregations, the Spirit transforms living souls and economic structures. In transforming lives, people change from being self-centered to God-centered and other-oriented. In transforming the economy, the economy shifts from being profit-driven to being value-driven, especially valuing people over profits.[37]

The role of the Holy Spirit in the economy can be interpreted as transformative in terms of freeing people from poverty and empowering them to live the "more abundant life" as a community. The Spirit also restores people, races, and communities from broken and/or oppressive relationships, reconciling them back to God and each other. Christian values, attitudes, and desires are additionally cultivated by the Spirit. All of these transformative events occur within a space graced by the Holy Spirit that makes shalom central to the new economy and community. Being holistic, transformation entails the "change in the whole of the person, material, social and spiritual as well as in the community, economics, social, and political."[38]

The Holy Spirit is key to illuminating the moral dimension of the economic. From a Pentecostal theology of the Holy Spirit and economic justice, the moral dimension to the economy must be engaged. A just economy is marked by just wages and just prices; this is an ethical issue. Rather than paying workers the lowest permissible wage, they should be paid a living wage; a wage that allows them to live with dignity and well-being. Rather than selling goods and services to the highest bidder, prices should be related to the actual cost of production; the profit margin should be in proportion to the cost of production.

The moral dimension of the economy factors in a calculation of the multiple dimensions within cost-benefit analyses. Financial,

---

[37] Definition from R.D. Winter *et al. Perspectives on the World Christian Movement. A reader* (Pasadena, CA: William Carey Library, 3rd ed., 1999) in Frederick Kakwata, "A Pneumatological Approach to Transformational Development: Implication for the Church," *Stellenbosch Theological Journal* 4.1 (2018), p. 199. https://www.semanticscholar.org/paper/A-pneumatological-approach-to-transformational-for-Kakwata/83faf5509064968eb865233f7989983 fo4aeefe5.

[38] Kakwata, "A Pneumatological Approach," p. 202.

social, cultural, political, ecological, emotional, and spiritual costs of goods and services must be assessed over against each of their benefits. A financial cost-benefit analysis alone is morally insufficient to determine the best economic policy or strategy. Clearly, a cost and benefits of these multiple dimensions are needed to make economic decisions in a holistic manner. From a theological perspective, the spiritual must be on par with the other dimensions.

Consumption and materialism are moral issues. Among Pentecostals, there is a vigorous debate about patterns of consumption and materialism biblically allowed to Christians. Some support over-consumption and crass materialism; conspicuous consumption are emblems of divine favor and blessings. Other required "ethics of frugality" and value simplicity of life; they are counter conspicuous consumption with what Ruth Marshall calls "a doctrine of morally-controlled materialism." With voluntary downward mobility as biblical mandate, Christians must learn to live on less in order to give more to the poor and others as well as the church. Yet, others, while affirming the "ethics of frugality," chose to turn "[t]he aspirations for health, happiness, decent housing, and running successful businesses" into collective ventures rather than individualistic projects. They seek communal solutions to their economic challenge rather than isolated individual ones. Their quest for communal solutions explores to empower congregations, communities, families, and individuals.[39]

While non-Pentecostal and even Christian communities might offer alternatives to the market logic of capitalism, how should a Pentecostal theology of the Holy Spirit and economic justice frame the chief obstacle to the "more abundant life." Since, according to Pentecostal theology, sin is the condition in which humans live, sin as constitutive to the human condition is probably the chief obstacle.

---

[39] Kate Meagher, "Trading on Faith: Religious Movements and Informal Economic Governance in Nigeria," *The Journal of Modern African Studies* 47.3 (Sep., 2009), p. 402; https://core.ac.uk/download/pdf/214287.pdf and Josiah Taru, "Pentecostal Charismatic Christianity and the Management of Precarity in Post-Colonial Zimbabwe," *Religion & Development* (February 2018), p. 14, https://www.rcsd.hu-berlin.de/de/publikationen/pdf-dateien/discussion-paper-2018-02_pentecostal_churches_zimbabwe.pdf/at_download/file.

What, then, is the expression of sin in the economy? Is it poverty since poverty is what seems to inhibit economic justice? From the perspective of some Pentecostals, we must confront poverty with God's word. To others like Daughtry, poverty must be addressed by reforming the economy and not merely dispensing charity; consequently, in this case, sin is social. According to even other Pentecostals, the expression of sin is self-interest, greed, or pride? From this perspective, sanctification or the cultivation of virtues would address vices as the expression of sin. By private poverty, the free market, and the banking system all seeking to maximize profit and minimize cost, they further breed self-interest, greed, and pride. The Holy Spirit's role in this case is to counter the market's breeding of these vices.[40]

Could the absence of social trust be an expression of sin in the economy? We trust in the grace of God and we learn to trust each other. According to the Harvard University scholar Robert Putnam, there was a strong correlation between high degrees of "social trust and cooperation" and economic prosperity. In other words, social trust is more key to a well-running economy than economic policy.[41]

Could lack of faith in God and the Bible be an expression of sin in the economy? This sounds quite farfetched. According to Harvard University economists Robert Barro and Rachel McCleary, "increases in some religious beliefs - notably in hell, heaven, and an after-life -tend to increase economic growth. There is also some indication that the stick represented by the fear of hell is more potent for growth than the carrot from the prospect of hell."[42]

If Barro and McCleary are correct, a Pentecostal theology of the Holy Spirit and economic justice can incorporate Pentecostal beliefs along with its related economic logic, and communal practices. As a haven in the midst of the economy, certain Pentecostal communities and their economic ministries become beacons of hope and communities of grace. A Pentecostal economic logic of the love of neighbor, generosity, and God's justice fashions a different kind of people

---

[40] Robert H. Nelson, "What Is 'Economic Theology'?," *The Princeton Seminary Bulletin* 25.1, 2004, p. 61.

[41] Nelson, "Economic Theology," p. 75.

[42] Nelson, "Economic Theology," p. 76, n 32; also see Rachel McCleary and Robert Barro, *Wealth of Religions: The Political Economy of Believing and Belonging* (Princeton: Princeton University Press, 2019).

and communities; it fashions a gospel-shaped people and community marked by love, care, compassion, support, forgiveness, restitution, and reconciliation. With this anchorage, these Pentecostal communities could be understood in the words Dr James Forbes, an African American practical theologian, as being attuned to the Holy Spirit "moving in the shadows of sacred places and the structures of secular institutions." As a generative and transformative presence, the Holy Spirit in this case moves and interacts outside and inside the boundaries of the economic structures.[43]

How is it that these Pentecostal communities supported by economic ministries exceed the sociological expectations and life outcomes of their locations? Especially, those in impoverished community, how are they not restrained by the sociological forces that predict their neighbors' plight. Additionally, how are these Pentecostals and their ministries not co-opted by the logic of the market economy? How are they able to operate according to a gospel set of logic, values, and practices?

Maybe a theological engagement of the sociologist insight of Donald Miller and Tetsunao Yamamori provide speculations to how these economic ministries operate. Miller and Tetsunao register how in their encountering of Pentecostalism globally that they found Pentecostal explanations and testimonies as a believable, convincing, and credible witness to a world that sociological theories failed to explain. To address this gap in sociological theory, Miller and Yamamori invented the concept "S Factor" to name what Pentecostals call the Holy Spirit. For them, the "S Factor" is a dimension beyond sociological factors that impact lives and communities.[44]

To paraphrase George Marsden's theological distinction in *The Outrageous Idea of Christian Scholarship*, we should theologically distinguish between the belief *that* the Holy Spirit acts in the economy and our actual ability to identify precisely *how* the Spirit operates in the economy. If God chose to be an economic actor, would we

[43] James A. Forbes, "Shall We Call This Dream Progressive Pentecostalism," *Spirit: A Journal of Issues Incidental to Black Pentecostalism* 1.1 (1977), p. 15.
[44] Donald Miller and Tetsunao Yamamori, *Global Pentecostalism: The New Face of Christian Social Engagement* (Berkeley: University of California Press, 2007), pp. 220-21.

theologically best register divine activity. Since we cannot precisely identify *how* the work of the Spirit operates within the economy, possibly we should frame our theological exploration in terms of divine absence rather than divine presence. Avoiding the binary of presence and absence, divine absence can be a form of divine activity, referring to spaces and moments where traces of divine activity remain. It could refer to the traces of the divine activity marking in the spaces and moments graced by God, signally the qualitative difference God makes by gracing a place, space, or moment. These traces with their lingering effects resemble the lingering scent of smoke after a fire, the fragrance of flowers, and the aroma of herbs; and, even, the trail of footprints after footfalls linger. In this case, the divine absence in terms of the traces of divine activity indicate spaces and moments which Christians and others negotiate. These grace-filled spaces exceed the possibilities historically present in a moment; rather than being limited by the possibilities of the historical moment, Christian communities operate beyond the sociologically defined historical possibilities.[45]

The economy becomes a vibrant arena where the Holy Spirit operates. The Holy Spirit "blows" through the economy as the Holy Spirit wishes in ways that are surreptitious, assertive, disruptive, subversive, reformative, redemptive, and/or transformative. A Pentecostal theology of the Holy Spirit and economic justice broadcasts an active God, even an interventionist God, who is recognized by the traces of divine activity. It witnesses to the God of the universe and beyond, a God who acts in history, including the economic sphere since no realm is beyond God's activity. According to a Pentecostal theology of the Holy Spirit and economic justice, as sites with traces of the divine activity, Pentecostal communities and their related economic ministries remain faithful to the gospel, empower people to live life in a more abundant way, and advance towards God's reign and justice, serving as grace-filled havens anticipating the transformed economy.

---

[45] George M. Marsden, *The Outrageous Idea of Christian Scholarship* (New York and Oxford: Oxford University Press, 1997), p. 95.

Conclusion

In this chapter, I have argued that Pentecostal economic ministries engage the economy in a variety of ways. While the first type of Winston and Adeyemi accepts the economy on its own terms, it challenges the way that the economy excludes and marginalizes the populations often attracted to Pentecostalism. Thus, the first type addresses economic exclusion by education, resourcing, and spirituality. It straightforwardly challenges the idea of the market logic of "unfettered" self-interest by introducing biblical virtues of generosity and debating "unrestrained" consumption with ethics of frugality.

The second type clearly challenges the way the free market economy works. It works to reform and, even, transform the economy towards economic justice. This type seeks a "guided" economy. More than expanding participation, this type works toward an economy with morals; it seeks for justice to be central to how the economy functions. The market logic of the economy is modified or even replaced with a biblical economic logic.

Both types that were discussed sought to expand economic participation of those often excluded from or marginalized by the economy. Since the expansion of participation within the economy of the formerly excluded can be deemed an issue of economic justice, both types are fighting against poverty and working for economic justice with different strategies. The theological approaches to the economy that Meeks developed offer insight in the different ways that these two types of economic ministries engage the economy beyond expanding participation.

Since Pentecostals believe that the Holy Spirit can operate in all spheres of life, the chapter explored the challenge of theologically framing how the Holy Spirit might operate within the economy as an economic actor. The discussion of divine activity in terms of tracing the lingering effect of divine absence offered a way to frame this theological conversation. As noted above the theological exploration of divine activity in terms of divine absence interprets divine absence in a manner that it is not simply the opposite of divine presence.

Theologically, the activity of the Holy Spirit impacts the economy as the Spirit operates in spheres that impinge on the economy such a value creation, inspiring biblical forms of economy, advancing the common good, and operating in way that Miller and Yamamori categorized as the "S Factor." According to this chapter, theologically, the activity of the Holy Spirit engages the economy in surreptitious, assertive, interventionist, disruptive, subversive, reformative, redemptive, and transformative ways.

Bibliography

Daughtry, Herbert, *Seize the Future: Two Speeches by Rev. Herbert Daughtry* (Brooklyn, NY: National Black United Front, 1981).

Forbes, James A., "Shall We Call This Dream Progressive Pentecostalism," *Spirit: A Journal of Issues Incidental to Black Pentecostalism* 1.1 (1977), pp. 12-14.

Kappstatter, Bob, "Busmen & Daughtry," *Daily News* (New York, NY; June 25, 1979), p. 341.

Liebermann, Mark, "Warn of New Fulton Street Boycott," *Daily News* (New York, NY; June 20, 1979), p. 576.

Marsden, George M., *The Outrageous Idea of Christian Scholarship* (New York and Oxford: Oxford University Press, 1997).

McCleary, Rachel and Robert Barro, *Wealth of Religions: The Political Economy of Believing and Belonging* (Princeton: Princeton University Press, 2019).

Meeks, M. Douglas, "Economy and Christianity: Ethics and Christian Theology" and "Economy and Christianity: Economic Studies of Christianity," in Daniel Patte (ed.), *The Cambridge Dictionary of Christianity* (Cambridge: Cambridge University Press, 2010).

Miller, Donald, and Tetsunao Yamamori, *Global Pentecostalism: The New Face of Christian Social Engagement* (Berkeley: University of California Press, 2007).

Miller, Donald E., Kimon H. Sargeant, and Richard Flory (eds.), *Spirit and Power: The Growth and Global Impact of Pentecostalism* (Oxford, UK: Oxford University Press, 2013).

Nelson, Robert H., "What Is 'Economic Theology'?," *The Princeton Seminary Bulletin* 25.1 (2004), pp. 61-76.

Quindlen, Anna, "Blacks Mourning the Death of Miller March to Wall Street in a Protest," *New York Times* (November 7, 1978), p. 49.

CHAPTER THREE

THE PROSPERITY GOSPEL AND THE OPTION FOR THE POOR

John Mark Robeck*

In May of 1985, an assembly of Pentecostal leaders from the Church of God (Cleveland, Tennessee) was held in St. Just, Puerto Rico. The meeting focused on "developing a Pentecostal pastoral model in the face of the Theology of Liberation."[1] There were at least three key points of emphasis. First and foremost, Pentecostals wanted to understand the teachings of the Theology of Liberation. Papers were presented such as *The Theology of Liberation: Objective Approach*, *The Theology of Liberation: Critical Approach* and *The Impact of the Theology of Liberation in the Base Communities in Latin America.*[2]

---

* John Mark Robeck (PhD, Claremont Graduate University) serves as Assistant Professor of Theology, Ethics, and Culture with specialization in the history of Pentecostalism in Latin America, and Latin American theologies at Vanguard University in Costa Mesa, California.

[1] Plutarco Bonilla A., "Presentación," *Pastoralia: Revista del Centro Evangélico Latinoamericano de Estudios Pastorales* 7.15 (diciembre, 1985), p. 7.

[2] These papers were later edited and published in the following journal belonging to the Latin American Evangelical Center for Pastoral Studies. *Pastoralia: Revista del Centro Evangélico Latinoamericano de Estudios Pastorales* 7.15 (diciembre, 1985).

The presentations shed light on the "new way to do theology,"[3] and its impact within the Base Ecclesial Communities.

Secondly, the assembly critically evaluated the Theology of Liberation. Ricardo Waldrop, author of *The Theology of Liberation*, warned the following, which is also relevant today.

> History shows that within every ecclesiastical movement there have been extremes that are not very healthy. Let's not forget that the Theology of Liberation represents a young movement. Nor should we forget that our own Pentecostal movement has suffered, and continues to suffer in some places, from fanaticism and extreme emphasis on the "most striking spiritual gifts" such as tongues, prophecies and miracles. We must measure others with the same yardstick with which we want to be measured and punished. We must go one step further, which would be to use our own analysis of the Theology of Liberation to correct our lack of commitment to a suffering continent that is hungry for peace and justice.[4]

In this chapter, I aim to strike a balance between observation and critique, honoring a movement that has sometimes leaned toward extremes.

A third purpose of the meeting was to consider the development of a new Pentecostal pastoral model in light of the Theology of Liberation (that is, to act). Something significant that came out of this meeting can be found in the following statement.

> We have to discard the idea that the proclamation of the gospel is only a matter of the proclamation of personal deliverance from sin. We need to be aware that we are "the guardian of our brother" throughout the world. The covenant of God is a "universal covenant" with all humanity and that is why we need to be in contact with the pains, sorrows and struggles of the people of God throughout the world ... Therefore, we cannot remain impartial.

---

[3] Gustavo Gutiérrez, *A Theology of Liberation: History, Politics, and Salvation,* (trans. Sister Caridad Inda and John Eagleson; Maryknoll, NY: Orbis Books, 1988), p. 11.

[4] Ricardo Waldrop, "*La Teología de la Liberación: Enfoque Critico,*" *Pastoralia: Revista del Centro Evangélico Latinoamericano de Estudios Pastorales* 7.15 (diciembre, 1985), p. 41.

We have been called to take the side of the oppressed, the sick, the homeless, the poor, the marginalized, that is, the side where Jesus is.[5]

Although the statement seems common today, it was quite radical at the time the above quote was written. Although since Pentecostalism's arrival in Central America shortly after the turn of the 20th century with a primary emphasis on the proclamation of the Gospel, and personal salvation,[6] the group in Puerto Rico was not alone in their thinking. Other Pentecostal gatherings in Salvador, Bahia, Brazil in 1988, concluded that "fulfilling their mission, the Pentecostal churches cannot fail to try to contribute to resolving the serious crisis through which our people are living in Latin America at the present time."[7] This apparent acceptance of an "option for the poor" highlights an important shift in the thinking of at least some Pentecostals, many of whom were poor themselves.

The notion that Pentecostalism arose "from the cultural, ecclesiological, and theological margins of American life"[8] has been well documented. Some have even argued that this emergence from the margins has served the movement well as evidenced by the following claim made in 1991, that while "the Catholic Church has made a preferential option for the poor, 'the poor seem to be making a preferential option for the Pentecostal sects [seitas]."[9] While this may be

---

[5] Aida Gaerán, "Teología de la liberación: Perspectiva de una Mujer Pentecostal," *Pastoralia: Revista del Centro Evangélico Latinoamericano de Estudios Pastorales* 7.15 (diciembre, 1985), pp. 90-91.

[6] See Douglas Petersen, *Not by Might Nor by Power: A Pentecostal Theology of Social Concern in Latin America* (Irvine, CA: Regnum Books International, 1996), pp. 24–25. Also see Daniel Ramirez, "Pentecostalism in Latin America," in Cecil M. Robeck, Jr and Amos Yong (eds.), *The Cambridge Companion to Pentecostalism* (New York: Cambridge University Press, 2014), p. 115.

[7] Gathering of Latin American Pentecostals, "Summary Report" (Salvador, Bahia, Brazil, 6-9 January 1998), p. 3.

[8] Zachary Tackett, "As a Prophetic Voice: Liberationism as a Matrix for Interpreting American Pentecostal thought and Praxis," *The Journal of the European Pentecostal Theological Association* 33.1 (2013), p. 42.

[9] Manuel A. Vasquez, *The Brazilian Popular Church and the Crisis of Modernity* (Cambridge; New York; Melbourne: Cambridge University Press, 1998), p. 73. Vasquez references the following when making this

true to a point, I side with Richard Mouw, former President of Fuller Theological Seminary, when he states that "I don't like the way that it is used to pit spiritual vitality against political-economic activism. It seems to pose a false choice between social activism and a vibrant spiritual life."[10] If we are to take the fullness of the life and work of the Spirit seriously, there must be room for both social activism and vibrant spirituality within the Spirit-filled Christian life.

The 1985 meeting in Puerto Rico, and it's conclusion that Pentecostal Pastors ought to side with the poor, oppressed, and disenfranchised of the world, also brought to light the fact that when considering the Theology of Liberation, and the preferential option for the poor, it "would be more accurate to use the phrase 'liberation theologies', because it is not a theology, but a family of theologies."[11] This brings up an important point when considering the Pentecostal Churches in Central America as a challenge for the Roman Catholic Church. The tendency to treat the movement as a single entity must be avoided.[12]

We need to approach the study of Prosperity Gospel within the Pentecostal and Charismatic movements in much the same way. It is essential that we recognize the diversity of the movements, the distinctions in socio-cultural contexts, the complexity of language, and the varied emphases on specific gifts and activities of the Holy Spirit, which sometimes give way to bizarre behaviors.

Pentecostal Transformations

The decade of the 1980's marks an important transitional period in the life of the Pentecostal Movement in Central America, and specifically in Guatemala. Although various Pentecostal

---

claim. Bishop Luciano Mendes de Almeida, interviewed by Renato Machado, April 17, 1991, Television program, "Noite e Dia."

[10] Richard Mouw, "Richard J. Mouw: Pentecostalism, Liberation Theology and Biblical Leadership." *Faith and Leadership*. Accessed November 03, 2016. https://www.faithandleadership.com/richard-j-mouw-pentecostalism-liberation-theology-and-biblical-leadership.

[11] Waldrop, "La Teología de la Liberación: Enfoque Critico," p. 31.

[12] Cecil M. Robeck Jr highlights several interesting distinctions found among Pentecostals in a brief article titled "Global and Local." *The Christian Century* 123.5 (Mar 7, 2006), p. 34.

denominations began to work in Guatemala as early as 1916,[13] the movement didn't really take off until much later. Pentecostal scholar Everett Wilson provides us with survey data that indicates the growth of the Pentecostal Movement according to the following figures.[14] In 1937 Classical Pentecostals numbered around 4,000, equaling 12% of the total Evangelical population. By 1956, the numbers had grown to 12,000 members, or 30% of the Evangelical population. By 1961, 15,000, or 32%, and by 1969, 22,000, or 30%. This reduction in percentage is presumably connected to the introduction of figures related to the arrival of Charismatics, who in 1969, numbered 3,000, or about 5% of the Evangelical movement. The addition of new statistics did not, however, limit the exponential growth of Classical Pentecostals or Charismatics in the years to come, during which they grew side by side. By 1982, Classical Pentecostals numbered 140,000 or about 42% of Evangelicals, and Charismatics numbered 76,000 or about 23% of Evangelicals. Wilson's final statistics in 1993 demonstrate the tremendous growth of both Classical Pentecostals and Charismatics with counts of 420,000, or 50%, and 150,000 or 18% respectively.[15] Among the Charismatic congregations listed in Wilson's research, Elim Christian Mission, El Calvario, Verbo, Bethany, Word in Action, El Shadai, and Christian Fraternity, some would now be considered "Prosperity" congregations.

This growth came at the same time as the Pentecostal movement began to try and make sense of its place within the socio-political landscape. Some scholars suggest that Pentecostals tend to remove themselves from society and create communities of their own so as to escape the rest of the world and were ultimately labeled as

---

[13] Everett Wilson, "Guatemalan Pentecostals: Something of Their Own," in Edward L. Cleary and Hannah W. Stewart-Gambino (eds.), *Power, Politics, and Pentecostals in Latin America* (Boulder, Colorado: Westview Press, 1997), pp. 139-62.

[14] It is important to clarify the use of specific vocabulary used by Everett Wilson. At the time of his writing it was not uncommon to indicate Classical Pentecostal by the use "Popular Pentecostal," I have opted to use the modern designation of Classical Pentecostal in this paper. It was also not uncommon to indicate Charismatic by the use of "Neo-Pentecostal," I have opted to use the modern designation of Charismatic in this study.

[15] Wilson, "Guatemalan Pentecostals," p. 152.

retreatist and other worldly.[16] Other's began to recognize the potential of the movement to affect social change. Luther P. Gerlach contends that "[w]e have examined Pentecostalism as an example of a religious movement which, in spite of conventional interpretations of its seemingly bizarre features, is in fact a movement for change, not a collection of sects, an opiate, or an anchor for tradition."[17] Can it be that both of these assumptions hold some truth? Will change come as a result of the collective option for the poor, or might it come as a result of individual faith claims associated with the prosperity gospel? In order to make sense of this, we must look at the history of the prosperity movement.

Prosperity

The prosperity gospel is not new, as evidenced by the work of Kate Bowler, Katherine Attanasi, Amos Yong, and Timothy Wadkins among others.[18] Its roots go all the way back to the 19th century and a pastor and radio evangelist by the name of E. W. Kenyon (1867-1948). Kenyon was groomed by his time spent both in Methodist and Baptist congregations, eventually becoming a Baptist minister around 1890.[19] Simultaneously, Kenyon was shaped by his time at the Emerson College of Oratory in Boston, which, according to Kate Bowler, was home to "the New England sage Ralph Waldo Trine and

---

[16] Christian Lalive D"Epinay, *Haven of the Masses: A Study of the Pentecostal Movement in Chile* (London: Lutterworth Press, 1969). Petersen, Douglas, *Not by Might Nor by Power: A Pentecostal Theology of Social Concern in Latin America* (Irvine, CA: Regnum, 1996).

[17] Luther P. Gerlach, "Pentecostalism: Revolution or Counter Revolution?," in Iwing I. Zaresky and Mark P. Leone (eds.), *Religious Movements in Contemporary America* (Princeton, NJ: Princeton University Press, 1974), p. 681.

[18] Kate Bowler, *Blessed: A History of the American Prosperity Gospel* (New York: Oxford University Press, 2013). Katherine Attanasi and Amos Yong, *Pentecostalism and Prosperity: The Socio-Economics of the Global Charismatic Movement* (New York, New York: Palgrave Macmillan, 2012). Timothy H. Wadkins, *The Rise of Pentecostalism in Modern El Salvador: From the Blood of the Martyrs to the Baptism of the Spirit* (Waco, Texas: Baylor University Press, 2017).

[19] Ron MacTavish. Unpublished Master's Thesis entitled "Pentecostal Profits: The Prosperity Gospel in the Global South," 2014, p. 20.

other metaphysical teachers...[which] certainly brought him into contact with the new age movement."[20] Due to such a diversity in experience and education, Kenyon presumably began to formulate his own theology, incorporating components of each of these influences.

Bowler provides us with a clear picture of Kenyon's developed theology when she writes that, "Kenyon appropriated New Thought's focus on mind, spirit, and universal laws to show that Christians could look to the cross not as a promise of things to come, but as a guarantee of benefits *already* granted."[21] All one needed to do was search the scriptures for the promises provided, and claim them as one's own. Linking God's use of the spoken word in creation, to a person's declaration of faith through the use of spoken words, Bowler concludes of Kenyon's theology, that the "power of the spoken word simply carried faith to its desired ends."[22] Though not a Pentecostal himself, Kenyon associated with members of the Pentecostal movement, such as William Durham, Aimee Semple McPherson, John G. Lake, and F.F. Bosworth.[23] He is even reported to have preached at more than one of McPherson's rallies.[24]

A wave of prosperity ministers followed E. W. Kenyon, all influenced in their own way by his theology. The resulting movement has sometimes been referred to as "Word of Faith," "Name it and Claim it," "Theology of the Seed," "Theology of the Pact," "Positive Confession," and even "Health and Wealth," an acknowledgement of the two central features of the expectation of the movements adherents.

Interestingly, non-prosperity Pentecostals have also historically emphasized God's faithfulness in the areas of health and wealth, though not to the same degree as the prosperity movement. Pentecostals recognize the believers role in the responsible stewardship of finances, "including the giving of tithes, offerings, and other sacrificial gifts."[25] Additionally, Pentecostals "emphasize God's promise

---

[20] Bowler, *Blessed*, p. 16.

[21] Bowler, *Blessed*, p. 17. Emphasis is Bowler's.

[22] Bowler, *Blessed*, p. 19.

[23] Bowler, *Blessed*, p. 21.

[24] MacTavish, *Pentecostal Profits*, p. 21.

[25] Cecil M. Robeck Jr, "Prosperity Theology and the Emergence of Neo-Pentecostalism," Unpublished lecture given at the Gregorian University in the spring of 2018, p. 1.

of faithfulness to supply the needs of those who put their trust in Him,"[26] as described in Proverbs 28.25. However, Pentecostal expectation of the faithfulness of God is not strictly associated with either financial gain or continued health, but is alternatively associated with the provision of basic human needs, and according to Cecil M. Robeck Jr, "a sense of well-being, purposefulness in life, the number of people who have come to the Lord as a result, and a genuine openness to others in need."[27] While Pentecostals do not necessarily relate ones' level of giving or faith with God's provision, proponents of the prosperity Gospel often do. One criticism of the movement makes this abundantly clear: "What generally unites the 'teachers of prosperity' is the teaching that the abundant life of the believer in the *now* includes health and material prosperity *without limits* ... Also, God is *obligated* to respond to my demand."[28] The correlation is striking.

At times it can be difficult to distinguish between the two movements. While some Pentecostals adhere to the tenets of prosperity theology, others reject it outright. The same is true of some prosperity leaders, as they work to distinguish themselves from Pentecostals. This tension has even led to the creation of new terminology used in the classification of various segments of the traditions. In the well-known book, *Global Pentecostalism: The New Face of Christian Social Engagement*, Donald E. Miller and Tetsunao Yamamori explain that many contemporary Pentecostals that accept the prosperity gospel are often referred to as Neo-Pentecostal. Elsewhere, authors simply acknowledge the complexity which they perceive to be associated with a "lack of standardization of the terms."[29]

---

[26] Robeck, *Prosperity Theology and the Emergence of Neo-Pentecostalism*, p. 1.

[27] Robeck, *Prosperity Theology and the Emergence of Neo-Pentecostalism*, p. 1.

[28] Eldin Villafañe, *Introducción al Pentecostalismo: Manda Fuego, Señor* (Nashville, Tennessee: Abingdon Press, 2012), p. 149. The emphasis is Villafañe's.

[29] Lindsey A. Huang and Gabe Ignatow, "The Prosperity Gospel and Individualistic Economic and Social Attitudes in Guatemala," *Interdisciplinary Journal of Research on Religion* 13 (2017), Retrieved from https://vanguard.idm.oclc.org/login?url=https://search-proquest-com.vanguard.idm.oclc.org/docview/1970247776?accountid=25359, p. 5.

It must also be acknowledged that at times, Pentecostals add to the confusion. Take for example the following critique of the prosperity movement.

It is clear that Latin American Pentecostals in the twenty-first century are at a crossroads. On one side there is a segment of the church that has become satisfied, established, and wealthy. This is the case of most neo-Pentecostal churches, which will continue to emphasize the conditions of prosperity as a result of true faith ... which may culminate in a post-Christian society ... The spiritual level of such congregations could reach a low level, where secularism supported by technological and information advances could endanger the heath of the church.[30]

This is a clear articulation of anti-prosperity sentiment, yet in the same manuscript the author provides a set of indicators of success within the Pentecostal community, which includes "overall prosperity."[31] What are we to gather from this apparent discrepancy? Is the notion of prosperity which leads the community to become satisfied, established, and wealthy a different prosperity than the one that indicates success? Or, is there another issue at stake here?

Though, it is difficult to trace the introduction of the prosperity gospel in Central America, it is clear that it has taken root and continues to grow. In an article titled "The Prosperity Gospel and Individualistic Economic and Social Attitudes in Guatemala," Lindsey A. Huang and Gabe Ignatow claim that while "82 percent of Pentecostals believe in the prosperity gospel, 71 percent of Charismatics and 68 percent of other Christians in Guatemala also adhere to this belief."[32] The numbers are surprisingly high. But what does this all mean? Has Guatemala become a stronghold of the prosperity gospel? Or, is there another explanation? Once again, I refer to Kate Bowler and her keen assessment of the prosperity gospel in the United States.

---

[30] Miguel Álvarez, *Beyond Borders: New Contexts of Mission in Latin America* (Cleveland, Tennessee: CPT Press, 2017), pp. 20-21.

[31] Álvarez, *Beyond Borders*, p. 215.

[32] Huang and Ignatow, "The Prosperity Gospel and Individualistic Economic and Social Attitudes in Guatemala," p. 5.

Given the controversies that swirl around the prosperity gospel, a few cautionary words should be kept in mind. First, I believe that, at a fundamental level, American desires for the "good life" are basic and ordinary. That is not to say that everyone has the same standards of adjudicating quality of life, but that when many people say "prosperity," they mean survival. People long for the necessities that sustain life and rejoice when those goods overflow.[33]

An important question comes out of this note of caution. What do we mean by prosperity, and how does it relate to either the prosperity gospel or the option for the poor? After all, both point to a hope for a better existence, and a belief that God can and does respond to human need.

Materiality of Salvation

Both the option for the poor and the prosperity gospel are grounded in the notion that salvation is more than simply a spiritual reality. Though not writing with the prosperity gospel in mind, Miroslav Volf argues that for both Pentecostal and liberation theology there is an emphasis placed on what he calls the "materiality of salvation."[34] As such, salvation "is not merely a spiritual reality touching only an individual person's inner being but also has to do with the *bodily* human existence."[35] He also correctly recognizes that this emphasis is "not a marginal theme but an essential constituent."[36] The materiality of salvation is a cornerstone for the development of both Pentecostal and liberation theology.

Following the lead of Amos Yong when writing about Christianity in Latin America, I would suggest that this emphasis exists within the prosperity movement as well. Yong states that "the masses see God's salvation as addressing the particularities of their physical,

---

[33] Bowler, *Blessed*, p. 8.

[34] Miroslav Volf, "Materiality of Salvation: An Investigation in the Soteriologies of Liberation and Pentecostal Theologies," *Journal of Ecumenical Studies* 26.3 (Summer, 1989), p. 448.

[35] Volf, "Materiality of Salvation," p. 448 (emphasis original).

[36] Volf, "Materiality of Salvation," p. 448.

material, and economic needs."[37] While this may be true of Christianity at large in the Latin America, Yong further clarifies his argument. "Christian redemption thus is not abstract but concrete, resulting in the overall prosperity and well-being of those who walk in the way of Christ and his Spirit."[38] It seems clear that the materiality of salvation is a significant component within all three traditions. Yet it must also be acknowledged that the option for the poor and the prosperity gospel originated in very different parts of the world.

Socialism vs. Capitalism

In his online article titled "The Prosperity Gospel: Dangerous and Different," Antonio Spadaro outlines the development of the "prosperity gospel," articulating its historical foundation in the United States, its relatedness to the so-called "American Dream,"[39] its emphasis on economic well-being and health, and its potential service to "the economic-political-philosophical concepts of a neo-liberal model."[40] A significant conclusion is found in the following statement.

> In truth, one of the serious problems that the prosperity gospel brings is its perverse effect on the poor. In fact, it not only exasperates individualism and knocks down the sense of solidarity, but it pushes people to adopt a miracle-centered outlook, because faith alone – not social or political commitment – can produce prosperity.[41]

---

[37] Amos Yong, "A Typology of Prosperity Theology: A Religious economy of Global Renewal or a Renewal economic?," in Attanasi, Katherine, and Amos Yong (eds.), *Pentecostalism and Prosperity: The Socio-Economics of the Global Charismatic Movement*. New York, New York: Palgrave Macmillan, 2012, 23.

[38] Yong, *A Typology of Prosperity Theology*, p. 23.

[39] Antonio Spadaro SJ - Marcelo Figueroa, "The Prosperity Gospel: Dangerous and Different," in *Civ. Catt.* English Edition, July 18, 2018, https://laciviltacattolica.com/the-prosperity-gospel-dangerous-and-different/.

[40] Spadaro, "The Prosperity Gospel."

[41] Spadaro, "The Prosperity Gospel."

While it would be easy simply to accept this critique, it is also important to reflect on the historical position of Pentecostals in relationship to the Theology of Liberation and the option for the poor. At this point it must be acknowledge that the option for the poor is not solely linked to the Theology of Liberation but has continued to be at the heart of the social doctrine of the Roman Catholic Church as clarified in the Vatican's two issued Instructions *Libertatis Nuntius* issued on August 6, 1984, and *Libertatis Conscientia* issued on March 22, 1986.[42] Most Pentecostals would be unaware of the distinctions, but to note the continued use of the option for the poor even after the Vatican's clarification of its position on the Theology of Liberation is important.

According to Pentecostal scholar Douglas Petersen, "Evangelical Christians have generally disavowed liberation theology, viewing it as Marxism garbed in theological language."[43] It seems that while scholars such as Spadaro see connections between the prosperity gospel, North America, and the neo-liberal agenda, others have made presumptions about potential connections between the Theology of Liberation, Marxism, and the potential of socialist or even communist ties.

Spadaro and various students of Pentecostalism share in some of their characterizations of the prosperity gospel. According to Spadaro the prosperity gospel is anthropocentric, placing "humans and their at the center."[44] In addition, through the use of the tools of globalization such as mass media, television, and theatrical displays of music, along with a charismatic presentation of a "fundamentalist and pragmatic reading of the Bible,"[45] the proponents of the prosperity gospel promote a "theological justification for economic neo-liberalism."[46] Likewise, as per Timothy Wadkins, the leaders of these congregations are charismatic men who "carry a worldly successful

---

[42] See Anselm Kyongsuk Min, *Dialectic of Salvation: Issues in Theology of Liberation* (Albany, NY: State University of New York Press, 1989).
[43] Petersen, *Not by Might Nor by Power*, p. 193.
[44] Spadaro, "The Prosperity Gospel."
[45] Spadaro, "The Prosperity Gospel."
[46] Spadaro, "The Prosperity Gospel."

persona,"[47] and the "churches all feature technological sophistica-
tion and high energy music."[48] In addition, "they are churches that
in one way or another embrace the ethos of the global economic culture and promote a kind of spiritual capitalism."[49] This seems to
place the prosperity gospel in a very negative light.

Reflecting on the significance of the theology of prosperity, Pentecostal author Darío López Rodríguez provides the following insight, which sounds very much like Spadaro.

> The tendency that these temporary "theological modes" have to
> an ideologization of the faith, which has led its enthusiastic pro-
> moters to religiously justify military dictatorships and democra-
> cies that impoverish the poorest every day, reveals that instead of
> helping to forge a theology from the historical context of poverty
> and exclusion in which thousands of Pentecostals live, their "the-
> ology" legitimizes the status quo and ignores the structural di-
> mension of sin and the social dimension of biblical doctrines
> such as justification by faith and holiness.[50]

With such condemnation, can any good come from the movement,
especially as it pertains to the poor?

Conclusion

On the one hand, Spadaro suggests that "the risk is that the poor
who are fascinated by this pseudo-Gospel remain dazzled in a sociopolitical emptiness that easily allows other forces to shape their
world, making them innocuous and defenseless."[51] On the other
hand, Miguel Álvarez points out that eventually "people get tired of

---

[47] Timothy H. Wadkins, *The Rise of Pentecostalism in Modern El Salvador: From the Blood of the Martyrs to the Baptism of the Spirit* (Waco, Texas:
Baylor University Press, 2017), p. 119.

[48] Wadkins, *The Rise of Pentecostalism in Modern El Salvador*, p. 119.

[49] Wadkins, *The Rise of Pentecostalism in Modern El Salvador*, pp. 120-
121.

[50] Darío López Rodríguez, *Pentecostalismo y Misiòn Integral: Teologìa
del Espìritu, Teologìa de la Vida* (Jesús María, Peru: Centro de
Investigaciones y Publicaciones (CENEP), 2008), p. 111.

[51] Spadaro, "The Prosperity Gospel."

the fallacies of the same rhetoric day after day."[52] The poor at not simply inactive participants that are entranced by the illusion of wealth and health, but are aware of the discrepancy of what is preached and what they experience. What can we conclude?

Although the emphasis of the prosperity gospel is placed on the individual's ability, by faith, to access the blessings of God, the Spirit-filled observer must not overlook that many of these churches also continue to hold to common theological tenants as classical Pentecostals. Classical Pentecostalism has always been a movement of upward social mobility, at least for some, even prior to the intro-duction of the prosperity component.

Also, members of the Pentecostal movement are members of var-ious social groupings, including families, small groups, congrega-tions, and neighborhood – each group impacted by the success or failure of its members. Douglas Petersen and others argue that Pen-tecostals have developed a theology of social concern.[53] Throughout Pentecostal history, the emphasis on personal and structural salva-tion, and the transformational power of the Holy Spirit have en-dowed local churches in the movement with potential to serve as spiritual-based social change agencies.

In conclusion, my theological project advances a theology of Pen-tecostal praxis with the "option for the poor" as a central theme. While North American Pentecostalism developed within the con-text of an individualistic, capitalistic society, it has a long religious history that bridges spirituality and concern about social problems with a goal of a better life for the Spirit-filled people.

Bibliography

Álvarez, Miguel, *Beyond Borders: New Contexts of Mission in Latin America* (Cleveland, Tennessee: CPT Press, 2017).

Attanasi, Katherine, and Amos Yong (eds.), *Pentecostalism and Prosperity: The Socio-Economics of the Global Charismatic Movement* (New York: Palgrave Macmillan, 2012).

---

[52] Álvarez, "Beyond Boarders," p. 21.

[53] See Petersen, *Not by Might Nor by Power,* and Miller and Yamamori, *Global Pentecostalism.*

Bonilla, Plutarco A., "Presentación," *Pastoralia: Revista del Centro Evangélico Latinoamericano de Estudios Pastorales* 7.15 (diciembre, 1985), p. 7.

Bowler, Kate. *Blessed: A History of the American Prosperity Gospel* (New York: Oxford University Press, 2013).

D'Epinay, Christian Lalive, *Haven of the Masses: A Study of the Pentecostal Movement in Chile* (London: Lutterworth Press, 1969).

Gaerán, Aida, "Teología de la liberación: Perspectiva de una Mujer Pentecostal," *Pastoralia: Revista del Centro Evangélico Latinoamericano de Estudios Pastorales* 7.15 (diciembre, 1985), pp. 90-91.

Gerlach, Luther P., "Pentecostalism: Revolution or Counter Revolution?," in Iwing I. Zaresky and Mark P. Leone (eds.), *Religious Movements in Contemporary America* (Princeton, NJ: Princeton University Press, 1974), pp. 669-99.

Gutiérrez, Gustavo, *A Theology of Liberation: History, Politics, and Salvation.* (Trans. Sister Caridad Inda and John Eagleson; Maryknoll, NY: Orbis Books, 1988).

Kyongsuk, Anselm, *Dialectic of Salvation: Issues in Theology of Liberation* (Albany, NY: State University of New York Press, 1989).

Petersen, Douglas, *Not by Might Nor by Power: A Pentecostal Theology of Social Concern in Latin America* (Irvine, CA: Regnum Books International, 1996).

Rodríguez, Darío López, *Pentecostalismo y Misiòn Integral: Teologìa del Espìritu, Teologìa de la Vida* (Jesús María, Peru: Centro de Investigaciones y Publicaciones. CENEP, 2008).

Robeck, Cecil M., Jr, "Prosperity Theology and the Emergence of Neo-Pentecostalism," Unpublished lecture given at the Gregorian University in the spring of 2018.

Tackett, Zachary, "As a Prophetic Voice: Liberationism as a Matrix for Interpreting American Pentecostal thought and Praxis," *The Journal of the European Pentecostal Theological Association* 33.1 (2013), p. 42-57.

Vasquez, Manuel A., *The Brazilian Popular Church and the Crisis of Modernity* (Cambridge: Cambridge University Press, 1998).

Villafañe, Eldin, *Introducción al Pentecostalismo: Manda Fuego, Señor* (Nashville, TN: Abingdon Press, 2012).

Volf, Miroslav, "Materiality of Salvation: An Investigation in the So-teriologies of Liberation and Pentecostal Theologies," *Journal of Ecumenical Studies* 26.3 (Summer, 1989), pp. 47-67.

Waldrop, Ricardo, *"La Teología de la Liberación: Enfoque Critico,"* *Pastoralia: Revista del Centro Evangélico Latinoamericano de Estudios Pastorales* 7.15 (diciembre, 1985), pp. 40-55.

Wadkins, Timothy H., *The Rise of Pentecostalism in Modern El Sal-vador: From the Blood of the Martyrs to the Baptism of the Spirit* (Waco, Texas: Baylor University Press, 2017).

Wilson, Everett, "Guatemalan Pentecostals: Something of Their Own," in Edward L. Cleary and Hannah W. Stewart-Gambino (eds.), *Power, Politics, and Pentecostals in Latin America* (Boulder, Colorado: Westview Press, 1997), pp. 139-62.

Racial/Ethnic Conciliation

CHAPTER FOUR

CONFRONTING WHITE NATIONALISM: MAKING SPACE FOR IDENTITIES, HISTORY AND CULTURAL MEMORY THROUGH A FRAMEWORK OF CHRIST-CENTERED LOVE

Tommy Cásarez*

Samuel P. Huntington offers a white nationalist argument in *Who Are We? The Challenges to America's National Identity.*[1] He builds his argument with conversations about culture, race, immigration, pluralism, and American public policy debates. Overall, Huntington argues that the best way to unite America is with one dominant cultural grouping that "gives rise" to the "greatness of America" – that is, as he sees it, the Anglo-Saxon Protestant Christian culture. He sees this as foundational to "unity in diversity." The unity consists of requiring all racial minorities to shed their cultural heritage and background for a "better one." Huntington dismisses the idea that whiteness[2] was a "tool of oppression" for more than 400-years. African, Native, Mexican and Chinese Americans were considered less

---

*Tommy Cásarez (PhD, Princeton Theological Seminary) currently serves as the Associate Dean of the Division of Theology and Professor of Systematic and Historical Theology at Vanguard University. He regularly teaches courses in the area of systematic theology, church history, and leadership studies. Dr. Cásarez also serves as an Associate Pastor at Templo Calvario Church of Santa Ana, CA.

[1] Samuel P. Huntington, *Who Are We? The Challenges to America's National Identity*, Simon and (Schuster: New York; 2004), p. 20.

[2] By the term "whiteness," I am referring to white superiority that framed races with white skin, culture, and ideas as superior to that of people who are not of Anglo-Saxon ethnic origin.

than human and incapable of "being white." Tunnel vision paramount to whiteness has historically limited rationality; ignoring that other societies and cultures existed and thrived long before the rise of white supremacy. Descendants of such societies and cultures have contributed profoundly to the development of the country we called the United States of America.

Notwithstanding, Huntington declares that "traditional" Anglo Americanism has won the national-cultural war, thus becoming the dominant culture to which everyone must assimilate. White nationalism disregards how Europeans gained superiority by excluding and even exterminating those who they enslaved. Notwithstanding, a contemporary, well-trained scholar like Huntington has the audacity to call for immigrants from all racial-ethnic backgrounds to submit and assimilate into the Anglo-Protestant cultural narrative. Oddly, he notes that in order for the immigrants to do so, they must pass the affirmation of the dominate culture. There is little room in his argument for the role of one's acceptance of or desire to insert oneself into the Anglo-Protestant narrative. Without acceptance there is no true insertion or participation in the benefits of living out the narrative. However, it makes sense that those who think like Huntington would shun acceptance because acceptance demands appreciation of otherness.

In *Who Are We?* Huntington primarily focuses on recent immigrant unwillingness and the Mexican American so-called stubborn refusal to assimilate. Huntington does not address the steps required to bring about his proposal. The result of such negligence functions to maintain structural inequality and racial oppression in America. As far as Huntington is concerned, the solution to the American identity crisis lies in the further exclusion and alienation of one's non-Anglo cultural identity through assimilation.

There are many fault lines running through Huntington's argument, but one in particular pertains to his concept of identity and identity formation. This chapter argues against Huntington's "purely constructivist" understanding of identity and identity formation. The blind spots present in his notion of identity and identity formation work to support his overarching purpose, but they also perpetuate an understanding of identity formation, which serves as an obstacle rather than a pathway to reviving (and reconfiguring I might add) American identity. A critical uncovering and exploration of these blind spots will follow after presenting his proposal. Charles Taylor's notion of identity formation and Anthony Appiah's understanding of the concept of "racial identity" will serve as primary conversation partners for my objections to Huntington's diabolical perspective. There are various difficulties whenever someone tries to insert themselves into the narrative of an "other." Does the one attempting to insert themselves fit the narrative? Are they accepted by the "other" as a participant in the narrative? These two points indicate the need to re-write the collective narratives that support cultural and racial identities through the framework of God's love. A theological framework of space-making love can provide both the grounds for properly remembering and correctly reconstructing historical narratives that constitute the collective American identity on the road to greater reconciliation and unity.

Huntington's Understanding of Identity

In Chapter 1 of his work entitled, "The Crisis of National Identity" Huntington suggests that "Americans of all races and ethnicities could attempt to reinvigorate their core culture." He goes on to as argue that this begins by recognizing that the U.S. is "primarily Christian ... adhering to Anglo-Protestant values, speaking English, maintaining its European cultural heritage, and committed to principles of the Creed."[3] This call comes right before his discussion of "Identities: National and Other." In the chapter on "Identities" he sets up the vehicle for accomplishing his goal as stated above – the "reinvigoration" of American culture by all Americans. His notion of identity and identity formation makes the goal stated above easily attainable; too easy in my estimation.

Ironically, this culturally conservative author chose to espouse a postmodern understanding of identity that parallels Charles Taylor's work, *Multiculturalism*, although Taylor's name is never mentioned. Strangely, some of the key features in Taylor's understanding of identity are present in Huntington's proposal, and I believe that those that are missing work to undermine Huntington's project. First, Huntington acknowledges that identities belong both to individuals and the groups that they identify with, but that

---

[3] Samuel P. Huntington, *Who Are We?*, p. 20.

identification is one that is self-consciously chosen by the individual.[4] In the same way that it is self-consciously chosen, he believes one may also easily reject it for another. Individual and group identities tell one's self that "I or we possess distinct qualities as an entity that differentiates me from you and us from them."[5] Individual identities result because one belongs to a particular group of people and has no other option but to identify with some, and differentiate one's self from others. The autonomous individual in Huntington's eyes is an unencumbered self, who consciously chooses to identify with the group in which one originates. Huntington fails to acknowledge the fact that the lack of choice in one's birth location or originating ethnic or social group already shaped that self-determination.

Group identities are significant for Huntington because they shape one's life plans. Sometimes going against the grain of one's identity is painful and may cause some confusion because one might begin to act in ways that contradict one's identity. If one believes oneself to be a scholar and begins to act like a politician, according to Huntington, then one may experience what he calls, "cognitive dissonance."[6] The outcome may be that the identity which one began with no longer is suitable to one's change in behavior. Therefore, one may have to exchange one identity for a more suitable one – one that is better suited to guide one's action and understanding of one's own self. This is both possible and necessary because identities are always changing. Also, "identities are overwhelmingly constructed"[7] and though one inherits ethnic and racial identity, they too can be rejected or redefined. Huntington never discusses the overwhelming difficulty and virtual impossibility of exchanging one racial identity for another. Racial identities differ radically from identities shaped by a profession, goals or interests.

Huntington posits that identities change in part because individuals change over time, but also because individual identities are hardly ever coextensive with group identities. Group identities function to shape individual identities because individuals interact within groups to shape their own identities. Although groups may

---

[4] Huntington, *Who Are We?*, p. 21.
[5] Huntington, *Who Are We?*, p. 21.
[6] Huntington, *Who Are We?*, p. 22.
[7] Huntington, *Who Are We?*, p. 22.

only have one primary identity, individuals tend to have multiple identities or groups that they identify with and draw from for the sake of their own identity. This also means that individual identities change depending on the situation and need at hand. Moreover, group identities change slowly in comparison to personal identities, and group identities may even disappear once the purpose for which the group identity was erected disappears or is fulfilled.

Lastly, probably the most promising remarks that Huntington makes in the whole book are located here in his discussion about how identities are formed. "[I]dentities are defined by the self but they are the product of the interaction between the self and others."[8] Though "the self" defines identity, identity arises out of encounters with an "other" – be it another individual or group. Huntington proceeds to draw out the ramifications of this line of argumentation in what I would suggest are the grounds for racial, social enclaves:

> How others perceive an individual or group affects the self-definition of that individual or group. If one enters a new social situation and is perceived as an outsider who does not belong, one is likely to think of oneself that way. If a large majority of the people in a country think that members of a minority group are inherently backward or inferior, the minority group members may internalize that concept of themselves, at which point it becomes part of their identity. Alternatively, they may react against that characterization and define themselves in opposition to it ... People can aspire to an identity but not be able to achieve it unless they are welcomed by those who already have that identity.[9]

Individual and group definition takes place in the shaping process of multiple encounters. That shaping process may work to produce positive or negative identities, which may then be internalized and become part of one's own identity. Moreover, regardless of how hard someone may aspire to a particular identity and desire to insert themselves in the narrative of a group different from their group of origin, unless that person is accepted by the other group, they will not achieve it. In order for the desire to achieve a new identity to be fulfilled, one must also be accepted by the group that inhabits that

---

[8] Huntington, *Who Are We?*, p. 23.
[9] Huntington, *Who Are We?*, p. 23.

new identity. The whole discussion of racial stigma and racial discrimination fits perfectly under this point. Even if Huntington himself does not take up the issue, his acknowledgement of it is positive and deserves to be further explored.

Huntington ultimately claims that people of all different ethnic and racial backgrounds can insert themselves into the American culture and way of life – values, beliefs and practices. For him, cultural identities are changeable but ancestral identities are somewhat stable and static. The assimilation process is crucial because Huntington claims that a unified culture is needed to sustain the greatness of the nation or the U.S. may come apart as fast as, and in the same way that Russia did. Huntington, therefore, explains that "People identify with those who are most like themselves and with whom they share a perceived common ethnicity, religion, tradition and myth of common descent and history."[10] These are all parts of what a common culture provides. Racial and ethnic minorities living in the U.S. are to be grafted into the Anglo-Protestant culture and its narrative as a means to preserving a greater end, "social security" – "the ability of a people to maintain their culture, institutions and way of life"[11]

Alternatives and Objections to Huntington's Notion of Identity and Identity Formation

Strangely, Huntington's analysis of identity and identity formation is partially true and partially false. For all his emphasis on partial truths, the most dangerous being that "the United States is a nation of immigrants" with immigrants defined specifically as those who arrived after 1790,[12] his own dependence upon a partial truth seems ironic. One fault in Huntington's argument emphasizes the extent to which one is consciously able to choose his or her identity, which

---

[10] Huntington, *Who Are We?*, p. 13.

[11] Huntington, *Who Are We?*, p. 180.

[12] Huntington suggests that the notion that the U.S. is nation of immigrants is a partial truth due to the misuse of the term immigrant. Only those newcomers who came to the U.S. after 1790 should be considered immigrants. These newcomers were immigrants to the new country because the settler community had already established a specified culture and way of life into which newcomers could immigrate (Huntington, p. 40).

is truly not as simple as Huntington claims. In fact, the choosing of one's identity in a "purely constructivists" sense overlooks the fact that identities are partly given and partly constructed. The inheritance of one's identity and the available resources from which to choose are both determined by forces outside of one's control – birthplace, parents, ancestry, gender, class, racial grouping. This prior determination contradicts Huntington's insistence that identities are "overwhelmingly constructed."

Moreover, collective identities provide scripts that afford individuals with materials to draw from for the purpose of constructing their own life plans. But these scripts are also used to guide the interaction and treatment between individuals to whom they apply. These scripts work like dramas that are enacted time and time again between individuals and groups. Positive scripts suggest positive behavior towards some, and negative scripts suggest detrimental behavior towards others. Huntington underestimates the role that racial and ethnic identities play in providing the scripts that shape one's life and self-perception. One cannot simply jump out of one racial identity and into another analogous to the way in which a person changes political parties. Racial identities are much more substantial than that, and they are also an aspect of one's social location. The dominant group's "acceptance" of those considered to be outside of the dominant group identity functions much more significantly in the process of one's identity formation than Huntington espouses. The lack of acceptance serves as an obstacle to identity formation and also limits the social context of life choices for those considered to be outsiders. Favorable acceptance of the formerly excluded, I suggest, would call for a rewriting of collective scripts which would result in facilitating a reconfiguration of American identity. I will now attempt to explicate the objections raised more fully.

Charles Taylor and Anthony Appiah provide an excellent alternative to Huntington's conceptualization of identity and identity formation. According to Charles Taylor, a central element of all human identity is that it possesses a personal and collective dimension that is "fundamentally dialogical."[13] Human identity is negotiated "through dialogue, partly overt, partly internal, with others."[14] Through dialogue with other people's understandings of who one is, one actually develops his or her own identity. Taylor contends that people are "self-interpreting animals" whose self-interpretation takes the form of a narrative.[15] They seek to understand themselves and to define their identity by acquiring "languages of expression." Also, these languages are "modes of expression whereby we define ourselves, including 'languages' of art, of gesture, of love, and the like."[16] They are not acquired on one's own but through interaction with "significant others" who function as the "crucibles of inwardly generated identities."[17] On a wider social level, inwardly generated individual identities are shaped in "open dialogue" with society as well.[18]

Although intimate others serve as the crucibles for individual identity, collective identities supplied by society also play an important role because they "provide the loose norms or models, which play a role in shaping the life plans of those who make these collective identities central to their individual identities."[19] Congruent to Taylor's "dialogical" emphasis above, K. Anthony Appiah claimed that one's individual identity is formed through dialogical relation between the individual and the ideas and practices supplied by the institutions of society, which are transmitted by one's own family in differing degrees. He highlighted the fact that "dialogue shapes the identity I develop as I grow up, but the very material out of which I form it is provided, in part, by my society, by what Taylor

---

[13] Charles Taylor, "The Politics of Recognition," in A. Gutman (ed.), *Multiculturalism: Examining the Politics of Recognition* (Princeton: Princeton University Press, 1994), pp. 25-74 (32).

[14] Taylor, "The Politics of Recognition," p. 34.

[15] Charles Taylor, *Human Agency and Language* (Cambridge: Cambridge University, vol. 1, 1985), p. 45.

[16] Taylor, "The Politics of Recognition," p. 32

[17] Taylor, "The Politics of Recognition," pp. 32, 36

[18] Taylor, "The Politics of Recognition," p. 36.

[19] K. Anthony Appiah, "Identity, Authenticity, Survival: Multicultural Societies and Social Reproduction," in A. Gutman (ed.), *Multiculturalism: Examining the Politics of Recognition* (Princeton: Princeton University Press, 1994), pp. 149-64 (155).

calls its language in a broad sense."[20] Appiah argued rightly that people create themselves from a predetermined set of options supplied by their culture and society. While people do decide for themselves which of the options, they personally choose in creating personal identities, they do not decide which options are actually available to them.[21]

Collective identities provide the "options" and "materials" for developing one's individual identity. They offer the narratives that individuals utilize to construct their own identities selectively. Enmeshed in the idea of "language in the broad sense" are collective identities, but this does not imply that they are determinative. Once someone acquires a mode of expression, he or she is not, therefore, fated to live in a particular fashion. Personal narratives are created in conversation with collective narratives because they provide the scripts from which personal narratives are selectively constructed. Collective identities provide the narratives that people employ in developing their "life plans and in telling their stories."[22] In fact, these narratives serve as "life scripts" that people use to create their own identities. They also utilize collective scripts to iterate their own stories within a larger story, which offers a sense of connectedness and meaning. Once again, in agreement with Appiah, I believe that collective identities should not be considered as deterministic restraints. Though negative scripts limit the shape of one's life plans and create an obstacle to be overcome, they do not inhibit self-determination and the possibility to reconstruct oneself in contrast to or as a variation of an over-arching collective identity. They are not in and of themselves fatalistic, but they do play a vital role in the construction of a person's identity by serving as a vital resource in the development of personal identity.

Furthermore, I would like to point out that these collective identities are based upon collective narratives of the past that are shared by a particular group and ultimately have their rooting in what is presumed to be the truth about that past. Even Huntington espouses teaching history as a necessary means to remember and to reinforce identity, "If, however, a nation is a remembered as well as

---

[20] Appiah, "Identity, Authenticity, Survival," p.154.
[21] Appiah, "Identity, Authenticity, Survival," p. 155.
[22] Appiah, "Identity, Authenticity, Survival," p. 160.

an imagined community, then people who are losing that memory are becoming something less than a nation."[23] With this statement Huntington wields a polemic against multicultural education. But is it really to teach the truth about history, or a one-sided story of a particular people that interests Huntington? As far as Huntington is concerned, recent trends towards multicultural education and ethnic studies programs at the college level have all worked to debilitate and erode American culture and identity. Though Huntington connects memory, history and national identity together, he refuses to acknowledge that the history to which collective narratives refer is a "shared" history that includes both conquerors and conquered, the colonizer as well as the colonized.

Dominant, collective identities, however, are usually written from the perspective of the conqueror at the expense of the conquered. Therefore, uncovering the truth about the historical past, and remembering it rightly, works to rectify a misconstrued collective narrative and to correct a group's own distorted sense of collective identity. False and negative scripts misrecognizing people in history unjustly create barriers to, instead of opportunities for, leading a socially respectable way of existence. Those whose internal self-image has been impaired by distorted narratives of the past face the added challenge of having to overcome negative internal self-images as they relate to themselves individually and as they relate to others. Even if one has successfully overcome the negative images of a distorted collective narrative, the path for doing so still creates an extra hurdle for leading a socially respectable way of life, which would not have been present if the narrative about the past had been correctly construed. In addition, distorted scripts also erect barriers to being dealt with as equals by other participants in society. When one's perception of another depends upon a misconstrued script of that other's collective narrative identity, then the treatment that follows, based upon the perceived negative script, influences how the other is treated by those outside of the collective group. Though one may overcome the view imposed by a negative script in relating to the other, the challenge for doing so is created by the existence of a false narrative depicting the other.

---

[23] Huntington, *Who Are We?*, p. 176.

It is unjust to project or present untrue images of a minority group's past, and it is equally unjust to demand that a minority group adopt a distorted reconstruction of their shared past proffered by a majority group for the purpose of assimilation. Misrecognizing and non-recognizing the truth about a minority group's past where injustice is concerned makes it difficult for those whose past is misconstrued to be true, faithful citizens when the official view of their past is untrue. Incorrect portrayals of a collective group's past forge an unjust obstacle to participatory citizenship when assimilation, according to Huntington's view, requires everyone to accept a one-sided narrative about the past. Throughout Huntington's own narrative he praises the accomplishments of the Anglo community but leaves out the struggles of many other people groups that were often the one's oppressed in the victories of that Anglo community. The whole story about the Anglo culture's rise to power is not being told even in his own work.

Ultimately, when the truth is revealed and remembered correctly, the people that identify themselves with that group's identity to construct their own will also be affected because the collective narrative they selectively employ to construct their personal identity will be based upon a more accurate account of the past. This is true for people from both majority and minority groups as they strive to draft a new narrative together. If, in order to insert oneself into the national identity one has to reject or forgo one's cultural identity, thereby, extinguishing it and its narrative all together, then the call to assimilation will truly be one that is unacceptable. A better proposal would entail the "reconfiguration of American identity" through the rewriting of scripts. Making space for the scripts of minority groups within the dominant, collective identity would call for a reshaping of the identity that is already given.

Huntington and Taylor both share a dialogical understanding of identity formation. Each holds the view that identities are constructed in interaction with others. Though both stress the interactive and dynamic nature of identities, Taylor broadens the interactive engagement to encounters that the self has with scripts provided by one's primary caregivers and the language "in the broad sense" that those caregivers provide. Individual identities also arise from the conversation with society and the collective identities provided by the society in which one finds oneself. This embeddedness and sense of belonging to a particular minority group functions simultaneously as a limitation and asset. As a limitation, an individual only has available whatever pre-existing resources are already contained in one's collective identity. Huntington overlooks the fact that "values, beliefs and practices" are all situated within a larger narrative cultural framework. Re-writing the larger cultural narrative is a necessary step in making space for minority cultures to inhabit the same cultural space. Writing more positive scripts to replace negative scripts embedded in a narrative – where a group is misrecognized or non-recognized – is a necessary strategy. The move to re-write negative scripts is a necessary strategy in creating a more just society and insuring that racial and ethnic minorities will be treated more fairly. If life scripts do shape one's behavior and life decisions, as well as the way one treats another, then the re-writing of scripts is essential because it will work to abate the dominant group's tendency to look down upon and treat minorities as outsiders and inferiors.

Huntington himself noted that when dominant groups treat minority groups as outsiders and as people who do not belong, then those who are treated as outsiders may internalize that identity and live out those scripts. Huntington also suggested that some identities may even disappear when their purpose is served or when the reason for which they were created disappears. I would simply like to point out that historically, the whole notion of race and the racialization of humanity was created by people of the white race to legitimize their conquest and enslavement of those from foreign lands. "Race" in America continues to function as a means of discerning between "us" and "them" with the white race serving as the standard of judgement or rule of thumb for evaluating others. When racial discrimination in contact as people relate to one another and contract in terms of formal social arrangements are factored in, race secures and sustains white Euro-Americans privileges while at the same time ensures that disadvantages are created for others. It is here that one of the most significant obstacles to the reconfiguration of American identity lies. With the majority of Euro-American citizens continuing to identify themselves predominantly as "white," the need persists for all those who are non-white to continue to have to grapple with their own raced-based identity.[24] This fault line in Huntington's proposal leads to having to deal with the continual shaping force of racial stigma and its expression in racial discrimination.

Remembering the Past: Making Space for Collective Memory, History, and Identity

The reconstructed past and collective memory impacts history and identity. Where the traces of history differ from memory, preference should be given to that which most resembles the reality represented by the traces of the past. Also, the Christian concept of love is the best framework within which to situate reconstructed identities. Importantly, the biblical concept of agape and self-donation love reveals that self-giving and other-receiving love is the work of the Holy Spirit.

First, there is a difference between the historical past, history, and memory. History and memory should both defer to the historical past in cases where the traces of history oppose one's account or recollection of the past.[25] The historical past here will be used to refer to the "way it really was" or that which is closest to the reality supported by the traces of history. History is, also, a critical reconstruction, while memory connotes the "identity shaping remembrance of the past."[26]

According to Maurice Halbwachs, all memory belongs to both an individual and a group.[27] While only individuals can remember, "one may say that the individual remembers by placing himself in the perspective of the group, but one may also affirm that the memory of the group realizes and manifest itself in the individual

---

[24] Huntington, "*Who Are We?*," p. 301.

[25] Miroslav Volf, *Exclusion and Embrace: A Theological Exploration of Identity, Otherness and Reconciliation* (Nashville: Abingdon, 1996), p. 240. This is especially true for recent white nativist narratives fueling hate in America which led to the mass killings in El Paso, Gilroy, and Charlottesville.

[26] Volf, *Exclusion and Embrace*, p. 240.

[27] Maurice Halbwachs, *On Collective Memory* (Chicago: University of Chicago Press, 1992), p. 171.

memories."[28] Although Halbwachs' concept of the distance between an individual's memory and that of the group leaves very little space for individuality, it is important to note the mutual interplay between individual and collective memory. In essence, when an individual remembers one does so by inserting oneself into a group, so that data, figures and ideas are not only recollected "via the structure intact for understanding them, but one also takes on the group's disposition toward them as well."[29] Here in lies the identity shaping aspect of the group's memory, for one inherently identifies with a certain group in order to remember.

Ultimately, Halbwachs advocated that group frameworks provided paradigmatic ways of remembering the past, which worked to form or shape a group's recollection of the historical past. In doing so he differentiated between group memory and the historical past, "Collective frameworks are ... the instruments used by the collective memory to reconstruct an image of the past which is in accord, in each epoch, with the predominant thoughts of the society."[30] Hence, each collective memory of the historical past is greatly influenced by the present-day frameworks involved at the time that reconstructing the past takes place. An extreme interpretation of Halbwachs' thesis would imply that every new reading was a further disconnect from the reality of the past because the outcome had been so influenced by the frameworks of its day. Jan Assman keenly noted another implication of Halbwachs' thesis by arguing that history itself is but the encasing of collective memory. Assman extended Halbwachs' idea of collective memory by taking it one step further to suggest that "cultural memory" is ultimately the concretization of group memory, which "comprises that body of reusable texts, images, and rituals specific to each society in each epoch, whose 'cultivation' serves to stabilize and convey that society's self-image."[31] History, then, is but one mode of cultural memory according to Assman. This idea concurs with Halbwachs' thesis that collective memory is a product of the frameworks at work in the time

---

[28] Halbwachs, *On Collective*, p. 40.

[29] Halbwachs, *On Collective*, p. 72.

[30] Halbwachs, On Collective, p. 40.

[31] Jan Assman and John Czaplicka, "Collective Memory and Cultural Identity," *New German Critique* 65 (1995), pp.125-133 (132).

of the memory's origination, but it points out how those memories are preserved and passed down from one generation to the next.[32]

I would like to suggest that where individual, collective and cultural memory differ from the representations of the historical past, society must give precedence to the "way it really was" of the historical past when the traces of history contradict memory. In the "Introduction" to *On Collective Memory*, Coser rightly noted that "collective memory has both cumulative and presentist aspects ... because it shows at least partial continuity as well as new readings of the past in terms of the present."[33] Basically, Coser highlighted that collective memory is a mixture of both "continuity and change" and that there are certain aspects of the historical past that remain in place despite the passage of time or the realization that one never "steps into the same river twice."[34] Building upon Coser's criticism, I suggest that priority be given to the continuity represented in the traces because regardless of the extent to which Halbwachs argues that history is rewritten by each generation because of a new reading, that process of rewriting history never occurs in a vacuum.[35] The affirmation of the historical past should always stand at the foundation of memory where that reality is known despite which generation takes a fresh look at the past.

Even if one disagrees with Halbwachs' explanation for how individuals remember the past, one must acknowledge some interplay between individual and collective memory and recognize that collective memory shapes positively or negatively the very memory that individuals possess. In addition to the idea that collective memory influences individual memory, collective memory itself is a product, to a large extent, of the social frameworks intact when groups formulate their memory of the past. Collective memories also serve a foundational role in the formation of cultural memory, which in essence is the concretizing of collective memory according to Jan Assman. History, then, is but one of many forms of cultural memory. However, when misguided or ill-intended social frameworks are active at the time of the formation of a collective memory, then the

---

[32] Assman and Czaplicka, "Collective Memory and Cultural Identity," p. 125.

[33] Halbwachs, *On Collective*, p. 66.

[34] Halbwachs, *On Collective*, p. 26.

[35] Halbwachs, *On Collective*, p. 34.

memory that the collective framework produces will also be misinformed and harmful. Hence, the memories produced by unjust and ill directed social frameworks are in need of transformation in the same way that the collective frameworks that produced them are in need of change.

Therefore, where biased social frameworks have functioned to produce misinformed collective and eventually cultural memories of the past, those distorted collective and cultural memories of the past must be rejected in the present. We should defer to the truth that is located in the historical representations of the past. Furthermore, the negatively slanted social frameworks that produced inaccurate collective and cultural memories must also be exchanged for a framework that aims at peaceful community by taking into account the perspective of the other. In order to transform misinformed memories of the past an "other-regarding" framework of love that entails forgiveness and reconciliation should be exercised to reconstruct and remember the past.

One could certainly object on the grounds that every social framework somewhat distorts or blurs one's collective memory of the past and interpretation of the data that represents history. Most collective frameworks do, to a certain extent, do injustice to the past and one's reconstruction of the past for the simple reason that not every detail of the past is accounted for and included in the reconstruction of the past. However, some frameworks are more suitable than others for accomplishing a better life for victims of violence, racial discrimination, and injustice.

As noted by Nietzsche in his condemnation of "historical justice" in order to do "strict" historical justice to the past was absolutely impossible and unjust.[36] The "hill" that serves as the vantage point from which one tries to judge the mountains and valleys of the past inhibits one's ability to do strict historical justice. In fact, interweaving isolated events into a "harmonious totality," which exist only in the imagination of the historian, according to Nietzsche, is the reason that he claims, "Objectivity and (strict historical) justice have nothing to do with one another."[37] He also emphasized that to recover and

---

[36] Friedrich Nietzsche, *Unfashionable Observations* (Stanford: Stanford University Press, 1995), pp. 102-108.

[37] Nietzsche, *Unfashionable*, pp. 126-27.

remember everything if one could actually do so, would be to "bring to light so much falsehood, coarseness, inhumanity, absurdity, and violence that the pious atmosphere of illusion in which alone everything that wants to live is actually capable of life, vanishes."[38] In other words, "strict" historical justice to the past for an individual is unhealthy for life and living in general. Cognizant of this reality Nietzsche suggests that every historical account of the past where injustice has occurred is in need of an "inner constructive impulse" or framework to guide it. "Only in love" Nietzsche adds, "does the human being create," for without love the human being withers or becomes "dishonest."[39]

Although I agree that the framework of love is most suitable for reconstructing and remembering the past, I do so for additional reasons beyond the notion that love will prevent one from becoming dishonest. First of all, within the framework of oppressed and oppressor lies the "inner constructive impulse" of liberation. If conqueror and conquered reign supreme as the only lenses one uses to perceive the other and the history of interaction with one another, then that outlook will create an illusion of one party's innocence over another, which will inevitably result in a "deceitful narrative."[40] For in truth, both parties involved in a conflict contributed to its outcome and either, actively wronged the other in the process of the struggle, or committed a wrong against others as a result. Instead of clearly defined lines of identifying one as victim and the other as victimizer, accounts of conflict are often messy. Even where the identification of perpetrator and perpetrated remain distinct, none are totally exempt from wrongdoing in the past or completely blameless where victimization has occurred. Though some may not have contributed to their victimization directly, none are completely passive. It is very likely that as a result of their tragic experience they may have allowed for the experience to brood hate in their hearts, adopted the false image of themselves reflected to them by their conquerors or possibly justified the committal of crimes against others because of their oppression.[41] In any case, viewing the past under the overarching concept of oppressed and oppressor lends itself to

---

[38] Nietzsche, *Unfashionable*, p. 131.
[39] Nietzsche, *Unfashionable*, pp. 131-32.
[40] Volf, *Exclusion and Embrace*, pp. 103-104.
[41] Nietzsche, *Unfashionable*, p. 177.

developing deceitful narratives that portray one party as completely innocent over another.

Second, if one were to situate the past in terms of oppressed and oppressors, even though the framework for viewing the past may very well be accurate and necessary, it is insufficient to stand alone.[42] This larger story is "ill-suited to bring about reconciliation and sustain peace between people and people groups."[43] When the intention for remembering is placed solely within the narrative of liberation, the inner-constructive impulse of freedom and justice guide the narrative so that the wrong of one party is highlighted at the expense of another in order to justify hostility or the call for hostility toward another. Consequently, justice and freedom alone as the driving impulse for recovering and reconstructing the past are insufficient for doing justice to the past. Many times they serve as instruments for justifying a victim's abuse of the victimizers.

Moreover, the umbrella concept of victim and victimizer supplies fuel to the fire of further resentment and future retaliation. This framework essentially locks people into association with the category of oppressed and oppressor, and thereby, makes re-negotiating or moving away from one's association with a particular category difficult. The question becomes, once the oppressed have been freed, how will they view their former oppressors? How then will the oppressed and oppressor live together in community once liberation is achieved? What kind of narrative will exist if the only outlook for viewing the other and a common past is one of conqueror and conquered? What, if anything, will keep the newly freed from newly oppressing their former oppressors? On the contrary, a framework of liberation alone works to justify further oppression of former oppressors rather than suppresses it.

An all-encompassing schema of oppressed and oppressors is inadequate for sustaining community and incapable of recovering the truth in such a way that refrains from doing injustice to one party over another because it will almost always lead to further injustice. As is often noted, history essentially embodies the perspective of the oppressor, the conqueror or the victimizer. Rarely are works of history produced from "below," and when they are, they are equally as

---

[42] Volf, *Exclusion and Embrace*, pp. 102-104.

[43] Volf, *Exclusion and Embrace*, p. 104.

unjust as an account of the same event from the other side, for both parties attempt to defend their own position while justifying their actions and condemning the actions of the other party. When a group does so, that group selectively remembers, and is blind to facts that weaken their position or debilitate their credibility. If the one-sided narrative is allowed to continue, it will inevitably lead to further injustice from the other side and vice versa. What kind of framework is needed? A framework of love is needed.

When love serves as the inner-constructive impulse for recovering and reconstructing the past, the goal is one of reconciliation that goes beyond liberation, and also entails doing justice to history. The Christian love that I will present begins with agape and ends with self-donation love, so that the "as God loves them" starts with agape as the guardian of the special relation and ends with God's space making love as the model. The features of agape form Christian love's main guidelines while the vision of God's reconciliation supplies the background and horizon within which love operates. In the following I will argue that one love others "because God loves" them and that one love others "as God loves" them.[44] Then, I will explain why a love that leads to reconciliation is preferred as an all-encompassing framework in which to situate recovering and reconstructing the past over the other paradigms previously mentioned. In order to highlight love's invaluable contribution to historical inquiry, I will delineate the shape of the Christian concept of agape and go beyond its boundary as a guardian for how to relate to others by advocating a model of self-donation love for establishing the truth about the past.

The warrant to love one another is rooted in the double commandment to love God and one's neighbor (Matt. 22.37-41). According to Gene Outka, these two commandments stand alone, and yet, the injunctions maintain "normative links." After all, the second commandment is similar to the first in the author's view. If one loves God, then one will desire what God desires and love whom God loves.[45] The ground for human beings to love one another, therefore,

---

[44] Gene Outka, *God and the Moral Life: Conversations in the Augustinian Tradition* (Oxford: Oxford University Press, 2007), p. 12.

[45] Gene Outka, "Universal Love and Impartiality," in E.N. Santurri and W. Werpehowski (eds.), *The Love Commandments: Essays in Christian*

is based upon God's "bestowal love," for God alone "makes His sun rise on the evil and on the good."[46] The fact that God loves both the just and the unjust, thereby, places before all humanity the grounds to be like God in one's love for others.[47] The "consequence" of God's "free love" is that "We love one another because God loves us, and we love one another as God loves us."[48]

Theologically, the model for how love is lived out by human beings in real life coincides with how God makes space within God's self to receive an antagonistic humanity into holy communion on the cross of Calvary.[49] God's reconciling humankind to God's self on the cross functions as the horizon at the forefront of humanity's struggle towards reconciliation with one another, and a backdrop that authorizes one to go and do likewise.

Gene Outka's extensive work, *Agape: An Ethical Analysis*, provides an excellent outline of the characteristic features that describe the Christian tradition's concept of neighbor-love. To begin, agape love essentially entails a unilateral and evaluative feature, which denote "an agent commitment and a recipient-evaluation."[50] According to Outka, in agape one has "unqualified" regard for the other,

---

Ethics and Moral Philosophy (Washington, DC: Georgetown University Press, 1992), pp. 1-10.

[46] Anders Nygren, *Agape and Eros* (trans. Philip Watson; London: SPCK, 1957), p. 66.

[47] Outka, *God and the Moral Life*, p.31. To love others "because" God loves them is generally agreed upon, but the definition of to love others "as" God loves them is fervently debated. Outka rightly suggests, "God's love in key respects serves as pattern and prototype. While we cannot and should not seek to love precisely as God loves the imitation of God's love has Biblical and traditional warrant" (p. 23). He has also noted correctly that the interplay between reciprocity and relationality play a crucial role in defining the ways in which we may and may not be like God. There are ways in which we should not attempt to be like God, while at the same time there are ways in which we ought to be like God. Even though the sinfulness of our humanity always seems to shine through when we do attempt to reflect God's actions and attitude towards others the struggle to do so ought not be discarded.

[48] Outka, *God and the Moral Life*, p. 31.

[49] Volf, *Exclusion and Embrace*, p. 100.

[50] Gene Outka, *Agape: An Ethical Analysis* (New Haven: Yale University Press, 1972), p. 10.

which means that one desires the best for the other outside of any idea that one will benefit from the progress of the other in return.[51] Moreover, the agent "unqualifiedly regarding" the other actually does so by including one's self in wanting what is best for the other. Contrary to altruism which is primarily committed to the good of the others, agape love includes the self of the agent in one's commitment to the other. Hence, I argue that in recovering the past agape love demands that the treatment of material be based upon one's "unqualified regard" for the other, which contradicts the pursuit of the historical past solely to justify one's own actions or condemn the actions of others. Although agape love does not require a mutual response from the recipient, it does hope for "mutuality," after all, the goal of love is communion between people.[52] In the end, by putting communion between one another as the goal, the project of reconstructing and remembering the past is shaped differently because the notions of freedom, liberation and justice remain integral to reconciliation, but not the sole result.

Next, to love one's neighbor is to have equal regard for the other which entails a non-discriminatory and non-preferential principle.[53] As Kierkegaard once put it, "When you open the door that you shut in order to pray to God and go out the very first person you meet is the neighbor."[54] So, caring for the other, or one's regard for the

---

[51] In a lecture given on September 27, 2001, Professor Outka equivocated the term "unqualified regard" and "equal regard" but advocated the usage of the term "unqualifiable regard" over and above the term "equal regard." *Agape: An Ethical Analysis* published in 1972 still contains the term "equal regard" for which I am substituting "unqualifiable regard" as well.

[52] Outka, *Agape*, p. 37.

[53] Outka, *Agape*, pp. 10-11.

[54] Søren Kierkegaard, *Works of Love*, H.V. Hong and E.H. Hong (eds.), Princeton: Princeton University Press, 1995), p. 44, 51. This quote captures Kierkegaard's sense of the universality of neighbor love and the strong command-like emphasis that he places on the verb shall, "It is in fact Christian love that discovers and knows that the neighbor exists and, what is the same thing, that everyone is a neighbor. If it were not a duty to love, the concept 'neighbor' would not exist either, but only when one loves the neighbor, only then is the selfishness in preferential love rooted out and the equality of the eternal preserved." Ultimately, the effect is that although one may deliberate about how an agent cares for the other, one may not deliberate whether another in need ought to be assisted.

other, is blind to any specific feature inherent to the other beyond the fact that the other is a human being. Therefore, in reconstructing the past, love requires that historical data not be granted special treatment or be overlooked to the detriment of one party over another, for love equally regards both parties. On the other hand, skepticism in the narrative of the dominant is allowable since the strong more than the weak have the means and the wherewithal to impose their perspective upon others. Yet, agape recognizes the other to be more than an enemy, he or she actually a neighbor, so that in doing so one will refrain from projecting demeaning images upon the other. Mirroring and reflecting God's love requires loving one's enemy and praying for those who cause one injury, for then the loving person is "like" the children of God (Matt. 5.44-45). Equal regard requires the narrative of the victim and victimizer to be regarded with equal importance and given proper consideration because each is a neighbor.

For my purposes, only after having forgiven will one be able to reconstruct the past so as to not use it as a means of excluding the other through injustice in a role reversal.[55] Forgiveness demands that the thirst for vengeance be set aside, but it does so by affirming justice and transcending it in order to make space for and approach the other.[56] This act works to remove the threads of hatred that must be exterminated, for otherwise, the cycle of victimization will continue unbroken.[57] What I described in demanding that a "forgiving disposition" be required in order to maintain the permanence of relationship stems from the concept of self-donation. It is here that the resources which enable one to do so lead the discussion to the narrative that serves as the model and goal of Christian love: God's reconciliation of humanity to God's self. Every other self is more than a victimizer, conqueror or oppressor in the paradigm of agape, for that same individual is also a neighbor. As a neighbor, he or she unconditionally and unilaterally warrants unqualifiable (to desire the best for the other), mutual (to treat as oneself), and equal (to treat all the same) regard.

---

[55] Volf, *Exclusion and Embrace*, p. 123.
[56] Volf, *Exclusion and Embrace*, p. 414.
[57] Volf, *Exclusion and Embrace*, p. 124.

However, I want to include within the framework of Christian love an unconditional and unilateral commitment to forgiveness as part of a space-making ethic that necessitates one to take into consideration the perspective of the other as a form of receiving the other. In an effort to receive the other, a movement of "self-giving" is required in which one goes outside of one's self to view the world from the perspective of the other and back. Forgiveness refers to the "other-receiving" aspect I discussed previously, so now I will return to the larger narrative from which self-donation originated in order to further explain what I mean by "self-giving" in relation to making space for the other. Although the concept of agape love supplies the guidelines and the parameters for how to reconstruct and remember the past, the source and the goal of the Christian concept of love are best exemplified in the Trinitarian act of "self-giving" and "other-receiving" love accomplished on the cross.

I would like to suggest that this self-giving and other-receiving love at work in the life of the believer is the work of the Spirit.[58] It is, after all, the case that "God's love has been poured out into our hearts through the Holy Spirit, who has been given to us."[59] The Spirit then empowers us to be space-making agents who embody this self-giving and other-receiving love by pouring out God's love into our hearts. As space-making agents filled with the Spirit we are able to make space for the other's – identity, social life, physical needs. I would add that the movement of God's love makes space for our participation in the life of God by the Spirit. We are then empowered through the Spirit to make space for others on the road towards reconciliation, which ultimately restores human communion in a world of "non-innocence."

---

[58] In a previous essay, I provided an extensive argument into the shape of Christian identity based on a social trinitarian model of the triunity of God in order to argue that human beings made in the image of God are to image, reflect or imitate God in creaturely ways. Portions of the current chapter were previously published, "The Spirit of Christ, Identity and the Undocumented in Our Midst: Towards a Space-Making Theological Ethic," in A.L. Harris, and M.D. Palmer (eds.), *The Holy Spirit and Social Justice: Interdisciplinary Global Perspectives Scripture and Theology* (Lanham: Seymour Press, 2019), pp. 128-47.

[59] Romans 5.5 (NIV).

That God's love is space-making is demonstrated by the space that Christ makes for humanity to participate in the divine life through the Holy Spirit – in the relation that is the Father, Son, and Spirit. Volf understands Christ as opening up humanity to the very life of God, so as to allow for the life of God to pour forth or overflow onto humanity through the Holy Spirit. It is here by the presence and power of the Holy Spirit that humanity is made to participate in the life that God enjoys. Jesus, therefore, as fully human and fully God makes space for humanity's participation in the life of the tri-une God. However, I would like to specify that it is in and through the Holy Spirit that we participate and become active space-making agents who embody God's self-giving and other-receiving love.

The focal point of Christ's space-making activity originates in the incarnation, and culminates in the crucifixion of Christ on the cross, but in my view, it is only realized and actualized for followers of Christ through the coming of the Spirit which Christ spoke of taking place after his departure (John 14,16). Just as Peter preached on the day of Pentecost, the fulfillment of Joel's prophecy ultimately makes space for humanity to be empowered by the Spirit since, "In the last days, God says, I will pour out my Spirit on all people."[60] The Holy Spirit makes our participation in the life of God possible, pours out the love God in our hearts, and empowers us to participate in the movement of God's of love as "space-making agents."

The central aim of the cross at Calvary was to restore communion between God and the creatures God made in God's own image.[61] The cross is what happened when the inner-Trinitarian love shared by the divine persons turned outward toward humanity and was met by a hostile community of human beings. Those human beings crucified the Son of God and executed Jesus of Nazareth on a wooden cross. In the Crucified, however, God refused to allow sin to serve as the reason for humanity's enmity with God and overcame it by sending His Son into the world (Jn.3.16). The distance that sin generates between God and God's own creatures was bridged in the incarnation of God, and through Christ's suffering. The space that sin creates, the division that sin makes, and the fellowship that sin breaks

---

[60] Acts 2.17 (NIV).

[61] Volf, *Exclusion and Embrace: A Theological Exploration of Identity, Otherness and Reconciliation*, 126-29.

between God and God's creation, were all overcome in the person and work of Jesus Christ. Christ, then, dealt with humanity's sin by taking it upon Christ's self, judging it as sin, and destroying it in His death. The distance between God and those creatures God created in God's own image was no longer a distance of separation due to sin, guilt and a just condemnation, but a distance of differentiation and of an appropriate reclamation of the space that a reconciled relationship between God and God's creatures entails.

On the cross, Christ accomplishes forgiveness of sin, but forgiveness was not the "culmination of Christ's relation to the offending other," for forgiveness was the "passage leading to embrace."[62] In the Crucified, Christ makes space within Christ's self – and therefore also in the divine community of persons – for humanity to dwell "in the Spirit," "in Christ" and "in God," because it was there on the cross that Christ embraced the "beloved other" at its worst.[63] The life, death, and resurrection of Jesus Christ are all part of a movement of God's love to make space for that which is not God. God divinely loves that which God created and determines not to be God without God's creation.

In other words, I would argue that the Holy Spirit opens the door for humanity to participate in the space that God possesses, inhabits, and creates within God's self in the divine life, while the forgiveness of sins that Christ accomplishes on the cross keeps that open door permanently in place. The movement of God's love is the Spirit of God to humanity so that God is the one who opens the door leading to participation in the divine spatial life. From another angle, divine space is opened up by the Holy Spirit to human space in the crucified in such a way that it becomes a shared space only through the Holy Spirit. That shared space enters into human space through the Spirit and provides human space a point of entry into the divine space through the presence and work of the Holy Spirit. Ultimately, God invites humanity to become a participant in the divine spatial existence of the triune God through the Holy Spirit.

God's activity towards humanity as a beloved other provides the guideline that suggests humanity make space within themselves for one another's perspective as a means of approaching peaceful

---

[62] Volf, *Exclusion and Embrace*, p. 126.
[63] Volf, *Exclusion and Embrace*, p. 126.

communion with the other as well. Take into consideration Christ's example:

> Instead of aping the enemy's act of violence and rejection, Christ, the victim who refuses to be defined by the perpetrator, forgives and makes space in Himself for the enemy. Hence, precisely as a victim Christ is the true judge: by offering to embrace the offenders, he judges both the initial wrongdoing of the perpetrators and the reactive wrongdoing of many victims.[64]

Self-giving and other receiving are part of the same movement of love. By giving of His life on the cross Jesus made space within the life of God for the perpetrator and the perpetrated as a victim who refused to imitate or repeat the victimizer's offense. On an earthly level, human being's actions of self-giving and other receiving are demonstrated by forgiveness and the desire for and openness towards receiving the other into oneself even if that other is an enemy. Although forgiveness breaks down the walls of division and hostility, it still leaves a gap between two parties, which would allow for coexisting tolerance, or the restoration of true communion. In one's love for the other, the invitation to communion is a form of openness that signifies the preference of mutuality with a former enemy over tolerance, which Christ himself exemplified.

Moreover, actually receiving the other into oneself requires one to "undertake a readjustment of one's identity in light of the other's alterity."[65] Making space for the other calls for taking within oneself the perspective of the other in the same way that God took within God's self the perspective of the victim by allowing Christ to be victimized and refraining from excluding the victimizer by making space for the victimizer within God's self as well. On the cross, the God of love and justice received both the victim and the victimizer within God's self, and judged the wrongs committed by affirming justice when God transcended justice through love. In recovering and reconstructing the past, love requires that after forgiving we make space within ourselves for the perspective of the other regardless if that perspective is the victim or the victimizer's point of view. One must make space within oneself for the other's self-perspective

---

[64] Volf, *Exclusion and Embrace*, pp. 126-27.
[65] Volf, *Exclusion and Embrace*, p. 110.

and for the other's perspective about them.[66] When an agent does so, the outcome of the process of receiving the other into oneself will inevitably shape and reshape the way one identifies oneself and the beloved other. The process of doing so may also shed light on some information or pre-existing resources in one's own background that could have been overlooked in the past, which would help reconstruct and remember the past more correctly.[67] Even though one makes the effort to see from the other's point of view, one should do so endeavoring that "competing perspectives may become converging perspectives and bring about an agreement."[68] On the other hand, the practice of viewing from the perspective of the other may require that one reject segments of the other's view.[69] Nonetheless, one's vision will be enlarged and therefore enhance recovering and reconstructing the past rightly.

In summation, to recover the past rightly involves allowing the traces of history that point back to the truth about the historical past to reign over one's individual, collective or cultural memory of that past. Cultural memory retained in the form of history must submit to the right of the historical past. Misguided social frameworks in play at the time of a particular collective memory, which was in turn concretized in the form of history, work to skew the truthfulness of that memory. This, therefore, discredits the correctness of the historical work that embodied the cultural memory. The term then is rightly used to refer back to that which most reflects the reality represented by the traces of the historical past and is given priority over the truthfulness of a collective or cultural memory. Furthermore, in order to discover the truth about the past so that it may be reconstructed and remembered rightly, a framework of love should be employed. The Christian concept of the love of God being poured out by God's Spirit unilaterally and unconditionally recognizes the other as a neighbor, and therefore, requires one to regard the other unqualifiedly, mutually and equally. Forgiveness, too, is inherent to self-donation biblical love that aims at reciprocity, for by doing so space is made to receive the other. A permanent commitment to peaceful communion is sought which extends beyond tolerance. In

---

[66] Volf, *Exclusion and Embrace*, pp. 214-15.
[67] Volf, *Exclusion and Embrace*, p. 213.
[68] Volf, *Exclusion and Embrace*, p. 213.
[69] Volf, *Exclusion and Embrace*, p. 213.

searching for the truth about the past, a space-making love for the other requires making space for the identity of the other through the power of the Spirit within one's self, which involves enlarging one's thinking. When we do so, we allow the voice of the other to echo within ourselves and we are open to the molding and changing of our view about ourselves and the other as a result.

Bibliography

Assman, Jan, and John Czaplicka, "Collective Memory and Cultural Identity," *New German Critique* 65 (1995), pp. 125-33.

Appiah, Anthony K., "Identity, Authenticity, Survival: Multicultural Societies and Social Reproduction," in Amy Gutman (ed.), *Multiculturalism: Examining the Politics of Recognition* (Princeton: Princeton University, 1994), pp. 149-64.

Appiah, Anthony K., and Amy Gutman, *Color Consciousness: The Political Morality of Race* (Princeton: Princeton University Press, 1996).

Cásarez, Tommy, "The Spirit of Christ, Identity and the Undocumented in Our Midst: Towards a Space-Making Theological Ethic," in Antipas L. Harris, and Michael D. Palmer (eds.), *The Holy Spirit and Social Justice: Interdisciplinary Global Perspectives Scripture and Theology* (Lanham, MD: Seymour Press, 2019), pp. 128-47.

Halbwachs, Maurice, *On Collective Memory* (Chicago: University of Chicago Press, 1992).

Huntington, Samuel P., *Who Are We? The Challenges to America's National Identity* (Simon and Schuster: New York, 2004).

Kierkegaard, Søren, *Works of Love* (ed. Howard V. Hong and Edna H. Hong; Princeton, NJ: Princeton University Press, 1995).

Loury, Glenn C., *The Anatomy of Racial Inequality* (Cambridge, MA: Harvard University, 2002).

Nietzsche, Friedrich, *Unfashionable Observations* (Stanford, CA: Stanford University Press, 1995).

Nygren, Anders, *Agape and Eros* (trans. Philip Watson; London: SPCK, 1957).

Outka, Gene, *Agape: An Ethical Analysis* (New Haven, CT: Yale University Press, 1972).

—"Universal Love and Impartiality," in E.N. Santurri and W. Werpehowski (eds.), *The Love Commandments: Essays in Christian Ethics and Moral Philosophy* (Washington, DC: Georgetown University Press, 1992), pp. 1-10.

—*God and the Moral Life: Conversations in the Augustinian Tradition* (Oxford: Oxford University Press, 2007).

Taylor, Charles, *Human Agency and Language* (Cambridge, MA: Cambridge University, 1985).

—"The Politics of Recognition," in Amy Gutman (ed.), *Multiculturalism: Examining the Politics of Recognition* (Princeton: Princeton University, 1994).

Volf, Miroslav, *Exclusion and Embrace: A Theological Exploration of Identity, Otherness and Reconciliation* (Nashville: Abingdon, 1996).

CHAPTER FIVE

DO BROWN IMMIGRANT LIVES MATTER?
THE SPIRIT IN JOHN AND SOCIAL JUSTICE

Rodolfo Galvan Estrada[*]

Does the comfort we give crying children depend upon the color of their skin? Would their immigration status determine the response of compassion and care to their suffering and plight? One would assume the love and compassion to the ethnically "other" is not dependent upon skin color or ethnic origin. However, on June 18, 2019, the United States Justice Department's attorney Sarah Fabian argued before a Ninth Circuit panel that children of immigrants who were seeking asylum did not need to have toothbrushes and soap while in custody. The judges were shocked with this argument and could not believe the case being presented.[1] Yet it was reported that many of these children had spent their time in custody in dirty diapers, drinking toilet water, and separated from their mothers. Women and children are forced to sleep on the floor in ice–cold

---

[*] Rodolfo Galvan Estrada (PhD, Regent University School of Divinity) is a New Testament Scholar. He serves as Director of Accreditation Processes at Fuller Theological Seminary in Pasadena, California.

[1] Helen Christophi, "Feds Tell 9th Circuit: Detained Kids 'Safe and Sanitary' Without Soap," *Courthouse News Service.* 18. June 2019; Mary Papenfuss, "Justice Department Argues Against Providing Soap, Toothbrushes, Beds to Detained Kids," *Huffington Post* (21 June 21 2019); See United States Courts for the Ninth Circuit, Case Jenny Flores v. William Barr,No.17–56297,accessedAugust 8, 2019, http://www.ca9.uscourts.gov/media/view_video.php?pk_vid =0000015907.

immigration detention centers, which are, in Spanish, called *hiel-eras* (freezers).[2] The conditions and treatment of Latinx immigrants has left United Nations officials deeply shocked, calling the situation a violation of international law, "cruel, inhuman or degrading treatment."[3]

Why so cruel? Is it to deter others from migrating to the United States of America? Would the United States of America treat refugees this way from Norway who have "white" skin? Would they do this to asylum seekers from Russia? Well, history does not suggest they would.

As if the mistreatment of immigrants were not cruel enough, August 4, 2019, the Latinx community faced another attack. A white supremacist from Allen, Texas drove nearly 10 hours to El Paso, Texas to kill Brown people at a shopping center. Choosing Texas was not a coincidence. This supremacist wanted to murder as many Latinx people as he could because he was convinced that they are, as he describes in his online manifesto, an "invasion," "race mixing," and adding too much diversity to the country.[4] The death of these Brown lives joins the continual and long American history of violence that the black community has experienced at the hands of white supremacy. Dealing with racism and hatred of foreigners is not something that is solely restricted to the pre–civil war and Jim Crow era. Michael Emerson and Christian Smith point out that racial practices that reproduce racial divisions are now more covert, embedded in normal operations of institutions, avoid direct racial terminology,

---

[2] Caitlin Dickerson, "There Is a Stench: Soiled Clothes and No Baths for Migrant Children at a Texas Center," *New York Times* (21 June 2019); Dan Frosch and Alicia A. Caldwell, "As Border Crisis Worsens, a Detention Center Designed for Children Has None," *The Wall Street Journal* (5 July 2019).

[3] Deanna Paul and Nick Miroff, "U.N. Human Rights Chief 'deeply shocked' by Migrant Detention Center Conditions in Texas," *Washington Post* (8 July 2019).

[4] See Tim Arango, Nicholas Bogel–Burroughs, and Katie Benner, "Minutes Before El Paso Killing, Hate-Filled Manifesto Appears Online," *New York Times* (3 August 2019); Yasmeen Abutaleb, "What's Inside the Hate–Filled Manifesto Linked to the Alleged El Paso Shooter," *Washington Post* (4 August 2019).

and are invisible to most whites.[5] Robin Diangelo also argues that today, we live in a white supremist culture. She explains that our culture positions "white people and all that is associated with them as ideal" and utilizes white people as the "norm or standard for human." As a result, people of color are considered a deviation from that norm.[6] Fear of losing white normalcy and seeing people of color gain equality sparks outrage and fear. In fact, Carol Anderson demonstrates that the hostile reaction toward our first black President, Barack Obama, emerged from an ethnonationalist rage and irrational fear that white people would soon be a minority in America.[7] Can this therefore explain the new wave of white supremacist violence and racism against the Latinx community?

There is a racial problem in America and sadly, the American Church has been a part of the problem instead of the solution.[8] Inflammatory rhetoric from political leaders, and the American Church's complicity with this rhetoric by their continual support of these leaders[9] has provided the environment for the boldness of

---

[5] Michael Emerson and Christian Smith, *Divided by Faith: Evangelical Religion and the Problem of Race in America* (Oxford: New York, 2000), p. 9.

[6] Robin Diangelo, *White Fragility: Why It's so Hard for White People to Talk about Racism* (Boston: Beacon, 2018), p. 33.

[7] Carol Anderson, *White Rage: The Unspoken Truth of our Racial Divide* (Bloomsbury: New York, 2017), pp. 169-73.

[8] See Jemar Tisby, *The Color of Compromise: The Truth About the American Church's Complicity in Racism* (Grand Rapids: Zondervan, 2019).

[9] In fact, the Pew Research finds that Trump receives his strongest support amongst White Evangelicals. Pew Research center finds that Trump still receives strong support from White Evangelicals (80% approval). See Gregory A. Smith, "Among White Evangelicals, Regular Churchgoers are the Most Supportive of Trump." Pew Research Center, Washington, DC, accessed April 26, 2017, http://www.pewresearch.org/ fact–tank/2017/04/26/among–white–evangelicals–regular–churchgoers– are–the–most–supportive–of–trump. For recent but similar results see also Alec Tyson, "Disagreements about Trump widely Seen as Reflecting Divides Over Other Values and Goals." Pew Research Center, Washington, DC; accessed 15 March 2018, http://www.pewresearch .org/fact– tank/2018/03/15/disagreements–about–trump–widely–seen–as–reflect– ing–divides–over–other–values–and–goals. Daniel Miller explains that evangelical support for Trump is a convergence of a single religious identity

white supremacist to terrorize ethnic lives. We must therefore ask, what does the Holy Spirit have to say about this racial hostility against Brown lives? Does the Spirit of God grieve, suffer, and provide us with some hope and direction to the problem of racism against the Latinx community?

Although it is common to draw upon Lukan pneumatology for discussions on the Spirit, this chapter focuses upon particular texts in the Gospel of John. In particular, we will focus on a rereading of John 3.1-10 and John 14.16-18 in light of the racial perceptions of the Latinx community which includes immigrants and Dreamers, also known as the Deferred Action of Childhood Arrivals (DACA). This chapter encourages a Spirit-filled Christian response to racism today in a two-fold manner. First, there is a need for self-awareness among local churches; the Church's primary spiritual identity is unity and that unity must be shared with all people from diverse ethnic origins. This is done by reminding believers of the common birth experience in the Spirit. Second, we must not be complicit or stand idle when it comes to oppressive injustice against the marginalized and abandoned. We must engage in advocacy for the oppressed because this is the same thing that the Spirit as the Paraclete, the defender of God's people, does for us. The struggle for justice and defense of the oppressed is a spiritual activity as well as a social one. In the end, my hope is that we can draw from these Gospel texts and recognize that the Spirit does have something to say about racism and how we view the Latinx community. It is imperative that the

---

that is both evangelical and political. See "The Mystery of Evangelical Trump Support?," *Constellations* (2018)), pp. 1–16; David Gushee notes that there were a variety of factors that attracted White Evangelicals to Trump. But he insists that regardless if the majority of White Evangelicals do not believe that they hold racists views, they are complicit with what he said about minorities and immigrants. See "Why Trump, and What Next? An (Ex-) Evangelical Response," in *Faith and Resistance in the Age of Trump* (ed. Miguel De La Torre; Maryknoll: Orbis, 2017), pp. 99–106; Racial sentiment against minorities nonetheless played a factor in Trump supporters. See David Norman Smith and Eric Hanley, "The Anger Games: Who Voted for Donald Trump in the 2016 Election, and Why?," *Critical Sociology* 44.2 (2018)), pp. 195–212; Thomas Pettigrew, "Social Psychological Perspectives on Trump Supporters," *Journal of Social and Political Psychology* 5.1 (2017)), pp. 107–116; Randall Balmer, "Under Trump, Evangelicals show their True Racist Colors," *Los Angeles Times*. August 23, 2017.

Church recognizes that racism and hostility against immigrants needs not just a moral solution, but a pneumatic response.

Latinx Immigrants and Being Born of the Spirit (John 3)

President Donald Trump has repeatedly generalized Latin American immigrants as "criminals," "rapists," "animals," and described as an "infestation" to be blocked from "invading" American soil through the building of a wall.[10] Undergirding such unwarranted allegations is an elitist assumption that brown people come from inferior countries and from inferior people. Notwithstanding, xenophobic and racial hostility are neither new nor limited to Latinx experiences. Stereotypes, racial slurs, threats of deportation, and caricatures of the "other" can be traced back through the Jim Crow era and American slavery to ancient Greek society.[11]

In the fourth century BCE, Hippocrates' early theories about people from other nations led to the Greek attitude of intellectual and strength superiority. Hippocrates said, "all things that grow in the earth assimilate themselves to the earth."[12] He reasoned that soft

---

[10] Julie Hirschfeld Davis, "Trump Calls Some Unauthorized Immigrants 'Animals' in Rant," *New York Times* (New York: NY), May 16, 2018; David Leonhardt and Ian Prasad Philbrick, "Donald Trump's Racism: The Definitive List," *New York Times* (New York: NY), 15 January 2018.

[11] Adrian Sherwin–White, *Racial Prejudice in Imperial Rome* (New York: Cambridge, 1970), p. 1; Mary Boatwright, *Peoples of the Roman World* (New York: Cambridge University, 2012), pp. 6–7; Denise McCoskey, *Race Antiquity and Its Legacy* (New York: Oxford, 2012), pp. 143–144; Benjamin Isaac, *The Invention of Racism in Classical Antiquity* (New Jersey: Princeton, 2004), pp. 1 37; Miriam Eliav Feldon, Benjamin Isaac, and Joseph Ziegler, "Introduction," in *The Origins of Racism in the West* (New York: Cambridge University, 2009), p. 9; Rebecca Kennedy, *Race and Ethnicity in the Classical World* (Indiana: Hackett, 2013), pp. xiii–xv; Contrary to the views of writers such as Ivan Hannaford, *Race: History of the Idea in the West* (Maryland: Johns Hopkins, 1996), pp. 4–8; Frank Snowden, *Blacks in Antiquity: Ethiopians in the Greco–Roman Experience* (MA: Cambridge, 1970), p. 2; *Before Color Prejudice; The Ancient View of Blacks* (MA: Cambridge, 1983), p. 63.

[12] Hippocrates, "all things that grow in the earth assimilate themselves to the earth. Such are the most sharply contrasted natures and physiques.

terrain produces weak people and those who reside in harsh climates are more courageous and intelligent.[13] Hippocrates' environmental views influenced both Plato and Aristotle's perception of foreigners. They advanced the assumption that Athens was divinely situated in a perfect region that gave birth to people with superior wisdom.[14] This view of foreigners is also echoed by the Roman writer

---

Take these observations as a standard when drawing all other conclusions, and you will make no mistake" (*Air, Water, Places*, 24.60).

[13] Hippocrates writes,

These are the most important factors that create differences in men's constitutions; next come the land in which a man is reared, and the water. For in general you will find assimilated to the nature of the land both the physique and the characteristics of the inhabitants. For where the land is rich, soft, and well–watered, and the water is very near the surface, so as to be hot in summer and cold in winter, and if the situation be favorable as regards the seasons, there the inhabitants are fleshy, ill–articulated, moist, lazy, and generally cowardly in character. Slackness and sleepiness can be observed in them, and as far as the arts are concerned, they are thick–witted, and neither subtle nor sharp. But where the land is bare, waterless, rough, oppressed by winter's storms and burnt by the sun, there you will see men who are hard, lean, well–articulated, well–braced, and hairy ; such natures will be found energetic, vigilant, stubborn and independent in character and in temper, wild rather than tame, of more than average sharpness and intelligence in the arts, and in war of more than average courage (*Air, Water, Places*, 24.40-59).

[14] Plato states, "So when, at that time, the goddess had furnished you, before all others, with all this orderly and regular system, she established your State, choosing the spot wherein you were born since she perceived therein a climate duly blended, and how that it would bring forth men of supreme wisdom" (*Timaeus*, 24c). He also observes that some regions "are naturally superior to others for the breeding of men of a good or bad type." Other areas are more suitable for living because the wind, sun, water, and soil not only affect the body but are "equally able to effect similar results in their souls as well" (*Laws*, 747d–e).

Likewise, we find Aristotle echoing similar remarks that reveal his view of Greek ethnic superiority. He states, "the Greek race participates in both characters, just as it occupies the middle position geographically, for it is both spirited and intelligent; hence it continues to be free and to have very good political institutions, and to be capable of ruling all mankind if it attains constitutional unity" (*Politics*, 7.1327b). Aristotle does not only turn

Vitruvius who stated, "the races of Italy are the most perfectly constituted in both respects – in bodily form and in mental activity."[15]
The Greeks and Romans presumed that the location of their birth
gave one an ethnic advantage over foreigners.[16] These perspectives

---

to environmental factors to justify the superiority of the Greeks, he makes
a close connection between the character of people and the region they
originate. He furthermore asserts that "those men who dwell in the north
have stiff hair and are courageous while those who dwell further south are
cowardly and have soft hair" (*Physiognomics*, 806b15).

[15] Vitruvius, *On Architecture*, 6.1.10–11; See also 6.1.3–5.

[16] The Greek historian Polybius also reflects an environmental view of
foreigners. When he explains the reason why the Arcadians are an austere
people he points to their cold and gloomy climate. He assumes that, "we
mortals have an irresistible tendency to yield to climatic influences. And to
this cause, and no other, may be traced the great distinctions which prevail
amongst us in character, physical formation, and complexion, as well as in
most of our habits, varying with nationality or wide local separation" (*Histories*, 4.21).

Environmental views are also found in the writing of Pliny. He points
out that a healthy mix of warm and cold climate creates people who are
moderate in size and color, which ironically describes those who live in
Rome. People in the northern and southern regions are described as "dull"
and "savage" because of their extreme climates. The empires that arise from
the middle of the world, as Pliny argues, include people who have gentle
customs, clear thought, and temperaments capable of understanding all of
nature. In reference to those who inhabit Rome and Greece he states, "they
have formed empires, which has never been done by the remote nations;
yet these latter have never been subjected by the former, being severed
from them and remaining solitary, from the effect produced on them by
their savage nature" (*Natural History*, 2.80); See also Cicero, "it is evident
that one's birth is more affected by local environment than by the condition
of the moon" (*De Divinatione*, 2.97), and Ptolemy,

For while the region which we inhabit is in one of the northern quarters,
the people who live under the more southern parallels, that is, those
from the equator to the summer tropic, since they have the sun over
their heads and are burned by it, have black skins and thick, woolly hair,
are contracted in form and shrunken in stature, are sanguine of nature,
and in habits are for the most part savage because their homes are continually oppressed by the heat; we call them by the general name Ethiopians. Those who live under the more northern parallels, those, I
mean, who have the Bears over their heads, since they are far removed
from the zodiac and the heat of the sun, are therefore cooled; but

formed the ideological bases for both Greek and Roman empires to promote the illusions that their intelligence and strength were superior to all others.

So, we can notice, ethnic supremacy is not new. It has been around for a long time. As it is today, people in the ancient world also recognized that the country of one's origin was important for the formation of one's identity and relationship with others. But does this give us the right to dehumanize them? Does it give us the right to slander the foreigners at our borders and treat them as animals by locking them in cages at our immigration prisons? Or should we continue to turn a blind eye toward the cruel and dehumanizing treatment of Latinx women and children because they are just that – immigrants?

When we turn to the Gospel of John 3.1-10, the teaching on being "born of the Spirit" is not just an evangelistic call to salvation. We must not fail to notice that this passage is also confronting the challenges of ethnic relations and views of ethnic superiority. And when we look more closely, we also notice that the discussion Jesus has with Nicodemus is also trying to reorient Nicodemus' understanding of ethnic identity and relations with others from the perspective of the Holy Spirit.

How does Jesus do this? He starts to talk about being "born of the Spirit." Why talk about a birthing from the Spirit? We must remember that when one is born from human means, one is born into an ethnic community.[17] Jesus uses this metaphor of "birth" to describe to Nicodemus how he should view his identity and membership in the family of God. In the ancient world, being born from a family granted certain ethnic privileges and rights. What were some of these benefits? Simply put, it included an association to land

---

because they have a richer share of moisture, which is most nourishing and is not there exhausted by heat, they are white in complexion, straight-haired, tall and well-nourished, and somewhat cold by nature; these too are savage in their habits because their dwelling–places are continually cold. The wintry character of their climate, the size of their plants, and the wildness of their animals are in accord with these qualities. We call these men, too, by a general name, Scythians (*Tetrabiblos*, 2.2).

[17] Jonathan Hall, *Ethnic Identity in Greek Antiquity* (New York: Cambridge University), pp. 24-25.

ownership, privileged rights of worship that were not granted to foreigners, and the right to rule others.[18] Inversely, those who did not have a proper ancestry did not share the rights and privileges that come with membership from a particular family or ancestor. Yes, Gentiles were known to convert to Judaism, but this did not mean that their ethnic birthing relations to ancestors became irrelevant. Scot McKnight and Shay Cohen find hints of this issue with the status of Gentile converts.[19] That is, even though there was a positive attitude toward Gentiles who desired to join the Jews community, converts were never seen as fully Jewish.[20] They lacked a Jewish ancestry! This is why we also find Paul in Roman 4 making the argument that we are all descendants of Abraham through our faith in Jesus. Paul is trying to help the readers recognize that Gentiles can be a part of the family of God through faith.

What then does it mean to be born of the Spirit in the Gospel of John? When Jesus tells Nicodemus that it is necessary for him to be "born of the Spirit," the exhortation aims to challenge his understanding of ethnic relations, including the systematic boundaries of segregation and exclusion that solely benefit the privileged. Jesus' exhortation is a pneumatic ethnic argument that informs Nicodemus of a new lineage that destabilizes his ethnic birth privilege. The

---

[18] K.C. Hanson points out that this is most expressed through genealogies. They do not have one simple meaning, function or compositional form, but are social constructs. He asserts that they establish a significant kinship group to which one belongs (2 Sam. 9.6), embody the honor of the family in a list of names (1 Sam. 9.1), make a political claim to leadership (1 Kgs. 13.2), assert an inheritance or family rights (2 Sam. 3.2-5; 5.13-16), establish membership in the religious group (1 Chron. 9.1; Ezra 2.59-63; 10.18-44), and establish the right to hereditary offices (Exod. 28.1; Lev 16.32). See "All in the Family: Kinship in Agrarian Roman Palestine," in *The Social World of the New Testament* (Peabody: Hendrickson, 2008), pp. 30-31.

[19] Scot McKnight, *A Light Among the Gentiles: Jewish Missionary Activity in the Second Temple Period* (Minneapolis: Fortress, 1991), p. 38; Shaye Cohen, *The Beginning of Jewishness* (Berkley: University of California, 1999), pp. 309-325; See also John Collins, *Between Athens and Jerusalem: Jewish Identity in the Hellenistic Diaspora* (Grand Rapids: Eerdmans, 2000), p. 262; Martin Goodman, *Judaism in the Roman World: Collected Essays* (Leiden: Brill, 2007), pp. 98-100; Louis Feldman, *Judaism and Hellenism Reconsidered* (Leiden: Brill, 2006), pp. 243-51.

[20] McKnight, *A Light Among the Gentiles*, p. 45.

language of being "born of the Spirit" challenges Nicodemus to re-discover what it means to ethnically join oneself to a community in which one has no privileged relation, superior ancestry, or ties to land. And Jesus does not argue for ceremonial conversion for Gentiles. He champions the need for all people to be maternally "born again" by the Spirit. This is a direct critique to those in power who uphold, benefit from, and presume ethnic superiority.

What this also does, especially for us today, is instill within the Christian faith a central belief that all disparate ethnic people can become bonded together into one family through the maternal birthing activity of the Spirit. In other words, by rooting our spiritual origin in the divine Spirit, the foreigner become our potential fellow kin. How then can hostile perceptions of foreigners be maintained by members of this Spirit–birthed family? Even more, how can we say that "God so loved the world" while also upholding hostile perceptions of foreigners and immigrants? This also suggests that nationalism and ethnocentric patriotism that fosters xenophobia and racial hostility toward foreigners are practices contrary to the Spirit. The Spirit desires to indiscriminately give birth to all people who believe in Jesus.

Perhaps for the readers of the Gospel, those who are observing, and still debating their relationship between Jews and Jewish Christian communities in the late first century, the teaching on being "born of the Spirit" had major ethnic significance. These readers of the Gospel may have had questions about the qualifications needed to be included within the family of God. However, in Jesus' teaching they are made aware that their membership in the family of God is grounded in the Spirit. The demagoguing of foreigners is thus not merely wrong for morality's sake, it is anti–pneumatic. We must prophetically speak to U.S. Christians that are complicit with the racism against the Latinx community and remind them of this central tenant of our identity. As believers who are born of the Spirit, there are no benefits and privileges in which we can base notions of ethnic superiority over immigrants or non–citizens. These are the false spirits that roam the earth and bring about division and animosity toward those whom the Spirit is open to include within the family of God through a new birth.

Defending Orphaned Latinx Dreamers and the Paraclete

Another aspect to explore in the Gospel of John is the implication of the Spirit's description as the Paraclete as it relates to social justice. But first, we must notice that what clearly separates the description of the Spirit from the other Gospels is this rare word "Paraclete."[21] This Greek word is difficult to translate. Some translations prefer the term "helper," "comforter," or "advocate."[22] Otto Betz remarks that the term originates from a courtroom context.[23] As such, a Paraclete is a "person called in to help, summoned to give assistance," or "helper in court."[24] We cannot ignore the forensic courtroom meaning that goes along with the description of the Spirit as a Paraclete. What then are the implications of this legal courtroom description of the Spirit? Primarily, it means that the Holy Spirit as the Paraclete

---

[21] The term παράκλητος is found on four occasions within John (14.16; 14.26; 15.26; 16.7) and once in the letter (1 Jn. 2.1). For a helpful analysis of the similarities and differences of the Spirit in the Gospel tradition see Craig Keener, *The Spirit in the Gospel's and Acts* (Peabody: Hendrickson, 1997).

[22] For example, the NRSV, NET, NLT, and NAB translate the term as "advocate." The NASB, NKJV, and ESV prefer "helper." The NIV and CSB translate παράκλητος as "counselor." The NJB prefers the transliteration "Paraclete" although the term is not an English word.

[23] Otto Betz, *Der Paraklet* (Leiden: Brill, 1963), p. 1; He insists that it "stammt aus der forensischen Sphäre" and is in reference to "den herbeigerufenen, Mann, der vor dem Richter für den Angeklagten spricht, den Fürsprecher, den Anwalt." In the Farewell Discourse different nuances and additional activities of the παράκλητος also emerge. The Spirit as παράκλητος is promised to be with the disciples forever, abiding with them and being in them (14.16-17). The παράκλητος will also teach and remind the disciples (14.26), testify (15.26-27), and convict the world (16.7); Johannes Behm agrees that παράκλητος is not used as a title for a professional legal adviser. But he finds that the history and concept of παράκλητος show that all subsidiary meanings were interwoven into the primary sense of advocate. See Behm, "παράκλητος," *TDNT* 5:814.

[24] Behm, "παράκλητος," pp. 801–803; Philo uses the term in reference to reconciliation with God (*Praem.* 1.166), the chief advisor Marco who is described as a παράκλητος for the emperor Tiberius (*Flacc.* 1.13, 22), and when the governor of Egypt Flaccus was exiled, it was Lepidus who interceded as a παράκλητος to help alleviate his banishment before Caligula (*Flacc.* 1.151, 181).

is a defender of God's people in a world filled with hatred (Jn 15.19), violence, and injustice (Jn 16.2). We must also notice that when Jesus promises to send the Paraclete to the disciples, the context is a pending abandonment. Jesus states, "I will ask the Father and he will send the Paraclete ... I will not leave you as orphans" (14.18). Jesus knew that his death would leave the disciples as orphans and thus promises to send the Paraclete. But why illustrate the reality of his departure with that of an orphan (14.18) – the most vulnerable and defenseless person in Greco–Roman antiquity?

The imagery of an orphan is a vivid metaphor that illustrates the grave consequences of abandonment that would befall the disciples. We may assume that orphans were those who only lost both parents, but this was not so in antiquity. Losing solely one's father would have classified a child as an orphan even though the mother was still alive.[25] There were many fatherless children in the ancient world given the high mortality rate and a tendency of men to marry late in life.[26] In fact, about one–third of all children within the Greco–Roman period would have lost their father by the age of fifteen.[27] Losing one's father brought economic disruption, placed one's inheritance in jeopardy, caused undue hardship and grief for the mother, and led to the possibility of becoming vulnerable to oppression and exploitation.[28] These challenges motivated many widows to immediately remarry.[29] Although guardians, older siblings, and extended family members often took it upon themselves to care for orphans, the harsh consequences of being orphaned were difficult to

---

[25] J.T. Fitzgerald, "Orphans in Mediterranean Antiquity and Early Christianity," *Act* 23 (2016)), p. 30.

[26] Sabine Hübner and David Ratzan, "Fatherless Antiquity? Perspectives on 'Fatherlessness' in the Ancient Mediterranean," in *Growing Up Fatherless in Antiquity* (ed. Sabine Hübner and David Ratzan; New York: Cambridge University, 2009), p. 9.

[27] Walter Scheidel, "The Demographic Background," in *Growing Up Fatherless in Antiquity* (ed. Sabine Hübner and David Ratzan (New York: Cambridge University, 2009), pp. 31–40.

[28] Hübner and Ratzan, "Fatherless Antiquity," pp. 10–13.

[29] Hübner, "Callirhoe's Dilemma: Remarriage and Stepfathers in the Greco-Roman East," in *Growing Up Fatherless in Antiquity* (ed. Sabine Hübner and David Ratzan; New York: Cambridge University, 2009), pp. 64–67.

alleviate. Orphans were the most vulnerable and easily marginalized, oppressed, and likely to experience injustice.

The difficult life of orphans is also noticed in Greek and biblical literature. Within the Homeric epics, an orphaned child was often put in a precarious and sometimes fatal situation.[30] Greek mythology also discusses their dire situation.[31] When we turn to biblical literature, the similar difficult experiences of orphans also emerge. Orphans in the Old Testament were defenseless in society.[32] They are most susceptible to being oppressed, murdered, sold as slaves, experience theft and financial distress, and denied justice.[33] Due to these harsh experiences, God is portrayed as their surrogate father and protector.[34] Although the New Testament rarely mentions orphans, the same command to care for orphans is assumed. In particular, Jesus demonstrates his ability to raise a dead orphan boy who was the only son of a widow in a town called Nain (Lk. 7.11-16). James describes true religion as "caring for the orphans and widows in their

---

[30] Georg Wöhrle, "Sons (and Daughters) without Fathers: Fatherlessness in the Homeric Epics," in Sabine Hübner and David Ratzan (ed.), *Growing Up Fatherless in Antiquity* (New York: Cambridge University, 2009), p. 174; Hübner remarks that it was the wealthy aristocrats who were able to provide guardians that served as father figures over the orphan's property. In other occasions, stepfathers would adopt orphans, welcome, and protect them. See "Remarriage and Stepfathers," pp. 80–81.

[31] Hesiod, *Op.* 327-34; Euripides, *Ion*, 25-35.

[32] Marcus Sigismund, "'Without Father, without Mother, without Genealogy': Fatherlessness in the Old and New Testament," in Sabine Hübner and David Ratzan (ed.), *Growing Up Fatherless in Antiquity* (New York: Cambridge, 2009), p. 87.

[33] Exod. 22.22; Deut. 10. 18; 14.28-29; 24.17-22; 26.12-13; 27.19; 2 Kgs 4.1; Job 24.9; 29.12; 31.17-22; Ps. 94.6; Prov. 23.10; Isa. 1.17, 23; Jer. 5.28; 7.6; 22.3; Ezek. 22.7; Zech. 7.10; Mal. 3.5.

[34] In the OT God is concerned about the status and welfare of orphans. God is depicted as their defender, promises to hear the cries, and avenge them (Exod. 22.22-27). God is described as executing justice for orphans (Deut. 10.18). The Psalmist also portrays God as a "helper of the orphan ... who inclines his ear to vindicate the orphan and oppressed" (Ps. 10.14, 17-18). Or as more poignantly described, "He is a father to the fatherless" (Ps. 68.5). And in Hosea the prophet claims, "For in you the orphan find mercy" (14.3). Even more, the Israelite community is given an injunction to protect and provide for them, not causing them any more undue hardship.

misfortune" (Jas. 1.27). And we find similar concerns within the context of caring for widows in Paul's letter to Timothy (1 Tim. 5.1-16).

How then does Jesus mitigate the pending orphaning caused by his death in the Gospel of John? Jesus tells the disciples that they will not be abandoned and promises to send the Paraclete. Simply put, the presence of the Paraclete is the presence of the Holy Spirit upon earth while Jesus is away. The sending of the Holy Spirit as Paraclete therefore compels us to bring the role of advocacy for the defenseless in our pneumatological imagination. Fighting for justice in this sense is just as spiritual as it is social. Defending God's people who experience abandonment and hatred is also the work of the Paraclete. Indeed, the Spirit as a Paraclete is not silent or absent. Jesus explains that the Spirit will be an advocate for the disciples, especially since they are warned that they would experience violence and hatred in the synagogue.

When we read this description of the Holy Spirit as a Paraclete through the context of the Latinx community, this also means that Jesus is promising to send the Holy Spirit to those who are defenseless and fatherless, includes Dreamers who are the legislatively orphaned children amongst us. Who are the Dreamers? The term "Dreamers" comes from the U.S. legislative bill S.1291 (2001), which was introduced by Senators Orrin Hatch (R) and Patrick Leahy (D). Later legislative bills such as the S.2205 (2007) and the S.3992 (2010) also used a similar acronym: Development, Relief, and Education for Alien Minors (D.R.E.A.M.). These bills aimed to cancel all deportation procedures of undocumented people under 30 years of age and who entered the United States of America before the age of 16. It would also adjust their status from "undocumented" to "temporary residents," with ongoing renewals every 10 years. The experience of Dreamers is unlike the experience of the first–generation migrants. The Center for American Progress and Tom K. Wong of the University of California San Diego finds that the average age that Dreamers came to the U.S. is 6 years old.[35] According to the Brookings Institute, almost one–third were 5 years or younger and more than two–

---

[35] Tom K. Wong, *et al.*, "DACA Recipients' Economic and Educational Gains Continue to Grow," Center for American Progress, accessed February 8, 2019, https://cdn.americanprogress.org/
content/uploads/2017/11/02125251/2017_DACA_study_economic_report_updated.pdf.

thirds were 10 or younger when they arrived.[36] In fact, their early arrival means that Dreamers are educated within public schools and have lived in the United States of America the majority of their lives.[37]

However, the Trump administration's hostility toward immigrants has taken a toll on the psychological wellbeing of Dreamers. Since Trump's presidency, field surveys reveal that Dreamers have experienced additional emotional distress given the new fear of being deported.[38] Luz Garcini found that 63% of undocumented young people between the ages of 18 to 25 are showing signs of psychological distress, which is the highest percentage of any age group. They not only experience chronic stress but also have an inner conflict as they contend with the reality that the U.S. does not want them even though the U.S. is their home.[39]

Dreamers are legislatively orphaned from their own land. Their home country which they have known their entire lives has rejected them, abandoned them, used them for political votes, and ultimately desires to exile them. Strikingly, the language for country in Greek is πατρίς (*patris*) which means to have a native land, hometown, or country. The term comes from the Greek word πατήρ (*pater*) which is translated as father. In antiquity it was understood that to have a native land is to have a fatherland.[40] And thus to be without a native land is akin to being fatherless, metaphorically orphaned without a place to call home. Jesus also knew what it meant

---

[36] Nicole Prchal Svajlenka and Audrey Singer, "Immigration Facts: Deferred Action for Childhood Arrivals (DACA)," Brookings Institute, accessed February 8, 2019, https://www.brookings.edu/research/immigration-facts-deferred-action-for-childhood-arrivals-daca.

[37] 72% of Dreamers are enrolled in college and pursue a bachelor's degree or higher. See Tom K. Wong, *et al.*, "Amid Legal and Political Uncertainty, DACA Remains More Important Than Ever," Center for American Progress, accessed February 8, 2019, https://americanprogress.org/issues/immigration/news/2018/08/15/454731/amid-legal-political-uncertainty-daca-remains-important-ever.

[38] Wong, *et al.*, "Amid Legal and Political Uncertainty," n.p.

[39] Cecilia Ballí, "Research: The psychological distress of Dreamers," *Houston Chronicle*. August 11, 2017.

[40] Homer, *Od.* 10.236; 20.193; 24.322; *Il.* 12.243; 24.500; Hesiod, *Scut.* 1, 2; Aristophanes, *Thesm.* 859; Aeschylus, *Sept.* 585; Demosthenes, *Cor.* 18.296; Plato, *Pol.* 3081.

to be a Dreamer. He knew what it meant to be orphaned from his own hometown. He called himself a prophet without a country (patris), rejected by his own people of Galilee.[41] We also find the writer of Hebrews metaphorically describing all the Jewish patriarchs as being orphaned from their own land. The writer affirms that they all died in faith as "strangers and exiles" even while they sought "a country (patris) that they could call their own" (Heb. 11.13-16). Thus, the experiences of Dreamers in the United States of America are not without parallel. Biblical literature includes people who had no homeland although they dwelled and lived upon the land their entire lives.

What then does the Paraclete have to do with Dreamers, those children who are orphaned from their own land? Or more specifically, how does the Paraclete's activity as a defender of the oppressed and those who experience injustice also shape our understanding of the orphaned Dreamers today, including migrant children in internment camps within the deserts of Texas? To put it simply, the Paraclete is a defender of God's people. The Paraclete moves to convict the world of its injustice and unrighteousness. How does the Paraclete do this? The Paraclete does this not only through convicting our consciousness, but also through the proclamation of justice. Indeed, the Paraclete is made manifest in the activity of advocacy. This must not only inform our spirituality; it must also shape how we view all social–political advocacy for the defenseless. Therefore, to engage in advocacy for justice and defend the oppressed is to imitate the work of the Holy Spirit. There are too many children who are denied their legal rights of asylum and opportunity to become citizens in the land in which they have lived their entire lives. Like the vulnerable experiences of orphans of antiquity, Dreamers today are legislatively abandoned by their own country (fatherland). Dreamers are not considered true children of this nation, even though they speak English just like any citizen. And it is also this current political climate that continues to leave them vulnerable to exploitation and oppression, a situation that would have come upon orphans in antiquity. We must engage in social advocacy for the most vulnerable. To do so is to join the movement and work of the Paraclete on earth, who, by definition is an advocate sent by the Father.

---

[41] Matthew 13.54-57; Mk. 6.1-4; Lk. 4.23-24; Jn. 4.44.

Our Call to Participate with the Spirit

Cornel West remarks that "race is the most explosive issue in American life precisely because it forces us to confront the tragic facts of poverty and paranoia, despair and distrust."[42] Yet the Church is challenged to revisit the Scriptures in order to engage the problem of race in society. Emerson and Smith notice that if anyone should be doing something about the race problem in America, it should be the Christians. But, as they notice, Christians are not addressing the fundamental divisions that exist in our current racialized society. Instead, they generally maintain these historical divides and recreate racial divisions and inequalities.[43] How do we change this? How do we prophetically speak to the Church so that it would regain its moral authority? And what must we do to participate in the Spirit's activity against racism and hostility against the Latinx community as we learn from the Gospel of John?

As I have done thus far in this reading of the Spirit from selected passages in John, the people of God must engage in ethnic justice, not only for the Latinx community, but for all people who are confronted with oppression because of their race or immigrant status. The people of the Spirit must recognize that membership into the family of God is only possible because of the birthing activity of the Spirit. This unity in the family of God should supersede the pride of being an "American." Our call to action must begin by seeing in one another the common birthing experience of the Spirit. Our minds need to be liberated from the demonic ideologies of racism. Racism thrives because there is a false assumption that one is superior to another because of one's ethnic identity. It is true, cultural diversity and differences exist. But this should not become the pretense for creating racial hierarchy. The Spirit of God is not racist. The divine breath extends the opportunity for all people from different ethnic identities and backgrounds to join the family of God. The Spirit of God is the breath of God that is inclusive and family embracing. Who are we, as people born of the Spirit, to create ethnic barriers and racial division where the Spirit has placed none? Did the Spirit only seek to provide a new birth to the Jews? Not at all. As we see in John 3, the Spirit of God moves where it pleases and will give birth

---

[42] Cornell West, *Race Matters* (Boston: Beacon, 2017), p. 107.

[43] Emerson and Smith, *Divided by Faith*, pp. 17–18.

to any person who believes in Jesus. We must not be afraid of the ethnically other but befriend them, welcome them in our communities, and honor them as equal members who are beloved and birthed by the Spirit. Yet this is a call to do more than just "befriend" the ethnically other. We must challenge communities and our Churches to tear down the systems that oppress people who look different. This involves a transformation on how we live in this world.

Second, the Holy Spirit as the Paraclete is concerned about the orphaned and marginalized amongst us. The presence and activity of the Paraclete is not only manifested in our spiritual experiences, it is also manifested in our advocacy for the abandoned such as the Latinx Dreamers amongst us. When Jesus was about to die, he promised that the Paraclete would come and be the defender of the disciples. Jesus was concerned about the disciples and the hardships they were about to encounter. We too, who are called to follow Jesus, must also be concerned about those who endure and experience political hardships because of their immigrant status. If we can recognize that the same Spirit that has embraced and welcomed us into the family of God also seeks to embrace immigrants and Dreamer amongst us, how can we continue to maintain or uphold unwarranted fears? How can we allow the dehumanization of immigrants continue within our churches and communities with racist rhetoric and policies? We cannot minimize the racial problem today nor fail to see how racism is also in our systems, policies, and structures in society. Fighting for justice and defending the oppressed and marginalized is to engage the same activity that the Holy Spirit has done for us. Without this Paraclete activity, we would all be alone and without the help from God. However, the fact that the Holy Spirit emerges as a defender of God's people compels us to imitate this activity and defend those who are orphaned amongst us. We look after the marginalized because this is what the Spirit does. We fight for justice because this is what the Paraclete does for those who are called and invited to be Jesus' disciples. This is what we do, because it is what the Spirit Paraclete has done for us. Our justice activity is not just social, it is a spiritual activity that imitates the Paraclete.

Our call to action therefore must join the Paraclete to push back against the anti–pneumatic xenophobia and racism that has emerged in our land, crept within our Christian communities, and continues to threaten the Latinx Church. Failure to stand up against racism is a failure to participate in the ongoing life–giving activity and presence of the Holy Spirit who seeks to draw and be with all people. We must recognize that none of us would or could be called "children of God" without the Spirit. Racism and hostility against the foreigner are at its core anti–pneumatic. We must never fail to reject or stand against racism and ethnic hostility against foreigners. To side with the racist and people who demonize the ethnically other is to stand against the Spirit who embraces all people and who fights for justice on earth as the Paraclete.

Bibliography

Abutaleb, Yasmeen, "What's Inside the Hate–Filled Manifesto Linked to the Alleged El Paso Shooter," *Washington Post* (4 August 2019).

Anderson, Carol, *White Rage: The Unspoken Truth of our Racial Divide* (Bloomsbury: New York, 2017).

Arango, Tim, Nicholas Bogel-Burroughs, and Katie Benner, "Minutes Before El Paso Killing, Hate–Filled Manifesto Appears Online," *New York Times* (3 August 2019).

Ballí, Cecilia, "Research: The psychological distress of Dreamers," *Houston Chronicle* (August 11, 2017).

Betz, Otto, *Der Paraklet* (Leiden: Brill, 1963).

Boatwright, Mary, *Peoples of the Roman World* (New York: Cambridge University, 2012).

McCoskey, Denise, *Race Antiquity and Its Legacy* (New York: Oxford, 2012).

Christophi, Helen, "Feds Tell 9th Circuit: Detained Kids 'Safe and Sanitary' Without Soap," *Courthouse News Service* (June 18, 2019).

Cohen, Shaye, *The Beginning of Jewishness* (Berkley: University of California, 1999).

Collins, John, *Between Athens and Jerusalem: Jewish Identity in the Hellenistic Diaspora* (Grand Rapids: Eerdmans, 2000).

Diangelo, Robin, *White Fragility: Why It's so Hard for White People to Talk about Racism* (Boston: Beacon, 2018).

Dickerson, Caitlin, "There Is a Stench: Soiled Clothes and No Baths for Migrant Children at a Texas Center," *New York Times* (21 June 2019).

Eliav–Feldon, Miriam, Benjamin Isaac, and Joseph Ziegler, "Introduction," in Eliav–Feldon, Miriam, Benjamin Isaac, and Joseph Ziegler (eds.), *The Origins of Racism in the West* (New York: Cambridge University, 2009), pp. 1-31.

Emerson, Michael, and Christian Smith, *Divided by Faith: Evangelical Religion and the Problem of Race in America* (Oxford: New York, 2000).

Feldman, Louis, *Judaism and Hellenism Reconsidered* (Leiden: Brill, 2006).

Frosch, Dan, and Alicia A. Caldwell, "As Border Crisis Worsens, a Detention Center Designed for Children Has None," *The Wall Street Journal* (5 July 2019).

Goodman, Martin, *Judaism in the Roman World: Collected Essays* (Leiden: Brill, 2007).

Hannaford, Ivan, *Race: History of the Idea in the West* (Maryland: Johns Hopkins, 1996).

Hall, Jonathan, *Ethnic Identity in Greek Antiquity* (New York: Cambridge University).

Hübner, Sabine, and David Ratzan (eds.), *Growing Up Fatherless in Antiquity* (New York: Cambridge University, 2009).

Isaac, Benjamin, *The Invention of Racism in Classical Antiquity* (New Jersey: Princeton, 2004).

Keener, Craig, *The Spirit in the Gospel's and Acts* (Peabody: Hendrickson, 1997).

Kennedy, Rebecca, *Race and Ethnicity in the Classical World* (Indiana: Hackett, 2013).

McKnight, Scot, *A Light Among the Gentiles: Jewish Missionary Activity in the Second Temple Period* (Minneapolis: Fortress, 1991).

Papenfuss, Mary, "Justice Department Argues Against Providing Soap, Toothbrushes, Beds to Detained Kids," *Huffington Post* (21 June 2019).

Sherwin-White, Adrian, *Racial Prejudice in Imperial Rome* (New York: Cambridge, 1970).

Snowden, Frank, *Blacks in Antiquity: Ethiopians in the Greco–Roman Experience* (MA: Cambridge, 1970).

Tisby, Jemar, *The Color of Compromise: The Truth About the American Church's Complicity in Racism* (Grand Rapids: Zondervan, 2019).

West, Cornell, *Race Matters* (Boston: Beacon, 2017).

TRUTH TO POWER

CHAPTER SIX

THE SPIRIT OF THE LORD IS FREEDOM: THE GOD OF THE GOSPEL AND THE ABOLITION OF MASTERY

Chris E.W. Green*

> The logic and practice of modern racism must be understood as a distinctly christological problem, requiring a christological solution.[1]

Not long after the infamous "witch" trials in Salem, a group of slaves in Boston founded the Religious Society of Negroes. Cotton Mather, the famous Puritan divine and a fierce defender of slavery, wrote the society's standards, including its covenant: "We, the miserable children of Adam and Noah ... freely resolve ... to become the Servants of the Glorious Lord."[2] Later, Mather published his *A Good Master Well Served*, which bore this gargantuan subtitle, "A brief discourse on the necessary properties & practices of a good servant in every-kind of servitude: and of the methods that should be taken by the heads of a family, to obtain such a servant." Mather made it unmistakably clear to the slaves in New England that they had only one

---

* Chris E.W. Green (PhD, Bangor University, Wales, UK) serves as Professor of Theology at Southeastern University in Lakeland, Florida, and Teaching Pastor at Sanctuary Church in Tulsa, Oklahoma.

[1] J. Kameron Carter, "Christology, or Redeeming Whiteness: A Response to James Perkinson's Appropriation of Black Theology," *Theology Today* 60 (2004), pp. 525-39 (532).

[2] Cotton Mather, "RULES For the Society of NEGROES. 1693. Evans Early American." No Page Numbers: Online.
https://quod.lib.umich.edu/e/evansdemo/R08350.0001.001/
1:1?rgn=div1;view=fulltext; accessed, 31 August 2019.

choice: either serve God and his servants (white and male) or serve the "black devil" and his minions (as the "black witches" had done).[3]

Mather believed that black people could have white souls if they were washed "White in the blood of the Lamb." Only this could save them from being "infinitely blacker."[4] But this meant that for Africans, salvation in Christ meant not full freedom but delivery from bondage to sin into a double slavery – first to God and then to their "earthly masters":

> First, Renounce, and, Forsake, the Service of those Invisible Masters, a Slavery to whom, is inconsistent, with the Service of the Lord Jesus Christ. Our Lord Jesus Christ hath said, in Math. 6.24. Ye cannot Serve God and Mammon. Thus, ye cannot Serve the Lord Jesus Christ, and Serve the World, the Flesh, and the Devil … Wretched Servants! Oh! That you were more sensible of your horrible Captivity; When will you be Aware, when will you be Weary of it! I tell you, a Turkish, or a Spanish Slavery, is not a thousandth part so miserable, as the Accursed Slavery of your Souls, to the Invisible Destroyers of your Souls. But will you at length take a Course, for your own Deliverance, O Wretched Servants, that you are?[5]

His views seem hateful to us now. But what if we still believe the essence of what he taught about mastery? What if we still hold the belief that God has ordered the world into superiors and inferiors, rules and ruled, greater and lessers? It seems to me that we do hold this belief, and that this belief is deeper than, and a root of, racism and white supremacy, sexism and misogyny, clericalism – and so many other evils. To cut out this root, we have to reimagine what we mean when we declare that Christ is Lord.

---

[3] Ibram X. Kendi, *Stamped from the Beginning: The Definitive History of Racist Ideas in America* (New York: Nation Books, 2016), pp. 61-62.

[4] Kendi, *Stamped from the Beginning*, p. 63.

[5] Cotton Mather, *A Good Master Well Served*, n.p. Available online: https://quod.lib.umich.edu/cgi/t/text/text-idx?c=evans;cc=ev-ans;view=text; idno=N00618.0001.001;rgn=div1;node=N00618.0001.001:3; accessed: 9 August 2019.

"Jesus Christ is Lord": A Good Confession?

To be clear, if we take the apostolic witness as definitive – as we should, of course – then the confession of Christ's lordship is integral to the proclamation of the gospel. But what does it actually mean? Which interpretations of the confession are most faithful?

Calling Jesus "Lord" usually serves two purposes. First, it is a way of acclaiming his *authority*, that is, his right to demand absolute allegiance and complete obedience from us. This right is usually believed to arise both from his natural superiority to us – he is God and we are not – as well as the fact that he created us "in the beginning." As his creatures, we are his property. As our owner, he always has the first and last word about us. Second, calling Jesus "Lord" is a way to acknowledge the fact that he has the power to *enforce* his demands on us. This recent Baptist confession frames the belief in familiar terms:

> The lordship of Jesus Christ is the singular, great confession of the Christian faith. When applied to the church, the declaration that "Jesus is Lord" is an absolute affirmation that the church and all that is associated with it belongs to Christ. The lordship of Christ is the belief that the church exists and functions in submission to the person and will of the resurrected Savior.[6]

But critical reflection turns up insuperable problems with this account of lordship. We cannot of course ignore the fact that the language of master and slave is given in Scripture. We should accept it as normative. But we must also insist it cannot be taken as affirmation either of the practice of slavery or of the ideology of mastery in any of its forms. Instead of taking our preconceptions of superiority and inferiority and mapping them onto our relation to God, we need to allow the revelation of God in Christ to draw an altogether different map of our reality. A new reality that saves us all from mastery and from all that we have done and continue to do with it.

---

[6] R. Stanton Norman, *The Baptist Way: Distinctives of a Baptist Church* (Nashville: Broadman & Holman Publishers, 2005), p. 33.

"But Not So with You"

We know that Jesus taught his disciples to reject the inequalities that others considered natural:

> The kings of the Gentiles lord it over them; and those in authority over them are called benefactors. But not so with you; rather the greatest among you must become like the youngest, and the leader like one who serves. For who is greater, the one who is at the table or the one who serves? Is it not the one at the table? But I am among you as one who serves (Lk 22.25-27).

And yet it has proven difficult for the church to take this teaching seriously. What Jesus seems to have forbidden, we continue to affirm. Or at least to excuse. But what if we were to take Jesus' words seriously? What if we refused to submit to the rules of mastery, wherever they are at play? What if we stopped trying to use them to our advantage?

At least on one reading, this is exactly what Paul called his churches to do:

> Let the same mind be in you that was in Christ Jesus, Who, though he was in the form of God, did not regard equality with God as something to be exploited, but emptied himself, taking the form of a slave, being born in human likeness. And being found in human form, he humbled himself and became obedient to the point of death – even death on a cross. Therefore God also highly exalted him and gave him the name that is above every name, so that at the name of Jesus every knee should bend, in heaven and on earth and under the earth, and every tongue should confess that Jesus Christ is Lord, to the glory of God the Father (Phil. 2.5-11).

This is a familiar passage, but I am convinced that it is almost always misread. Jesus, Paul says, does not exploit his divinity, the "form of God," but empties it – pours it into – his humanity, into the "form of a slave." That does *not* mean Christ became less divine. That is not even a meaningful concept. God is infinite: he cannot be less or more. God is perfect: he can never improve or backslide. So, in the taking of flesh, Christ does not de-divinize himself. He divinizes his humanity instead. Christ takes the form of a slave because that is the only form of life (as death has made it) that could receive the fulness he intends to give all creatures. In the world as we know it, nothing and no-one is as much like God as the person we have treated as less human than we are. And if even the form of the slave has been humanized by God, then all human beings are transfigured by the work of Christ.

We misread this passage because we assume that God needs to limit himself in order to live a human life. As if his divinity is incompatible with creation. We misread this passage because we assume that for God to become human is for God to humiliate himself. But the incarnation, as Bonhoeffer says, is not God's humiliation.[7] It is his revelation. He does not rid himself of the form of God but fills the form of a slave with the form of God. Theologically, *that* is what kenosis means. Not emptying out, but filling up.

Christ does humble himself, to be sure. But the humiliation, as Scripture describes it, comes in his obedience to *death*, not God. "And being found in human form, he humbled himself and became obedient to the point of death – even death on a cross" (Phil. 2.8). Notice, Christ does not merely obey *to the point of death*. He submits *to dying*, and so to death itself. In this way, we might say that Christ exposes death, *not God*, as the source of our conceptions and practices of lordship and submission. He exposes death in the same way that he reveals God, thus showing that slavery and mastery are antithetical to the character of God. Not creations of the Spirit, but irruptions of evil. And so slavery, as well as any and all prejudices and discriminations – including racism, misogyny, and clericalism – that assert the superiority of some and the inferiority of others, are exposed as anti-Christ.

Jesus has been given "the name that is above every name" (Phil. 2.9). But not in the sense that he is "the greatest," the one "at the top," the "last one standing." He has been given a name beyond all names because he has finally overcome the rivalry inherent in naming. He has "made captivity itself a captive" (Eph. 4.8), and in so doing, has overcome mastery once for all. J. Kameron Carter has it exactly right: YHWY performs mastery differently.[8] That is why, in him, we are "more than conquerors" (Rom. 8.37): both conquering

---

[7] See Dietrich Bonhoeffer, *Who is Christ for Us?* (Minneapolis: Fortress Press, 2002).

[8] J. Kameron Carter, *Race: A Theological Account* (Oxford: Oxford University Press, 2008), p. 323.

and being conquered have been done away with, just as mastery and slavery have been.

One of Jesus' stranger parables – and they are all strange – tells the story of a wealthy landowner who pays all of his workers the same wage at the end of the day in spite of the fact that they did not all work the same hours. Some, in fact, came only at the very end of the day, and worked only the last hour. Unsurprisingly, those who had worked the longest complained against the others. This is how the lord in the parable replies: "Friend, I am doing you no wrong ... Are you envious because I am generous?" And then Jesus add this coda to his story: "So the last will be first, and the first will be last" (Mt. 20.16). In saying that, Jesus makes his intentions clear: he means to do away with the very possibility of lasts and firsts. *He is the first and the last* (Rev. 1.17), which means no one can ever dominate or be dominated again. He is Lord, and so we are neither masters nor slaves, neither superiors nor inferiors. We are to one another what we are to him: friends, family.

Performing Lordship Differently

In his homilies on Ecclesiastes, Gregory of Nyssa condemns slavery in the starkest terms. This condemnation is all the more startling given that his older brother, Basil of Caesarea, and their friend, Gregory of Nazianzus, both accepted slavery as a kind of necessary evil.[9] As Carter explains, Nyssan's repudiation of slavery begins by "calling into question the chief supposition of the slaveholding system: the anthropological distinction between superior and inferior that grounds the logic of mastery and slavery."[10] Because they are made in God's image, made for a common share in Christ(likeness), all human beings – all, without exception – are free and self-determining (οὐ ἐλευθέρα ἡ φύσις καὶ αὐτεξούσιος).[11] All, without exception, are equal.

In making his case, Gregory first argues that slaveowners (like the Preacher) arrogate to themselves what belongs to God alone. "If [your slave] is in the likeness of God, and rules the whole earth, and

---

[9] Carter, *Race*, p. 232.
[10] Carter, *Race*, p. 236.
[11] PG, XLIV, col. 664 D.

has been granted authority over everything on earth from God, who is his buyer, tell me? Who is his seller? To God alone belongs this power."[12] Having established that point – all human beings are equally endowed with authority over all creation – Gregory makes an astonishing move:

> To God alone belongs this power; or rather, *not even to God him-self.* For "his gracious gifts," it says, "are irrevocable" (Rom. 11.29). God would not therefore reduce the human race to slavery, since he himself, when we had been enslaved to sin, spontaneously re-called us to freedom. But if God does not enslave what is free, who is he that sets his own power above God's?[13]

In this astonishing passage, Gregory is letting his Christological commitments take him to their logical end: the power of enslave-ment, the power of mastery, does not belong even to God because it is utterly at odds with the character of God.[14] God is free and freeing. Indeed, that is the key to understanding the whole of salvation his-tory. God established creatures in freedom in the beginning. And even after they had fallen into bondage, he freed them anew and gave us them his own share in the freedom that is his nature, his life so that they could never be enslaved again.

All that to say, for Nyssa, on this side of Easter, there is no more possibility of superiority and inferiority between human persons than there is between the divine persons. And – this is the critical point – there is no superiority and inferiority, no mastery and slav-ery, in our relation to God. Gregory leaves no doubt: God is not a master; we are not slaves. This, I believe, is the heart of the matter for Gregory's theological vision. Christ *is* Lord. That is a good con-fession. But the spirit of his lordship – its essence, its purpose – is

---

[12] Gregory of Nyssa, *Homilies on Ecclesiastes* (New York: Walter de Gruyter; 1993), p. 74.

[13] Gregory of Nyssa, *Homilies on Ecclesiastes*, p. 74. Emphasis added.

[14] J. Cameron Carter, "Between W.E.B. Du Bois and Karl Barth: The Problem of Modern Political Theology" in Vincent Lloyd (ed.), *Race and Political Theology* (Stanford: Stanford University Press, 2012), pp. 83-111, sees in Barth's *Römberbrief* an argument similar to Gregory's. In rebellion against God, striving to be like God (*sicut deus*), human beings now body forth the absurdity of mastery and slavery, which is the absurdity of sin it-self. Jesus, as the one human who is truly God, exposes it as absurd.

freedom. When the will of Christ is done "on earth as it is in heaven," there can no longer be "slave or free" – or any thoughts or practices that even suggest such distinctions. "Where the Spirit of the Lord is, there is freedom" (2 Cor. 3.16).

It is that latter point that sets Gregory's preaching apart, not only from his contemporaries but from the larger Christian tradition. Unlike others, who would of course agree that in Christ all are *spiritually* equal but that for now "nature" requires social and domestic inequalities, Gregory insists that our lived lives must bear out the proclaimed truth of the gospel *historically*. We cannot, as Mather and the vast majority of other Christian teachers have done, claim that Christ delivers us only in spiritual matters, leaving our societal and domestic and ecclesial orders unchallenged. If the ground is level at Calvary, how can it not be leveled everywhere else, too?

"Slaves, Obey Your Masters"

Needless to say, Scripture, in both testaments, gives directives to slaves and to masters. And in so doing, it seems to affirm the rightness, or at least the necessity, of mastery and slavery. Even a casual reading of the New Testament makes clear that both Peter and Paul, the pillars of the church, expected slaves to obey their masters – even the cruel ones – and to do so genuinely, whole-heartedly, as nothing less than an act of devotion to God.[15]

So, what are we to make of this? Overwhelmingly, Christians have read these texts, and others like them, as divine allowance if not outright affirmation of radical human inequality. Howard Thurman states the truth bluntly, but accurately: "too often the weight of the Christian movement has been on the side of the strong and the powerful and against the weak and oppressed."[16] That presents us with a problem. If we do not dismiss them altogether, is there a way to read

---

[15] "Slaves, accept the authority of your masters with all deference, not only those who are kind and gentle but also those who are harsh" (1 Pet. 2.18). "Slaves, obey your earthly masters with fear and trembling, in singleness of heart, as you obey Christ; not only while being watched, and in order to please them, but as slaves of Christ, doing the will of God from the heart" (Eph. 6.5-6).

[16] Howard Thurman, *Jesus and the Disinherited* (Boston: Beacon Press, 1976), p. 31.

them differently, perhaps redemptively? Is there a way to receive the spirit of these texts without the letter killing us?

We should begin with the fact that the Scriptures also contain claims transcending "all barriers of race and class and condition."[17] These transcendent claims suggest what William Webb calls a "redemptive trajectory" away from the social status quo .[18] Perhaps, then, taken as a whole, what the apostles and prophets say about mastery indicates that God is working in time to lead his people into a future in which full equality is realized as the norm. At any given moment in history, God's people may own slaves, and even justify it by appeals to God's will, but God is always working against it, leading his people toward deep, abiding equality.

But it may also be true that these master/slave texts, these "household codes," are inspired precisely to prove our hearts.[19] In this way, all of these passages might work for us something like Paul's letter was meant to work for Philemon, an early Christian slave-owner. N.T. Wright has argued that in his letter to Philemon "Paul is reconciling master and slave by taking on himself the role of Christ."[20] But Wright concludes the apostle is *not* demanding or even requesting his friend, Philemon, to grant Onesimus his freedom. He means only that when Onesimus again takes up his tasks in Philemon's household, he should not be expected to do so as "merely a slave."[21] Apparently, Wright believes that Paul believes – and that Paul wants Philemon and Onesimus to believe – that Onesimus is first and foremost a "brother" who just so happens also to be a slave.

I do not think Wright's reading is radical enough to do justice to the proclamation of the gospel. His reading mutes, if it does not out-and-out silence, the goodness of the good news. There is so much more to Paul's "even more" (v. 21)! Elsewhere, the apostle promises

---

[17] Thurman, *Jesus and the Disinherited*, p. 33.

[18] See William J. Webb, *Slaves, Women & Homosexuals: Exploring the Hermeneutics of Cultural Analysis* (Downers Grove, IL: IVP Academic, 2000).

[19] See my *Sanctifying Interpretation: Scripture, Holiness, Vocation* (Cleveland, TN: CPT Press, 2014).

[20] N.T. Wright, *Colossians and Philemon* (TNTC; Downers Grove, IL: InterVarsity Press; 1986), p. 193.

[21] Wright, *Colossians and Philemon*, p. 192.

that God purposes nothing less than his own fulness for us (Eph. 3.19; Col. 2.10). So, we have reason to ask: what would God's fulness mean for Onesimus and Philemon in this case? It seems obvious to me that Paul's "even more" to Philemon can only truly be fulfilled by Onesimus' deliverance into full equality. If there is anything less than perfect mutuality with his former master, then there is still "more" that can be done for the slave. And so, I believe that the best way to read Paul's letter to Philemon is as an invitation to fulness: Philemon *can* offer his former slave a share in the same equality the Father shares with the Son and the Son shares with his church. Nothing less than that is possible. And so, nothing less than that is needed.

Divine Power, Divine Humility

In the first volume of her systematics, Kate Sonderegger puts forward a creative reworking of the doctrine of divine omnipotence. She rejects the (Augustinian) notion that power is about doing whatever one wants, so that absolute power gives God the ability always to get his way. And she rejects the (Schleiermacherian) notion that power is about causation. Instead, Sonderegger argues that "Perfect Power is Holy Humility,"[22] and that talk about divine omnipotence must be removed from causal categories altogether. God does not *have* power. God *is* power. God is his own power, just as he is his own space, his own time.[23] And so he in no way violates creaturely integrity. He is as incapable of violence as he is of lying.

For Sonderegger, the revelatory event *par excellence* is Moses' encounter with God at the burning bush. The bush burns, but it is not consumed. The divine fire presents itself, but the bush is not undone by it. And *that,* she argues, is the definitive sign of God's power and presence: the creator presents himself without violating the creature. God reveals both himself and the creature. In Sonderegger's own words: "Almighty God is life, vitality, fire, utterly hidden in the dynamism in this world, poured out into the creaturely realm as its

---

[22] Katherine Sonderegger, *Systematic Theology: The Doctrine of God* (Minneapolis: Fortress Press, 2015), p. 176.

[23] See Matthew Wilcoxen, *Divine Humility* (Waco, TX: Baylor University Press, 2019), pp. 156-68.

own power, objective, humble; yet never the creature, never contained and confined, always explosive, holy, personal."[24]

God's power, then, is radically unlike what we have imagined it to be.[25] When we talk about God's power, we are saying that God is simply himself with us and toward us. He has no need of force. He does not need to make anything happen. Therefore, as Sonderegger says, he remains "utterly hidden in the dynamism in this word." This is at least in part what we mean when we say that God is "invisible," and why only faith can grasp what God has done.

I take time to draw attention to God's power in relation to his humility because I think we need to see how our presuppositions about divine power continue to underwrite, to sustain, our conceptions of mastery – long after we have rejected the practice of slavery. Even now, "woke" as we imagine ourselves to be, we find it virtually impossible to think of God and our relationship to God in any terms except those of power and submission, strength and weakness, greater and lesser. So much so that we force these dynamics into the Father-Son relation, as if the Son's obedience is the subservience of an inferior to a superior. Is that not how we understand Jesus' saying, "The Father is greater than I" (Jn 14.28)? But that understanding, if we hold it, is deeply problematic.

"The Father is Greater than I"

Traditionally, this statement is taken to be about the Son's humanity in relation to the Father's divinity. So read, this saying affirms the very presuppositions I am calling into question. But what if we did not read it that way? What if we were to understand that the Father is "greater" not in the sense that he is superior to the Son but in the

---

[24] Sonderegger, *Systematic Theology*, p. 209.

[25] Here, Sonderegger's critiques of the tradition are exactly right, it seems to me. As Wilcoxen (*Divine Humility*, p. 176) explains, if God were absolute cause, then

> his relation to creation would itself be absolutely necessary; he would be metaphysically dependent upon his effects. On the other hand, were God's power rooted in his ability to do whatever he wills, his power itself would be abstracted, severed from his goodness – a theological incoherence from the perspective of divine unicity and a severe problem for faith.

sense that he is the source of the Son's equality? This seems to be the logic of an earlier saying in the Gospel:

> Jesus said to them, Very truly, I tell you, the Son can do nothing on his own, but only what he sees the Father doing; for whatever the Father does, the Son does likewise. The Father loves the Son and shows him all that he himself is doing; and he will show him greater works than these, so that you will be astonished. Indeed, just as the Father raises the dead and gives them life, so also the Son gives life to whomever he wishes. The Father judges no one but has given all judgment to the Son, so that all may honor the Son just as they honor the Father (Jn 5.19-23).

Whatever it means to say the Father is "greater," it *cannot* mean that the Son is less than equal with him in any sense (humanly or divinely). When Jesus says, "the Father is greater than I," He does not mean, "I am less than the Father." Just the opposite is true, in fact. It is precisely *because* the Father is "greater" that Jesus can say "I and the Father are one" (Jn 10.30).

What do I mean? I mean that the divine nature is "greater" even than itself. That is, the Triune life is always excessive, always "greater" in such a way that nothing is "lesser" but everything – including God's own life – is more and more itself. This is why Jesus tells his disciples that they should rejoice: "If you loved me, you would rejoice that I am going to the Father, because the Father is greater than I" (Jn 14.28). Ascending into the Father's "greater," Jesus' "going away" turns out to be nothing but a more blessed "coming to." After all, the one who is omnipresent can never be absent: he can only be differently present. And the same holds true of the one who is divine by nature and shares that nature with us. By telling us that the Father is "greater," Jesus is telling us that the Father, like the Son, is infinite, and infinitely gracious.

Theologically, then, this is the bottom line: to understand what Jesus is saying, we have to think both trinitarianly and pneumato-logically. The Father loves the Son and the Son loves the Father, but this is not a self-enclosed relationship. God is the God he is because the Spirit, as the essence of the love between the Father and the Son, frees them from it and for it. As Rowan Williams explains,

> The single life of the Godhead is the going-out from self-identity into the other; that cannot be a closed mutuality (for then the

other would be only the mirror of the same); the love of one for other must itself open on to a further otherness if it is not to return to the same; and only so is the divine life "as a whole" constituted as love (rather than mutual reinforcement of identity).[26]

These are dense claims, obviously, but the truth is apparent enough. The Spirit is the essence and abundance, the flow and the overflow of the love of the Father for the Son and the love of the Son for the Father. Because these three "subsistent relations" constitute the divine life, our God's character is revealed to be a movement from "greater" to "greater" – without there in any sense ever being a "lesser." This is true of God's life *ad intra* and so of God's life *ad extra*. Given that this is true, we should never again think of superiority and inferiority, mastery and slavery, as descriptive of either God's life with God, or God's life with us, or our life with one another, or our life with the other creatures.[27]

Conclusion

Christ has performed Lordship differently, and in so doing, he has set us free to live in full freedom. In making Christ Lord in the Spirit, the Father has established our equality which radically reconfigures the very meaning of lordship so that superiority and inferiority are done away with for good. Christ makes not only the end of slavery, but also the abolition of mastery. And therefore, we now can – and therefore we *must* – perform *our* lives differently. As Gregory said to his audience on one Easter Sunday:

> You masters have heard; mark my saying as a sound one; do not slander me to your slaves as praising the day with false rhetoric, take away the pain from oppressed souls as the Lord does the

---

[26] Rowan Williams, "The Deflections of Desire: Negative Theology in Trinitarian Discourse" in Oliver Davies and Denys Turner (eds.), *Silence and the Word: Negative Theology and Incarnation* (Cambridge: Cambridge University Press, 2004), pp. 115-35 (117).

[27] This does *not* mean that there are no differentiations of roles; no one leading, no one following; no one holding authority over another. It *does* mean that such differentiations must be rooted in true equality, not inequality, just as Christ's obedience arises from his oneness with the Father, and the disciples' obedience arises from their friendship with Christ.

deadness from bodies, transform their disgrace into honour, their oppression into joy, their fear of speaking into openness; bring out the prostrate from their corner as if from their graves, let the beauty of the Paschal feast blossom like a flower upon everyone.[28]

We can summarize Nyssan's message in these terms: what makes Easter Easter is that it is equally good news for everyone. Is it not to our shame, and more importantly to others' hurt, that we have allowed Easter to be better news for Philemon than it is for Onesimus?

Without in any way being naive about either our own limitations or the reach of evil, we can and should be working to change how the world "works." We cannot establish the kingdom of God through our efforts, but we do not have to resign ourselves to the corruption, the injustice, the scarcity, the stockpiling, the bad faith, the meaninglessness that destroys life as we know it. We do not have to accept the domestic, ecclesial, and societal patterns of mastery and slavery, superiority and inferiority in our day-to-day lives.

For Christians, the ethical vision is cast by hope. As Jenson would say it, we can know that if it *shall be* true in the Fulfillment, then it *can be* true in some anticipatory way here-and-now. To focus on just one such problem: racism, and the white supremacy that it justifies, is bound up with beliefs about and practices of superiority. And those beliefs and practices *can* be changed. Racism is not simply ineradicable. It is not natural, and it is not graced. Hence, we do not have to submit to its claims to power. Again, as people who share in the divine nature, people led by the Spirit and at one with Christ, we have the power and the authority – which is to say, the *responsibility* – to alter reality. That is what it means, really, to say that Christ is Lord.

Bibliography

Bonhoeffer, Dietrich, *Who is Christ for Us?* (Minneapolis: Fortress Press, 2002).

Carter, J. Kameron, "Between W.E.B. Du Bois and Karl Barth: The Problem of Modern Political Theology," in Vincent Lloyd (ed.),

---

[28] Gregory of Nyssa, *The Easter Sermons* (Cambridge, MA: Philadelphia Patristic Foundation; 1981), p. 9.

Race and Political Theology (Stanford: Stanford University Press, 2012), pp. 83-111.

—"Christology, or Redeeming Whiteness: A Response to James Perkinson's Appropriation of Black Theology," *Theology Today* (60) (2004), pp. 525-39.

—*Race: A Theological Account* (Oxford: Oxford University Press, 2008).

Green, Chris E.W., *Sanctifying Interpretation: Vocation, Holiness, Scripture* (Cleveland, TN: CPT Press, 2014).

Gregory of Nyssa, *The Easter Sermons* (Cambridge, MA: Philadelphia Patristic Foundation, 1981).

—*Homilies on Ecclesiastes* (New York: Walter de Gruyter; 1993).

Kendi, Ibram X., *Stamped from the Beginning: The Definitive History of Racist Ideas in America* (New York: Nation Books, 2016).

Mather, Cotton, *A Good Master Well Served*, n.p. https://quod.lib.umich.ed u/cgi/t/text/text-idx?c=evans;cc=evans;view=text;idno=N00618.0001.001 ;rgn=div1; node=N00618. 0001.001:3.

Sonderegger, Katherine, *Systematic Theology: The Doctrine of God* (Minneapolis: Fortress Press, 2015).

Norman, R. Stanton, *The Baptist Way: Distinctives of a Baptist Church* (Nashville: Broadman & Holman Publishers, 2005).

Thurman, Howard, *Jesus and the Disinherited* (Boston: Beacon Press, 1976).

Webb, William J., *Slaves, Women & Homosexuals: Exploring the Hermeneutics of Cultural Analysis* (Downers Grove, IL: IVP Academic, 2000).

Wilcoxen, Matthew, *Divine Humility* (Waco, TX: Baylor University Press, 2019).

Williams, Rowan, "The Deflections of Desire: Negative Theology in Trinitarian Discourse," in Oliver Davies and Denys Turner (eds.), *Silence and the Word: Negative Theology and Incarnation* (Cambridge: Cambridge University Press, 2004).

Wright, N.T., *Colossians and Philemon* (TNTC; Downers Grove, IL: InterVarsity Press; 1986).

CHAPTER SEVEN

HEARING WHAT THE HOLY SPIRIT SAYS TODAY: PROPHETIC PROCLAMATION AGAINST ABUSE OF POWER

Daniel Morrison[*]

Over the past few years, the Christian church in the United States has had black congregants departing from a variety of mostly white Churches. After the initial failure of the Southern Baptist Convention to denounce the Alt-right Movement and its embrace of racist ideologies, the Reverend Doctor Lawrence Ware noted his plan to depart from the Convention.[1] After multiple edits to the resolution which called on the body to denounce the Alt-right, along with numerous rounds of voting, news outlets could finally report the Convention's condemnation of the movement on that Wednesday of the 2017 meeting.

While ministers like Ware face the difficulties of serving in their denominations, black lay members encounter the disappointment associated with the inactivity of those to whom they look for leadership and spiritual guidance. The *New York Times* reports,

> Black congregants – as recounted by people in Chicago, Los Angeles, Atlanta, Fort Worth and elsewhere – had already grown uneasy in recent years as they watched their white pastors fail to

[*] Daniel O. Morison (PhD, McMaster Divinity College, Ontario, Canada) serves as Assistant Professor of New Testament & Expository Preaching at the Assemblies of God Theological Seminary in Springfield, Missouri.
[1] Lawrence Ware, "Why I'm Leaving the Southern Baptist Convention" (2017) <https://nyti.ms/2uqoonj>.

address police shootings of African-Americans. They heard prayers for Paris, for Brussels, for law enforcement; they heard that one should keep one's eyes on the kingdom, that the church was colorblind, and that talk of racial injustice was divisive, not a matter of the gospel.[2]

These churches have abandoned the fellowship of the Holy Spirit and the like-mindedness that accompanies such fellowship (Phil 2.1-2). Instead, the congregations have conformed to the practices of the government and unlovingly and insensitively attempted to exercise authority over community members who already feel the pain of injustice. The attempt to silence their voices by delegitimizing their statements as "not a matter of the gospel" reveals that they have failed to recognize that "Christian love of the neighbor and justice cannot be separated, for love implies a demand for justice."[3]

Some churches inform their constituents that "the Scriptures call for civic loyalty,"[4] caution against open acts of civil disobedience,[5] and have in the past threatened to revoke the ministerial status of those who speak against the government.[6] They leave little room for standing against governments that violate the rights of others within the church – those from every tribe, language, people, and nation (Rev. 5.9). Instead of standing with those who experience the abusive power of the government, many churches have historically affirmed the activities of the government and attempted to join the government in silencing and refusing to acknowledge the voices of marginalized members of congregations.[7]

---

[2] Campbell Robertson, "A Quiet Exodus: Why Black Worshipers Are Leaving White Evangelical Churches?" (2018) <https://nyti.ms/2De9fnP>.

[3] Veli-Matti Kärkkäinen, *Christology: A Global Introduction* (Grand Rapids: Baker Academic, 2003), p. 222.

[4] General Council of the Assemblies of God, "War and Conscientious Objectors,"<https://ag.org/Beliefs/Topics-Index/War-and-Conscientious-Objectors>.

[5] General Council of the Assemblies of God. "Civil Disobedience" <https://ag.org/Beliefs/Topics-Index/Civil-Disobedience>.

[6] Edith L. Blumhofer, *Restoring the Faith: The Assemblies of God, Pentecostalism, and American Culture* (Champaign, IL: University of Illinois Press, 1993), p. 148.

[7] Joe Newman, *Race and the Assemblies of God: The Journey from Azusa Street to the "Miracle of Memphis"* (Youngstown, NY: Cambria Press, 2007),

While some majority white churches in the United States commit the sin of partiality (Jas. 2.9) by favoring law enforcement over ethnic minorities in their congregations, practice the sin of racism, and join oppressive systems in attempting to suppress the voices of victims, the Spirit calls the church to another way of life. The Apocalypse recalls the Spirit's declaration to the churches regarding both conformity to culture and power abuse. The Ephesian congregation's adoption of practices modeled by the broader culture demands a prophetic confrontation where the Spirit prophetically inspires John to challenge the church in Ephesus regarding its behavior and promises to reverse the effects of the abusive practices the congregation has embraced (Rev. 1.10; 2.1-7). The message to the church in Ephesus issues a Spirit-inspired prophetic proclamation against power abuse, noting that those who conform to the ungodly, abusive practices of their governments will have no part in God's eschatological kingdom. Given the present cultural climate in the United States, congregations must heed the call to hear what the Spirit continues to say to the churches.

Sociocultural Situation

The current cultural setting of the United States maintains various parallels with the city of Ephesus during the composition of the message to the congregation. The sociocultural situation in Ephesus reveals that the city exercised some of the most, if not the most, power among the cities within Asia Minor.[8] The city maintained a position of power and prominence as the largest in the region. It also served as a center of Roman administration.[9] The imperial cult found a prosperous place for its propagation in Ephesus; the location maintained a temple dedicated to Augustus.[10] The city's status

---

p. 108. Newman notes that the *Pentecostal Evangel*, the weekly publication of the Assemblies of God fails to mention the Civil Rights Movement during the 1950s.

[8] Ben Witherington, *Revelation* (Cambridge: Cambridge University Press, 2003), p. 95.

[9] David E. Aune, *Revelation 1–5* (Word Biblical Commentary, 52A; Dallas, TX: Word Books, 1997), p. 136.

[10] Craig R. Koester, *Revelation: A New Translation with Introduction and Commentary* (New Haven: Yale University Press, 2014), p. 259.

as a political, religious, and cultural center made it one of the most influential cities in Asia Minor.[11]

In addition to the city's leadership in the area of politics and culture, Ephesus possessed significant economic power. It was the most extensive commercial center in Asia.[12] The worship of Artemis significantly contributed to the city's culture and economy.[13] The Artemision's operation as a financial institution within Ephesus directly connects the cult of Artemis with the financial influence of the city.[14] While the people of the city worshiped other local deities, such as Apollo, Athena, and Zeus, the Ephesians understood themselves to have a special relationship with Artemis.[15]

These combined factors consistently made the congregation in Ephesus susceptible to interaction with some form of alternative teaching. As with the Christians in Ephesus as noted in the writings of the Apostle Paul (1 Tim. 1.3-11; 4.1-8; 2 Tim. 3.1-17), those receiving John's writing must face the toil of addressing those who rise up among the group bringing a false teaching to the congregation (Acts 20.28-32). The book of Revelation encourages the assembly to exhibit faithful resistance to the empire and the cults that contribute to its sociocultural contexts.[16]

The problem for this congregation comes in how it demonstrates resistance. When considering how the Roman Empire functioned, history reveals that "the Roman Empire promulgated a sort of

---

[11] Lähnemann, *Die Sieben Sendschreiben*, p. 525.

[12] Strabo, *Geographica*, p. 895.

[13] Michael Immendörfer, *Ephesians and Artemis: The Cult of the Great Goddess of Ephesus as the Epistle's Context* (Tübingen: Mohr Siebeck, 2017), p. 283.

[14] David Braund, *Greek Religion and Cults in the Black Sea Region: Goddesses in the Bosporan Kingdom from the Archaic Period to the Byzantine Era* (Cambridge: Cambridge University Press, 2018), p. 126.

[15] Craig S. Keener, *Revelation* (Grand Rapids: Zondervan, 2000), p. 106; Joseph L. Trafton, *Reading Revelation: A Literary and Theological Commentary* (Macon, GA: Smyth & Helwys, 2005), p. 32.

[16] François Bovon, "John's Self-Presentation in Revelation 1:9-10," *Catholic Biblical Quarterly* 62 (2000), pp. 693–700 (699); Greg Carey, *Elusive Apocalypse: Reading Authority in the Revelation to John* (Macon, GA: Mercer University Press, 1999), pp. 24–25; Michael J. Gorman, *Reading Revelation Responsibly: Uncivil Worship and Witness: Following the Lamb Into the New Creation* (Eugene, OR: Cascade, 2011), p. 1.

'Roman imperial theology' based on violence, power, domination, and material prosperity."[17] These kinds of approaches were central to the expansion and maintenance of the empire. They stand in contradiction with the teachings of Christ.[18] Abandonment of Christ's teachings and the implementation of such power abuse results in the prophetic confrontation presented by the Spirit to the congregation.

Textual Analysis

The congregation in Ephesus exercises power in the midst of internal conflict.[19] Moreover, the manner by which the congregation does this reflects its abuse of power. The congregation performs multiple works for which it receives a commendation.[20] While the assembly displays behavior that highlights its Christian dedication, some of their internal attitudes reflect a rejection of the Spirit's transforming work. As a result, they experience the challenge of functioning as a group that maintains Christian fidelity in the midst of a culture to which some community members may assimilate.[21] Like the majority church in America, in an attempt to demonstrate their faithfulness, the Ephesian congregation ultimately fails to show Christian dedication.

The congregation goes to an extreme to maintain their fidelity and finds itself failing to exhibit love toward those they should engage as brothers and sisters in the faith.[22] The message presents an

[17] Johnny Bernard Hill, *Prophetic Rage: A Postcolonial Theology of Liberation* (Grand Rapids: Eerdmans, 2013), p. 109.

[18] Warren Carter, "Matthew and Empire," in Porter and Westfall (eds.), *Empire in the New Testament*, pp. 90–119 (111).

[19] Rick Strelan, *Paul, Artemis, and the Jews in Ephesus* (New York: de Gruyter, 1996), p. 109.

[20] Grant R. Osborne, *Revelation* (Grand Rapids: Baker Academic, 2002), p. 116.

[21] Trebilco, Paul. *The Early Christians in Ephesus From Paul to Ignatius* (Grand Rapids: Eerdmans, 2007), pp. 235–36.

[22] M. Eugene Boring, *Revelation* (Louisville, KY: John Knox, 1989), p. 92; Richard E. Oster, *Seven Congregations in a Roman Crucible: A Commentary on Revelation 1–3* (Eugene, OR: Wipf & Stock, 2013), p. 98; Elisabeth Schüssler Fiorenza, "Apocalyptic and Gnosis in the Book of Revelation and Paul," *Journal of Biblical Literature* 92 (1973), pp. 565–81 (568); Rebecca

assembly that abandons love and abuses power. The congregation adopts the ways of the Empire and unlovingly exerts power over those who exhibit disagreement with the majority position within the congregation. The Holy Spirit prophetically challenges the congregation for the ungodly attitude it exhibits in its attempt to demonstrate faithfulness to God. He urges the assembly to maintain its allegiance to the Kingdom of God by abandoning the abusive practices of the Roman empire. If the congregation demonstrates its ability to love others, the community will experience the fullness of the relationship people experienced prior to humanity's rebellion against God. If the congregation fails, the community will experience rejection.

A Prophetic Presentation of Divine Power

While many people recognize the power of the government, the Spirit reminds the audience that Christ exercises ultimate power and authority over his congregations.[23] He reveals Christ as "the one who holds the seven stars in his right hand, the one who walks in the midst of the seven golden lampstands" (ὁ κρατῶν τοὺς ἑπτὰ ἀστέρας ἐν τῇ δεξιᾷ αὐτοῦ, ὁ περιπατῶν ἐν μέσῳ τῶν ἑπτὰ λυχνιῶν τῶν χρυσῶν, 2.1). This language parallels John's initial vision of Jesus in Rev. 1.13, 16 where he describes Christ as a divine, royal figure.[24] Additionally, Jesus' proximity to and activity among the stars and lampstands highlight his relationship with the congregations. According to David Machin and Andrea Mayr, "distance signifies social relations,"[25] reflecting an indirect correlation between relationships and spatial

---

Skaggs and Priscilla C. Benham, *Revelation* (Dorset, UK: Deo, 2009), p. 33. Boring, Oster, Schüssler Fiorenza, and Skaggs and Benham recognize the evil people in Rev 2.2 as Christians. Though Boring identifies them as those from outside the local community, Skaggs and Benham explain that Paul warned of such individuals coming from both outside of and within the community (Acts 20.28–31).

[23] Ben Witherington, *Revelation* (Cambridge: Cambridge University Press, 2003), p. 95.

[24] Robert H. Mounce, *The Book of Revelation* (Grand Rapids: Eerdmans, 1977), p. 68.

[25] David Machin, and Andrea Mayr. *How to Do Critical Discourse Analysis: A Multimodal Introduction* (London: Sage, 2012), p. 97. Though Machin and Mayr explain correlation when discussing images, they explain that this parallels real life, which written texts portray.

proximity unless other factors of the text speak to the contrary.[26] Based on his relationship with the community, Jesus confronts the Ephesian congregation.

Holding the Seven Stars and Walking Among the Lampstands
Though reminiscent of John's first description of Jesus (Rev. 1.16), the language of Rev. 2.1 uses slightly different verbiage. When depicting Jesus' possession of the seven stars in the inauguration of the vision, John uses the term ἔχω (to have, 1.16). When the Spirit speaks, he uses the term κρατέω (to hold, 2.1).

This shift in terminology reflects more than mere possession of the angels of the churches (Rev. 1.16). The language of the Spirit connects Christ with the concepts of power, strength, authority, and the exercise thereof.[27] The association of Christ with the term κρατέω reinforces the understanding that he has authority over the assemblies.[28] This construal of authority reminds the congregation that even though it lives within the geographic realm of a worldly empire, Jesus maintains authority over them.

Jesus' activity among the seven golden lampstands reinforces his authority. Just as there exists a distinction in language between the first description of Jesus with the seven stars (Rev. 1.16) and how he now appears in relation to them (Rev. 2.1), the same disparity holds true for Jesus' activity among the lampstands. The latter portrayal depicts him as more than merely present. He is present and active among the churches.

In Revelation 1, John's vision portrays Christ "in the midst of the lampstands" (ἐν μέσῳ τῶν λυχνιῶν, 1.13). When the Spirit speaks to the congregations, Christ "walks among the lampstands"

---

[26] Linda R. Waugh *et al.* "Critical Discourse Analysis: Definition, Approaches, Relation to Pragmatics, Critique, and Trends," in A. Capone and J.L. Mey (eds.), *Interdisciplinary Studies in Pragmatics, Culture, and Society* (Switzerland: Springer International Publishing, 2016), pp. 71–135 (85).

[27] Paige Patterson, *Revelation* (Nashville: B&H, 2012), p. 83; J.P. Louw and E.A. Nida. *Greek-English Lexicon of the New Testament Based on Semantic Domains* (New York: United Bible Societies, 1988), p. 473. In this entry in Louw and Nida, the term κρατέω relates to the concept of someone or something possessing control of another. Another example of this appears in Acts 2.24, when Peter explains that it was impossible for Christ to be held by death.

[28] Peter J. Leithart, *Revelation 1–11* (London: Bloomsbury, 2018), p. 145.

(περιπατῶν ἐν μέσῳ τῶν ἑπτὰ λυχνιῶν, Rev. 2.1). The Spirit's language reveals more than Christ's presence among the churches; it reveals Christ's power. The association of Jesus with this activity demonstrates his authority over the assemblies he prepares to confront.

Ecclesial Interactions

The Spirit's challenge exposes the shortcoming of the community and reveals that the congregation engages in the abuse of power over those it encounters. The engagement of the church with "evil people" (κακούς, 2.2) depicts the congregation as the aggressors against these people. The congregation's works fall into two categories: "toil" (κόπον) and "patient endurance" (ὑπομονήν, 2.2).[29] The assembly's toil reflects the activity between the congregation and those they encounter, while its patient endurance highlights its attitude related to its interactions.[30]

The group's labor reflects its exercise of power through actions and discernment while interacting with those they encounter. The assembly demonstrates its power over those with whom it interacts by consistently acting on those they encounter. The message declares to the congregation "you cannot bear evil people" (οὐ δύνῃ βαστάσαι κακούς, 2.2), "you tested those who call themselves apostles" (ἐπείρασας τοὺς λέγοντας ἑαυτοὺς ἀποστόλους, 2.2), and "you found them false" (εὗρες αὐτοὺς ψευδεῖς, 2.2).[31] The portrayal of the congregation in each clause presents it performing actions that impact those with whom they interact. Such construal reflects the church's exercise of power over these people.[32]

In contrast to the congregation, John depicts the evil people as powerless. They try to exercise power by speaking, but the text reveals their lack of power in comparison to the Ephesian congregation. When this group speaks, they do so only regarding themselves,

---

[29] Grant R. Osborne, *Revelation* (Grand Rapids: Baker Academic, 2002), p. 112.

[30] Pierre Prigent, *Commentary on the Apocalypse of St. John* (trans. Wendy Pradels; Tübingen: Mohr Siebeck, 2001), p. 157.

[31] David E. Aune, *Revelation 1–5* (Word Biblical Commentary, 52A; Dallas, TX: Word Books, 1997), p. 220. Aune asserts that the use of this term functions as juridical language, communicating that the assembly has evaluated these individuals.

[32] Lynne Young and Brigid Fitzgerald. *The Power of Language: How Discourse Influences Society* (London: Equinox, 2006), pp. 24–25.

and the text mentions no parties as the recipients of their speech. Though they speak, their speech has no impact on others. The text also presents them as liars since they are not apostles as they present themselves to be (Rev. 2.2). This depiction delegitimizes and discredits these people's speech.[33] Their impotent speech parallels the silencing of alternative voices in contemporary society through the present-day church's refusal to listen to them and attempt to prevent them from being heard, stripping them of any power they may have to address issues of abuse.

In addition to the discussion of the congregation's actions, the message expounds upon the community's attitude when discussing the church's patient endurance.[34] The group hears "you have patient endurance" (ὑπομονὴν ἔχεις, 2.3), "you bear up on account of my name" (ἐβάστασας διὰ τὸ ὄνομά μου, 2.3), and "you have not grown weary" (οὐ κεκοπίακες, 2.3). All of these clauses reveal that the Ephesian congregation has remained faithful in their dedication to Jesus.

Further elaboration on the attitude of the church reflects a deficiency in bearing the fruit of the Spirit (cf. Gal. 5.22-23). The congregation hears "you abandoned your first love" (τὴν ἀγάπην σου τὴν πρώτην ἀφῆκες, 2.4).[35] This reveals the congregation's practice of abuse, highlighting an illegitimate exercise of power.[36] This departure from their first love holds great significance, as love appears at the beginning of the clause of the Greek text.[37] While extensive discussion surrounds the object of this love,[38] the congregation's

---

[33] Christopher Hart, *Discourse, Grammar, and Ideology: Functional and Cognitive Perspectives* (London: Bloomsbury Academic, 2014), p. 8.

[34] Louw and Nida, *Greek-English Lexicon of the New Testament*, pp. 292–93.

[35] This term, like the expressions of the congregation's patient endurance, occurs in the semantic domain of Attitudes and Emotions.

[36] Martin Luther King, Jr, "Where Do We Go from Here?," in Washington (ed.), *A Testament of Hope: The Essential Writings and Speeches of Martin Luther King, Jr*, pp. 245–52 (247). King argues that "Power without love is reckless and abusive."

[37] John Christopher Thomas, *The Apocalypse: A Literary and Theological Commentary* (Cleveland, TN: CPT, 2012), p. 116.

[38] Though some assert that Christ functions as the object of their love, the congregation stands firm in its commitment to Christ, as noted by their actions and tenacity to stand against evil. Additional support for this idea

treatment of others in the community identifies those the church opposes as the object of the love the assembly abandons.[39] The actions of the church impact its relationship with others. The lack of love reflects the congregation's failure to live as part of the kingdom of God and fully identify as people of the Spirit. Instead, their adoption of the government's practices makes them appear as faithful citizens of the empire. The deficiency in love makes those in the congregation at Ephesus unrecognizable as faithful Christians, for others recognize Jesus' followers by the love they have for one another (cf. Jn 13.35). Their lack of love calls into question their love for God and their allegiance to his kingdom, as one cannot fail to love another person yet love God (cf. 1 Jn 4.20).

In contrast with how the congregation should not behave, the end of the message once again commends the assembly for its attitude; the church manifests hatred.[40] Since the church lacks love, their manifestation of hatred should not surprise readers. The congregation hates the works of another group known as the Nicolaitans. The text notes the hatred of their works and not those who perform the works, reflecting a New Testament model of hating lawlessness and unrighteous actions (cf. Rom. 7.15; Heb 1.9). The connection between the congregation's hatred and lack of love leaves one open to question whether or not the hatred of people's actions leads to standing firm against them, but when unfettered, leads to an abuse of power.

Divine Confrontation

The congregation's abuse of power leads to a confrontation where the community receives a divine reprimand based on its treatment of others. The Spirit reveals the relative nature of this congregation's

---

comes from the fact that within the messages, Christ never functions as the recipient of any human actions, as he exhibits ultimate authority.

[39] Craig R. Koester, *Revelation: A New Translation With Introduction and Commentary* (New Haven, CT: Yale University Press, 2014), p. 269.

[40] Willem S. Vorster, "In What Sense is the Louw/Nida Dictionary Authoritative?," *HTS Theological Studies* 47 (1991), pp. 26–38 (30). Vorster rightly critiques Louw and Nida for not listing the term μισέω in the semantic domain of Attitudes and Emotions. Given the relationship between the terms, they should appear in the same semantic domain.

power.[41] The community abuses power when interacting with others, but it possesses minimal authority compared to Christ. Within the context of this confrontation, the congregation has its shortcomings exposed and is guided toward repentance. In addition to the evaluations and instructions, the group receives threats, based on its compliance with the instructions it receives. The Spirit never speaks regarding his thoughts or actions regarding those the text calls evil. He concerns himself with the abusive actions of the congregation and its conformity to the government by engaging in the abuse of its power. The presentations of such power urge the assembly to submit to the words of the Spirit instead of conforming to the abusive culture of the empire.

Divine Actions Toward the Church

The Spirit's declaration to the church in Ephesus parallels the instructions Jesus gave his disciples about loving others (e.g. Mt. 5.44; 19.19; Jn 13.34; 15.12). The Ephesian church received exhortation regarding love on other occasions as well. The text explains that "bearing with one another in love" (ἀνεχόμενοι ἀλλήλων ἐν ἀγάπῃ, Eph. 4.2) functions as part of their calling.[42] When speaking of how they should not fall prey to false teaching, the message also notes they should be ἀληθεύοντες ... ἐν ἀγάπῃ (speaking the truth in love, Eph. 4.15). The words of Jesus, as well as the Pauline instruction to the church in Ephesus, reveal the failure of this congregation and provide an explanation for the commands issued and the promises of requital made for any potential disobedience.

Admonition
Even as the church exerts power over others, the Spirit reveals Christ's authority over the assembly through a series of commands.[43] In light of the community's failure to exhibit love, the congregation

---

[41] Karen Stanbridge and Howard Ramos, *Seeing Politics Differently: A Brief Introduction to Political Sociology* (Oxford: Oxford University Press, 2012), p. 3.

[42] F.F. Bruce, *The Epistles to the Colossians, to Philemon, and to the Ephesians* (New International Commentary on the New Testament; Grand Rapids, MI: Eerdmans, 1984), p. 334.

[43] Young and Fitzgerald, *Power of Language*, pp. 75–76.

receives a call to love those it opposes. The community hears three commands: "remember from where you have fallen" (μνημόνευε οὖν πόθεν πέπτωκας, Rev. 2.5), "repent" (μετανόησον, Rev. 2.5), and "do the first works" (τὰ πρῶτα ἔργα ποίησον, Rev. 2.5). The call to remember from where it has fallen suggests that the church had a former state where its current activity devoid of love did not exist.[44] The command to repent urges a change in attitude, which should result in a change in actions. As a result, the final command urges the church to follow through with its repentance by interacting with others as it did before. The call to do the works it did at first relates to the quality, not quantity, of the works previously performed. Since the failure of the church relates to its lack of love, the prophetic message mandates that love accompany the community's activities.[45] The commendation reveals that the church continued to work with the quality of love lacking from its works, its activities lacked the potency that the congregation should have had within the church and with the broader culture.[46]

Requital

The commands do not function as impotent suggestions for the church. If the church fails to exhibit love, the Spirit declares that the church's relationship with God will come to an end. He declares, "I will come to you and remove your lampstand from its place, unless you repent" (ἔρχομαί σοι καὶ κινήσω τὴν λυχνίαν σου ἐκ τοῦ τόπου αὐτῆς, ἐὰν μὴ μετανοήσῃς, 2.5b). Immediately following this threat, the text reveals that which the assembly possesses the power to do if they wish to avoid such judgment – simply repent. First, the message declares that Jesus will come to the church. Depending on where one stands with Christ, his coming can have either a positive or negative effect. For the church in Ephesus, a lack of repentance leads to a negative result of Christ coming – eternal punishment.[47] Disobedience will result in the removal of the church's lampstand from its place.

---

[44] Mounce, *Book of Revelation*, p. 94.

[45] Thomas, *Apocalypse*, p. 118.

[46] Skaggs and Benham, *Revelation*, p. 34.

[47] Matthew Streett, *Here Comes the Judge: Violent Pacifism in the Book of Revelation* (London: T. & T. Clark, 2012), p. 48.

Various writers propose ideas regarding the meaning of the removal of the lampstand. Gregory Beale asserts that the removal of the lampstand relates to the loss of the church's witness,[48] while Grant Osborne argues that the removal of the lampstand reflects a loss of the community's standing as a church.[49] While these are plausible assumptions, the question of from what Christ will remove the lampstand aids in explaining the promise of requital.

While the term "place" may refer to status,[50] the text refers to the place as the location of the lampstand.[51] Both Rev. 1.16 and Rev. 2.1 connect the location of the lampstands to Christ's location. These passages note Jesus "in the midst of" (ἐν μέσῳ) the lampstands. As a result, while discussions of the removal of the lampstand revolve around status and function, the text makes clear, based on the lampstand's current location, that impenitence results in Christ exercising his authority and removing the lampstand from his presence.[52] Even as Jesus' proximity to the lampstands signifies relationship, the removal of the lampstand signifies rejection.[53] If the church fails to exhibit appropriate relationships with others, the divine relationship with the congregation will come to an end. Those who think they stand secure in God while abusing others should heed this warning that the Spirit proclaims to the churches.

Identification with the Church

Though the church receives criticism for its abandonment of the love it previously had, Christ identifies with the church in its hatred by noting "I also hate" (κἀγὼ μισῶ Rev. 2.6) the works of the Nicolaitans. Though it might appear ironic that the Spirit would inspire

---

[48] Gregory K. Beale, *John's Use of the Old Testament in Revelation* (Sheffield: Sheffield Academic, 1998), p. 154.

[49] Osborne, *Revelation*, p. 118.

[50] Walter A. Bauer, *et al.*, *A Greek-English Lexicon of the New Testament and Other Early Christian Literature* (Chicago, IL: University of Chicago Press, 2000), pp. 1011–12.

[51] Bauer, *Greek-English Lexicon of the New Testament*, p. 1011.

[52] Paul Decock, "The Works of God, of Christ, and of the Faithful in the Apocalypse of John," *Neotestamentica* 41 (2007), pp. 37–66 (41); Alexander E. Stewart, *Soteriology as Motivation in the Apocalypse of John* (Piscataway, NJ: Gorgias, 2015), p. 128.

[53] W. Gordon Campbell, *Reading Revelation: A Thematic Approach* (Cambridge: James Clarke and Co., 2012), p. 276.

a rebuke and threaten the church for its lack of love, the Spirit identifies the congregation with Christ in its hatred. This hatred targets the works of the Nicolaitans, not the Nicolaitans themselves. This approach of hating sinful behavior models how all churches should interact with those engaged in sin. They should love people, even when they hate those people's actions.

Promise to the Conqueror (Rev. 2.7)
The promise to the conqueror stands in contrast with the promise of requital that the congregation receives for its failure to live as God's people. As opposed to rejection and separation, the promise to the conqueror offers an eternal relationship with God reminiscent of that which humanity had with him in the Garden of Eden.[54] The Spirit once again testifies about Christ and reveals his power over those in the church. The message declares "I will give to [the conqueror] to eat from the tree of life, which is in the paradise of God" (δώσω αὐτῷ φαγεῖν ἐκ τοῦ ξύλου τῆς ζωῆς, ὅ ἐστιν ἐν τῷ παραδείσῳ τοῦ θεοῦ, 2.7b). Christ exercises power as the social agent who performs the activity of giving the overcomer to eat from the tree of life. This promise displays the power of God and Christ and reminds those in the congregation that there are those who have greater power than it possesses and can impact the present state of the church and its eternal fate.

Textual Summary

While the congregation in Ephesus takes a stand for Christ and exercises power over self-proclaimed apostles who are not whom they claim to be, it abandons the life of the Spirit and embraces the ways of the empire by attempting to enforce a majority position through a means that the Spirit condemns. While this congregation's actions demonstrate the community's support of God's kingdom, the attitude it exhibits when interacting with others demonstrates disloyalty to the Kingdom of God. The Spirit issues a prophetic proclamation against this congregation and provides corrective measures regarding how it should function as a segment of his kingdom. He calls the church to love others.

---

[54] Brian K. Blount, *Revelation: A Commentary* (Louisville, KY: Westminster John Knox, 2009), p. 52.

Intertextual Analysis

Just as older denominations in the US have remained silent regarding or have adopted the government's practices of racism, younger segments of the church, like Pentecostals have followed the examples of their predecessors. When discussing the Pentecostal Movement's history concerning racism, Iain MacRobert explains,

> Just as infants are unconscious of racial and colour distinctions until those who are "older and wiser" infect them with prejudice in their childhood, so also the Pentecostal movement enjoyed several years of racial harmony until the divisions on the basis of colour, which had split the older denominations in America, led to the segregation of white from black Pentecostals.[55]

Much like the power abuses that occur in the church today, the power abuse demonstrated by the church in Ephesus did not begin with the local congregation but was learned from the sinful ideologies of predecessors.

The message to the church in Ephesus alludes to the language of the Genesis narrative regarding access to the tree of life. The allusion to Genesis recalls the sin of humanity, marked by the first biblical account of power abuse.[56] Further examination reveals that 2 *Enoch* also speaks of God moving about in Paradise where the tree of life is located. The intertextual features of the text recall the language of the Genesis narrative and bookend the message. Christ walking among the seven golden lampstands (Rev. 2.1), paralleled by the Spirit's activity among the churches (Rev. 2.7), connects John's audience with the Genesis narrative when God walks in Paradise (Gen. 3.8). The mention of the tree of life (Rev. 2.7; cf. Gen. 2.22) serves as another common feature of the texts. Along with the parallels above, the location of the tree in paradise (Rev. 2.7; cf. Gen. 3.8) supports the idea that the message alludes to the narrative. These texts also maintain a parallel structure in which the divine being walks, evaluates and judges the people, and discusses access to the tree of life.

---

[55] Iain MacRobert, *The Black Roots and White Racism of Early Pentecostalism in the USA* (London: MacMillan Press, 1988), p. 87.

[56] Ian Boxall, *The Revelation of Saint John* (Peabody, MA: Hendrickson, 2006), p. 48. While Boxall asserts the connection between Rev 2.1 and Gen 3.8, his argument that it may serve as reassurance for Christians facing a dominant culture finds no support from the text.

When looking at the text of Genesis, the material reveals that the confrontation between the Lord and humanity takes place because the humans have illegitimately exercised their power. Genesis 1.28 (LXX) notes God's commands to the man and woman. He tells them to "lord over" (κατακυριεύσατε) the earth.[57] Though God had given humanity authority over the earth, he also limited their power by instructing Adam not to eat of the tree of the knowledge of good and evil (Gen. 2.17). In Gen. 3.6, both the man and the woman eat of the forbidden fruit. The exercise of power to violate the commands of the Lord constitutes an abuse of power that leads to their confrontation with God when he reveals that their actions will lead to an inequality between them where the man will rule over the woman.[58] This perpetuates the abuse of power among humanity that continues today. Because of their actions, God expels the man and the woman from the paradise.

When comparing the Genesis narrative with the message to the congregation in Ephesus, it becomes apparent that while both texts have common features, the text of Revelation speaks regarding gaining access to the tree of life, not losing access to it. Beyond the scope of Revelation, other writings speak of future access to the tree of life. The text of Ezek. 47.7-12 discusses access to the tree of life.[59] The text of 1 Enoch discusses the restoration of humanity's access to the tree of life after eschatological judgments have occurred, noting the preservation of the fruit of the tree for "the righteous and holy" (1 En. 25.4-5). 2 Enoch also mentions the restoration of humanity's access to paradise. In 2 Enoch, which also speaks of God moving about in paradise (2 En. 8.1-3),[60] readers discover that this location is reserved for the righteous who endure offense (2 En. 9.1), not those who in self-righteousness offend others.

The intertextual dimension of analysis reinforces the idea that those who illegitimately use, and abuse power will not have access

---

[57] Susan Ann Brayford, *Genesis* (Leiden: Brill, 2007), p. 224.

[58] Walter Vogels, "The Power Struggle Between Man and Woman (Gen 3, 16b)," *Biblica* 77 (1996), pp. 197–209 (197).

[59] Steve Moyise, "Genesis in Revelation," in Menken and Moyise (eds.), *Genesis in the New Testament*, pp. 166–80 (170).

[60] Paul Swarup, *The Self-Understanding of the Dead Sea Scrolls Community: An Eternal Planting, a House of Holiness* (London: T. & T. Clark, 2006), p. 30.

to the tree of life. For this reason, the message discourages readers and hearers from following their government's ungodly model of exercising power. Instead, the community receives encouragement to exercise the power it has with love.

Intratextual Analysis
Since this community has adopted the empire's abusive practices of power, Rev. 21.9–22.5 portrays access to the tree of life for those who resist embracing the empire's abusive behavior. Access to the tree of life reveals the reversal of the effects of the empire's abusive practices. It also provides a model to the congregation regarding how it should behave as it encounters others, demonstrating that the assembly should utilize its power to bring healing to those who have been abused by worldly systems of government.

The vision of the tree of life in Revelation 22 depicts the fulfillment of the promise to the conqueror in Rev. 2.7. While both Rev. 2.7 and Rev. 22.2 mention the tree of life, the message and the description of the city's geography maintain multiple common features. In addition to the mention of the tree of life, Christ appears in the midst of the lampstands and the Spirit of Christ acts among the congregations (Rev. 2.1, 7; Rev. 22.2), while the throne of God has its home in the midst of the holy city where the people will dwell. The message promises that the conqueror will receive food to eat from the tree of life (Rev. 2.7), while the tree produces fruit (Rev. 22.2), which people can eat for food. These common features reveal that these portions of the Apocalypse speak about gaining access to the tree of life.

The message to the church in Ephesus uses the language of paradise, reminiscent of the Garden of Eden. This vision transforms the garden into a city. This city stands in contrast with Babylon (Rome).[61] Additional support for this contrast comes from the personification of these cities as women. John refers to Babylon as the prostitute (Rev. 17.1), while he identifies the new Jerusalem as the bride, the wife of the Lamb (Rev. 21.9).

In addition to the tree's production of fruit, the leaves of the tree are for the healing of the nations. The necessity of healing stems

---

[61] Barbara R. Rossing, "Healing, Kairos, and Land in the New Testament: Eschatology and the End of Empire," in Harker and Johnson (eds.), *Rooted and Grounded: Essays on Land and Christian Discipleship*, pp. 61–76 (72).

from Rome's abuse of the nations. Revelation depicts Rome's abuse and oppressive dominance. The prostitute, who represents Rome,[62] sits on many waters (Rev. 17.1), which represent peoples, multitudes, nations, and languages (Rev. 17.15). Her position on these groups reflects her dominance. The text depicts her power when she makes all the nations drink of the wine of the passion of her sexual immorality (Rev. 14.8). She also deceived the nations with her sorcery (Rev. 18.23). These demonstrations of her power based on her activity in relation to the nations necessitate the healing that the nations will receive through the leaves from the tree of life.

The empire has obtained "peace" through power abuse and the exertion of military might.[63] The Spirit declares through John that the individuals who dwell in the holy city will never have to worry about functioning as victims of abuse or military might. The open gates of the city signify that they will have peace and never have to concern themselves about invasions or the abuse of another empire (Rev. 21.25).[64]

Ultimately, the tree of life and the paradise bring life and peace to those who dwell in the holy city. This depiction of the holy city presents a model for the congregation's behavior. This depiction of life in the eschatological kingdom guides churches regarding how they should live as a group of citizens in the Kingdom of God and refuse to conform to the practices of the worldly empires in which they live.

Conclusion

The message to the church in Ephesus challenges local assemblies regarding the exercise of power and power abuse. While legal debates currently abound within the church regarding the relationship between ethnic minorities and the local government, congregations have an obligation and biblical mandate to hear the cries of their

---

[62] Elisabeth Schüssler Fiorenza, *Revelation: Vision of a Just World* (Minneapolis: Fortress, 1991), p. 89. Support for this also comes from the closing of 1 Peter when he sends greetings from the one in "Babylon" (5.13).

[63] Kathy Ehrensperger, *Paul At the Crossroads of Cultures: Theologising in the Space Between* (London: Bloomsbury T. & T. Clark, 2013), p. 109.

[64] Eric J. Gilchrest, *Revelation 21–22 in Light of Jewish and Greco-Roman Utopianism* (Leiden: Brill, 2013), p. 267.

brothers and sisters and to reclaim their prophetic voices within the public sphere. As long as congregations affirm and adopt the ungodly practices of exhibiting partiality toward one group over another, the perpetuation of power abuse and power struggles will continue among those who should demonstrate love toward one another. May God's people hear the prophetic proclamation against power abuse that the Spirit says to the churches.

Bibliography

Aune, David E., *Revelation 1–5* (Word Biblical Commentary 52A; Dallas, TX: Word Books, 1997).

Bauer, Walter A., *et al.*, *A Greek-English Lexicon of the New Testament and Other Early Christian Literature* (Chicago, IL: University of Chicago Press, 2000).

Beale, Gregory K., *John's Use of the Old Testament in Revelation* (Sheffield: Sheffield Academic, 1998).

Blount, Brian K., *Revelation: A Commentary* (Louisville, KY: Westminster John Knox, 2009).

Blumhofer, Edith L., *Restoring the Faith: The Assemblies of God, Pentecostalism, and American Culture* (Champaign, IL: University of Illinois Press, 1993).

Boring, M. Eugene, *Revelation* (Louisville, KY: John Knox, 1989).

Bovon, François, "John's Self-Presentation in Revelation 1:9-10" *Catholic Biblical Quarterly* 62 (2000), pp. 693-700.

Boxall, Ian, *The Revelation of Saint John* (Peabody, MA: Hendrickson, 2006).

Braund, David, *Greek Religion and Cults in the Black Sea Region: Goddesses in the Bosporan Kingdom from the Archaic Period to the Byzantine Era* (Cambridge: Cambridge University Press, 2018).

Brayford, Susan Ann, *Genesis* (Leiden: Brill, 2007).

Bruce, F.F., *The Epistles to the Colossians, to Philemon, and to the Ephesians* (New International Commentary on the New Testament; Grand Rapids, MI: Eerdmans, 1984).

Campbell, W. Gordon, *Reading Revelation: A Thematic Approach* (Cambridge: James Clarke and Co., 2012).

Carey, Greg, *Elusive Apocalypse: Reading Authority in the Revelation to John* (Macon, GA: Mercer University Press, 1999).

Decock, Paul, "The Works of God, of Christ, and of the Faithful in the Apocalypse of John," *Neotestamentica* 41 (2007), pp. 37–66.

Ehrensperger, Kathy, *Paul At the Crossroads of Cultures: Theologising in the Space Between* (London: Bloomsbury T. & T. Clark, 2013).

General Council of the Assemblies of God, "Civil Disobedience," Accessed August 23, 2018. https://ag.org/Beliefs/Topics-Index/Civil-Disobedience.

General Council of the Assemblies of God, "War and Conscientious Objectors," Accessed August 25, 2018. https://ag.org/Beliefs/Topics-Index/War-and-Conscientious-Objectors.

Gilchrest, Eric J., *Revelation 21–22 in Light of Jewish and Greco-Roman Utopianism* (Leiden: Brill, 2013).

Gorman, Michael J., *Reading Revelation Responsibly: Uncivil Worship and Witness: Following the Lamb Into the New Creation* (Eugene, OR: Cascade, 2011).

Hart, Christopher, *Discourse, Grammar, and Ideology: Functional and Cognitive Perspectives* (London: Bloomsbury Academic, 2014).

Hill, Johnny Bernard, *Prophetic Rage: A Postcolonial Theology of Liberation* (Grand Rapids: Eerdmans, 2013).

Immendörfer, Michael, *Ephesians and Artemis: The Cult of the Great Goddess of Ephesus as the Epistle's Context* (Tübingen: Mohr Siebeck, 2017).

Kärkkäinen, Veli-Matti, *Christology: A Global Introduction* (Grand Rapids: Baker Academic, 2003).

Keener, Craig S., *Revelation* (Grand Rapids: Zondervan, 2000).

Koester, Craig R., *Revelation: A New Translation With Introduction and Commentary* (New Haven, CT: Yale University Press, 2014).

Leithart, Peter J., *Revelation 1–11* (London: Bloomsbury, 2018).

Louw, J.P., and E.A. Nida, *Greek-English Lexicon of the New Testament Based on Semantic Domains* (2 Vols.; New York: United Bible Societies, 1988).

Machin, David, and Andrea Mayr, *How to Do Critical Discourse Analysis: A Multimodal Introduction* (London: Sage, 2012).

MacRobert, Iain, *The Black Roots and White Racism of Early Pentecostalism in the USA* (London: MacMillan Press, 1988).

Mounce, Robert H., *The Book of Revelation* (Grand Rapids: Eerdmans, 1977).

Newman, Joe, *Race and the Assemblies of God: The Journey from Azusa Street to the "Miracle of Memphis"* (Youngstown, NY: Cambria Press, 2007).

Osborne, Grant R., *Revelation* (Grand Rapids: Baker Academic, 2002).

Oster, Richard E., *Seven Congregations in a Roman Crucible: A Commentary on Revelation 1-3* (Eugene, OR: Wipf & Stock, 2013).

Patterson, Paige, *Revelation* (Nashville: B&H, 2012).

Prigent, Pierre, *Commentary on the Apocalypse of St. John* (trans. Wendy Pradels; Tübingen: Mohr Siebeck, 2001).

Schüssler Fiorenza, Elisabeth, "Apocalyptic and Gnosis in the Book of Revelation and Paul," *Journal of Biblical Literature* 92 (1973), pp. 565-81.

Schüssler Fiorenza, Elisabeth, *Revelation: Vision of a Just World* (Minneapolis: Fortress, 1991).

Skaggs, Rebecca, and Priscilla C. Benham, *Revelation* (Pentecostal Commentary; Dorset, UK: Deo, 2009).

Stanbridge, Karen, and Howard Ramos, *Seeing Politics Differently: A Brief Introduction to Political Sociology* (Oxford: Oxford University Press, 2012).

Stewart, Alexander E., *Soteriology as Motivation in the Apocalypse of John* (Piscataway, NJ: Gorgias, 2015).

Streett, Matthew, *Here Comes the Judge: Violent Pacifism in the Book of Revelation* (London: T. & T. Clark, 2012).

Strelan, Rick, *Paul, Artemis, and the Jews in Ephesus* (New York: de Gruyter, 1996).

Swarup, Paul, *The Self-Understanding of the Dead Sea Scrolls Community: An Eternal Planting, a House of Holiness* (London: T. & T. Clark, 2006).

Thomas, John Christopher, *The Apocalypse: A Literary and Theological Commentary* (Cleveland, TN: CPT, 2012).

Trafton, Joseph L., *Reading Revelation: A Literary and Theological Commentary* (Macon, GA: Smyth & Helwys, 2005).

Trebilco, Paul, *The Early Christians in Ephesus From Paul to Ignatius* (Grand Rapids: Eerdmans, 2007).

Vogels, Walter, "The Power Struggle Between Man and Woman (Gen 3, 16b)," *Biblica* 77 (1996), pp. 197-209.

Ware, Lawrence, "Why I'm Leaving the Southern Baptist Convention" (2017), accessed 20. August 2018. https://nyti.ms/2uqoonj.

Waugh, Linda R., *et al.*, "Critical Discourse Analysis: Definition, Approaches, Relation to Pragmatics, Critique, and Trends," in A. Capone and J.L. Mey (eds.), *Interdisciplinary Studies in Pragmatics, Culture, and Society* (Switzerland: Springer International Publishing, 2016), pp. 71–135.

Witherington, Ben, *Revelation* (Cambridge: Cambridge University Press, 2003).

Young, Lynne, and Brigid Fitzgerald, *The Power of Language: How Discourse Influences Society* (London: Equinox, 2006).

PROPHETIC CONSCIOUSNESS

CHAPTER EIGHT

SHE IS CLOTHED WITH STRENGTH AND DIGNITY: HOLY DRAG AND THE PROPHETIC SOCIAL CONSCIOUSNESS OF THE BLACK PENTECOSTAL HOLINESS TRADITION[*]

Dara Coleby Delgado[*]

In the second edition of the book *African American Religion: Varieties of Protest and Accommodation*, Hans A. Baer and Merrill Singer explore the relationship between Black Holiness Pentecostalism and social activism. Ultimately, the authors conclude this portion of their study by asserting that "the vast majority of African American conversionists sects [among which they include Black Holiness-Pentecostalism] remain apolitical in their posture toward the larger society."[1] The idea is that Black Holiness Pentecostals tend to put more emphasis on socially approved behaviors, attitudes, work

---

[*] An earlier version of this article was published, Dara Coleby Delgado, "The Practicality of Holiness: A Historical Examination of Class, Race, and Gender within Black Holiness Pentecostalism, Bishop Ida Bell Robinson, and the Mount Sinai Holy Church of America," *Pneuma* 41.1 (2019), pp. 50-65.

[*] Dara Coleby Delgado (PhD, University of Dayton) was an AAUW American Dissertation Fellow. She also served on the faculty at both the University of Dayton and Roberts Wesleyan College. Her research interests include the history and theology of American Pentecostalism, as well as the role of race, gender, and popular culture in American Christianity during the modern era.

[1] Hans A. Baer, and Merrill Singer, *African American Religion: Varieties of Protest and Accommodation* (Knoxville, TN: University of Tennessee Press, 2002), p. 182.

ethic, and styles of dress than on engaging in socio-economic and political affairs.

This chapter considers Baer and Singer's claim that historically Black Holiness Pentecostals tended to be apathetic towards worldly concerns, and puts that claim in conversation with the life and work of Ida Bell Robinson, founder of the Mount Sinai Holy Church of America [1925-1946]. I explore the issues of class, race, and gender in relation to holiness. Moreover, I contend that the distinct practices of early Black Holiness Pentecostals proved critical to living a sanctified, or clean, life and also determined the ways local churches addressed and worked to remedy problems around poverty (both social and economic) and power in their communities.

Mount Sinai Holy Church of America (MSHCA) was founded by a black woman whose life and ministry included the black experience in the United States in the first four decades of the twentieth century. Therefore, it is not surprising that MSHCA developed into a ministry that was both woman-centered[2] and race-conscious. To say that under Bishop Robinson's leadership, MSHCA was woman-

---

[2] It is important to note that the word-phrase, "woman-centered," which denotes a subjective structural commitment to having women at the highest level of leadership in the MSHCA, is preferred to the more objective phrase "woman-oriented." I contend that the former highlights MSHCA's distinct and intentional practice of absolute gender equality and inclusion within a mixed-gendered congregation, while the latter does not. In other words, "woman-centered" points to MSHCA having been both founded by a woman and subsequently led by women, but not to the exclusion of men, as compared to "woman-oriented" which signifies a more female-dominated and gender-exclusive institution. In his book, *Passionately Human, No Less Divine*, historian Wallace D. Best, examines women's religious work in Chicago during the migration era and offers Lucy Smith and All Nations Pentecostal Church as one such example of a "woman-oriented" community. Unlike Robinson's, Smith's congregation was so singular in its focus that it operated as "female sacred world" and thus remained "overwhelmingly feminine" with a 4 to 1 female to male membership ratio. *Wallace D. Best, Passionately Human, No Less Divine: Religion and Culture in Black Chicago, 1915-1952* (Princeton and Oxford: Princeton University Press, 1998), pp. 175, 161. I am most grateful to Emilio Alvarez, Jr, PhD for his critique of this claim of woman-centeredness, and for his suggested feedback encouraging me to distinguish between "woman-centered" and "woman-oriented."

centered is not to suggest that it ministered and catered to women only, because that was not the case; in fact, MSHCA has always been a mixed gendered religious community. Instead, by choosing to characterize the ministry as woman-centered, I am recognizing a distinct characteristic of MSHCA, namely, its commitment to maintaining female leadership at the highest levels of ecclesial authority.[3] Similarly, by characterizing MSHCA as race-conscious, I am not negating the significance of Robinson having led a mixed-race congregation at the height of segregation in the United States; rather, I am noting that as a religious community, even one that attracted white followers, MSHCA remained unapologetically and characteristically Black in its performance, sociopolitical rhetoric, and epistemic framework.

Because Bishop Robinson's life and work via MSHCA were woman-centered and race-conscious, it is imperative that I consider Baer and Singer's claim in light of the complexities that surround power when black and holy women assert their agency in response to their spirituality and in defense of their human dignity. To that end, I employ styles of dress as a critical lens through which to examine how the Black Holiness Pentecostal tradition, vis-a-vis MSHCA, used dress, particularly holy dress, as a means of subversion and reclaiming power. As such I intend to show how black and holy women, in general, and the women of MSHCA, in particular, used so-called "holy drag" to recover their black and holy bodies as sites of cultural and sexual inscription.

The Great Migration and the Social Prophetic Consciousness of Bishop Ida Bell Robinson

That Ida Bell Robinson was a woman pastor is a testament to the acceleration of industrialization and the progress of Progressivism,[4]

---

[3] Historically, this was not the case for other Holiness Pentecostal denominations founded by women. In fact, six of the nine original church elders were women and the organization had consistent female bishops from 1924 to 2001.

[4] Mt. Sinai Holy Church of America, Inc., *Yearbook of Fourteenth Annual Convocation of the Mt. Sinai Holy Church of America, Inc* (September 27, 1925), p. 22. Just because progress was taking place does not mean that Robinson's efforts went unchallenged. On day five of MSHC's first

but that Ida Bell Robinson founded a Black Holiness Pentecostal denomination is a testament to the correlation between the Great Migration and the emergence of the sanctified church in the urban North. Within this social-historical context, Robinson claimed a personal revelation that allowed her to transcend the supposed impediments of having been born both black and a woman by likening herself to Moses. Via this personal revelation and its concomitant mandate to "Come out on Mount Sinai" and *loose the women*,[5] Robinson embodied a metaphysic that not only problematized notions of gender heteronormativity and blackness, but also affirmed her as one called of God. Undoubtedly to the chagrin of the dominant anti-black racist and sexist culture that actively sought to malign her body as inferior, savage, and vile, Robinson persisted and cultivated a movement that would provide women the same type of freedom and agency from within a complicated space of intersectionality in the social history of the United States of America.

Although little is known about why Ida Robinson and her husband Oliver migrated North to Philadelphia,[6] we can assume that she, like many other African Americans between 1916 and the late 1960s, set out in the hopes of finding better economic security and

---

convocation Elder Mary Jackson shared the story of how Robinson began the MSHC. In it, she notes that "[Robison] appeared before lawyers, judges, and notaries concerning this work to get the charter...This being a very rare thing, these officials whom she was before said one to the other: "This is a lot of power to give a woman."

[5] Mt. Sinai Holy Church of America, Inc., *Celebrating our Legacy* – Mt. Sinai Holy Church of America, Inc (Philadelphia, PA: Mt Sinai Holy Church of America, vol. 1, 1999), p. 139. According to MSHCA's denominational history, "1924 became a significant year in the life of [then] Elder Ida Robinson. On several occasions, God had revealed Himself through visions and dreams. He had made her to know the she was to be an instrument in His hand and to establish a church that would allow full clergy rights to women."

[6] Beyond her sister's invitation to join her in Philadelphia. See, Harold Dean Trulear, "Ida B. Robinson: The Mother as Symbolic Presence," in J.R. Goff, Jr, and Grant Wacker (eds.), *Portraits of A Generation: Early Pentecostal Leaders* (Fayetteville, AR: The University of Arkansas Press, 2002), p. 312.

a haven away from the violence and oppression of the South.[7] Unfortunately, Philadelphia was not exactly the Promised Land, and it fell woefully short of providing its new residents with a welcome basket flowing with milk and honey. Instead, southern black migrants found the "prospect of economic success and social well-being constantly undermined by discrimination in the housing and labor markets."[8] Like other Black Holiness-Pentecostal leaders whose churches were in black urban neighborhoods, Robinson worked intentionally and diligently to respond to the variety of challenges posed by urban living.

Philadelphia, where Robinson lived and led the Mount Sinai Holiness Church of America until her death in 1946, was "a world where the working poor and the impoverished live[d] in neighborhoods lacking the political might and resources to secure the amenities of a stable and salubrious, family-oriented environment."[9] As such, nurtured a ministerial presence and program rooted in a prophetic social consciousness distinctive to Black Holiness Pentecostalism.

Robinson's prophetic social consciousness as a Black Holiness-Pentecostal was likely cultivated during her time as preacher and pastor in the United Holy Church of America (UHCA), one of the oldest Black Holiness Pentecostal denomination in the United States.[10] Based on William C. Turner, Jr's study of the UHCA, we can

---

[7] Deidre Helen Crumbley, *Saved and Sanctified: The Rise of a Storefront Church in Great Migration Philadelphia* (Gainesville, FL: University Press of Florida, 2012), p. 7.

[8] Crumbley, *Saved and Sanctified*, 37. Crumbley notes that this disappointment and concomitant economic hardship was exacerbated by the Great Depression, which that ultimately "hit Black people with doubled force."

[9] Crumbley, *Saved and Sanctified*, p. 54.

[10] Estrelda Y. Alexander, *Limited Liberty: The Legacy of Four Pentecostal Women Pioneers* (Cleveland, OH: The Pilgrim Press 2008), p. 121. Also see Trulear, "Ida B. Robinson," p. 312. After Robinson arrived in Philadelphia in 1917, she fellowshipped with the Church of God (TN). However, in 1919, she severed ties with the denomination and began to fellowship with UHCA, where she was ordained to the ministry and eventually assumed the pastorate of Mt. Olive Holy Church (Philadelphia). Mt. Olive plays an important role in the histories of both denominations. For the UHCA, Mt Olive was one of the founding congregations of the Northern District of the United Holy Church of America. Robinson was a gifted preacher, teacher,

surmise that Robinson as a black and holy person formed in the tradition, would have been fully committed to the tripartite work of
holiness, spiritual empowerment, and prophetic social consciousness.[11] This system of checks and balances would have encouraged
Robinson, as a religious leader to (1) take notice of the world in
which she and her congregants lived (2) assume a sense of responsibility for ameliorating social and cultural woes that oppressed the
community, and (3) fight the evils of systemic racism, poverty, and
the like.[12] Moreover, from Turner we gather that as black and holy
people, Robinson's followers would have been called upon to sacrifice time, money, and resources to ensure that the gospel was
preached, that schools were erected, and "the world [was] helped."
Essentially, as black and holy people, they were to focus on a life of
sobriety, "strict discipline, [and] deep devotion," but also social responsibility and selfless service.[13] For these reasons, it comes as no
surprise that Robinson used her position of authority to assert her
pacifism and decry World War II, pastor a racially mixed congregation at the height of segregation in the US, and address social issues

---

and singer; she was also a highly respected and valued member of UHC's
clergy. Under her charismatic leadership, the congregation grew so much
that it had to relocate three times. Nevertheless, as questions concerning
women preachers came to a head, UHCA made the decision to no longer
ordain women to the ministry publicly. According to Harold Dean Trulear,
by 1924, women in the UHCA were having difficulty achieving ordination
and those that were ordained were relegated to private ceremonies and limited access to leadership roles (Trulear, "Ida B. Robinson," p. 312). A MSHCA
Yearbook from 1938 notes that two UHCA leaders, Elders Williams and
Spann, attended MSHCA Annual Convocation that year, and were publicly
recognized. It is unknown whether they were permitted to address the audience Robinson decided to sever ties with the organization. Based on their
decision to attend and the warm welcome they received, it appears that
Robinson and UHCA parted amicably and remained friendly toward one
another [see, MSHCA *Yearbook* (September 23, 1938), p. 24]. Because the
split was over gender equality, Robinson retained much of UHCA's polity,
doctrine, and practices. See, Alexander, *Limited Liberty*, p. 125.
[11] William C. Turner, Jr, *The United Holy Church of America: A Study in
Black Holiness Pentecostalism* (Piscataway, NJ: Gorgias Press, 2006), p. 114.
[12] Turner, *The United Holy Church of America*, p. 128.
[13] Turner, *The United Holy Church of America*, p. 10 and p. 19.

such as racism (specifically lynching and white supremacy) and economic disparity.[14]

Ultimately, beyond taboos around dress codes and uniforms, divorce and remarriage, alcohol and narcotics, and secular entertainment, MSHCA's holiness identity included a prophetic social consciousness that embodied the "sense in which the Holiness Movement was for the poor"[15] – those poor in body and spirit. Being *for* the poor conveys the notion of attraction and mission. Said differently, while many of the urban poor were attracted to Black Holiness Pentecostal churches in the North, like those affiliated with MSHCA, the prophetic social consciousness of these churches compelled adherents to serve the poor and to express their perfect love for God and humanity among them.

Under Robinson's leadership, MSHCA's concern for the poor resulted in the formation of individual service departments within the denomination like missions, education, and the young women's holiness home. In 1925, Home Missionary and sister to Bishop Ida Robinson, Sister Edna Jordan, shared that loving and serving the poor meant "Soliciting aid for the poor from the public, going out into the streets and lanes, bringing in the poor down and outs to be fed and clothed, and to hear the Word and be saved."[16] From Jordan's brief account of what serving the poor meant to her, we learn how affiliate churches of MSHCA not only expressed regard for and engaged with their local communities but also committed to practicing material works of mercy. Early sources confirm that the ministries associated with MSHCA readily provided shelter and food for the poor, visited the hospitalized and the imprisoned, buried the dead, and educated the ignorant, all as a means of ministering to the physical needs of the human person and conveying the practicality of holiness.

---

[14] Ida Robinson, "The Economic Persecution," *The Latter Day Messenger* 3 (May 23, 1935), p. 2. Bettye Collier-Thomas, *Daughters of Thunder: Black Women and Their Sermons: 1850-1979* (San Francisco, CA: Jossey-Bass, 1998), pp. 203-205.

[15] Turner, *The United Holy Church of America*, p. 9.

[16] MSHC, *Yearbook* (September 28, 1925), pp. 24-25.

Family: Social Betterment and Survival

Within the Black Holiness Pentecostal tradition, family is immediate, extended, and spiritual. One way to tell the story of Black Holiness Pentecostalism is from the vantage point of family. Specifically, one that has settled in the urban North, is living among a host of black southern migrants, and is occupying a variety of storefronts, home prayer groups, and church buildings. Such a story would reveal how individuals, having made the decision to be saved, sanctified, and Holy Ghost filled, believed themselves to be adopted into the family of God, and thus voluntarily open to embracing a new community of strangers as their brothers and sisters. Undoubtedly, if a history of Black Holiness Pentecostalism were told from a familial context, we would learn many things. But none more important than how "families" like Mount Sinai Holy Church of America believed that it was unequivocally antithetical to true holiness to either ignore the world or disregard opportunities to mitigate the pain and suffering of the oppressed.

This notion of family does not mean that Baer and Singer were not correct, even if only in part, in their assessment of Black Holiness Pentecostal organizations like MSHCA, as many sanctified communities did/do in fact place a great deal of emphasis on clean living via socially approved behaviors, attitudes, work ethic, and styles of dress. However, conceding this point should not suggest that Baer and Singer did not overreach by claiming that this focus has been to the detriment of Black Holiness Pentecostals' sociopolitical involvement. If Baer and Singer are reducing sociopolitical engagement to policy and programming, like that which is common to historical black Protestant denominations such as the Baptists and Methodists, then Black Holiness-Pentecostalism falls woefully short.

However, if sociopolitical involvement includes community sustainment through street missions, soup kitchens, clothes distribution, literacy programs, and employment opportunities, then Black Holiness Pentecostalism fits the bill.[17] To claim that Black Holiness

---

[17] Giggie, *After Redemption,* p. 4 and p. 7. Giggie, having noted a similar list in his text, notes that "southern migrants flooded northern cities and introduced new styles of music and worship to Black urban congregants,

Pentecostals are so busy looking to the heavens in anticipation of the *Parousia* that they neglect their own families – biological, spiritual, and racial – is to misunderstand the spiritual lives of black Americans living in a violent and uncertain world. Furthermore, such a claim grossly misrepresents the practicality of their message of holiness. It seems that Baer and Singer's conception of sociopolitical engagement is too narrow to appreciate fully how Black Holiness Pentecostals "find in their sacred beliefs and practices a mediating space through which to respond to the ambiguities, horrors, and hopes of life."[18]

Historically speaking, the practicality of holiness played an invaluable role, not only in how early Black Holiness Pentecostals responded to the alternations of *"living while black* in America,"[19] but also in how they practiced self-defense, and subsequently, communal preservation. Black Holiness Pentecostalism's strict guidelines about entertainment and commensality are excellent examples of how Black Holiness Pentecostals used holiness as a mechanism for social betterment and security. In other words, holiness codes around prohibitive practices and restrictive activities reflect a general conviction that although God was faithful to protect God's Holy People, it was best for the saints to spend "most of their free time at church and avoiding worldly activities." The rationale behind this was rather straightforward: "the church [is a safe place] where there are no penalties for being black and poor."[20] This point, which stressed avoiding being in the wrong place at the wrong time, was concerned about limiting contact with any person, group, or thing – e.g. police, KKK, and warring gangs – capable of threatening the overall welfare of the family.[21]

Ultimately, Black Holiness Pentecostals' sociopolitical engagement is born out of a notion of holiness wherein the three defining

---

formed Holiness Pentecostal storefront churches, and tested ideas about racial self-help made famous through the philosophy of Marcus Garvey."

[18] Giggie, *After Redemption*, p. xvii.

[19] Crumbley, *Saved and Sanctified*, p. 11.

[20] Deidre Helen Crumbley, "Raising Saints in Exile: Intergenerational Know-ledge Transfer in a Storefront-Sanctified Church," in Cheryl Waites (ed.), *Social Work Practice with African-American Families: An Intergenerational Perspective* (New York: Routledge, 2008), p. 83.

[21] Crumbley, *Saved and Sanctified*, p. 154. Also see Turner, p. 130.

aspects of prophetic social consciousness are scaffolded by a commitment to morality (being) and public engagement (doing). In other words, fully sanctified lives, guided by the work of the Spirt and committed to its righteousness peace, and joy (e.g. social justice) must focus on a life of sobriety, "strict discipline, [and] deep devotion," as well as social responsibility and selfless service.[22] For this reason, Black Holiness Pentecostals like Bishop Ida Bell Robinson, concerned for safety, security, and prosperity of the entire community, rejected sociopolitical passivity. It is not surprising, therefore, that even quotidian matters such as sartorial choice, not only played a role in religious identity politics but also black women's ongoing struggle for betterment and survival, vis-à-vis, agency and autonomy.

Fighting Jezebel: Holy Drag and the Black and Holy Woman

Styles of dress is another example of how practitioners attended to the family and used holiness as a mechanism for its overall safety and preservation. Within Mount Sinai Holy Church of America both women and men had to adhere to a specific dress code.[23] To be sure, the dress code prescribed to women was more intricate and imposing than the one assigned to men, but of course, this was not without a gendered and socially-constructed reason. Briefly, clothing, specifically women's "clothing signified one's moral status, as well as class." For a woman to be viewed and subsequently valued as someone who was moral, chaste, and pious she had to be wholly covered up.[24]

Consistent with most holiness traditions, MSHCA's strict dress code for women mandated both plainness and layers of clothing. Specifically, women were not to wear makeup, jewelry, braided hair or short dresses; but they were expected to wear either plain, long,

---

[22] Turner, *The United Holy Church of America*, pp. 10 and 19.

[23] Arthur Huff Fauset, *Black Gods of the Metropolis: Negro Religious Cults of the Urban North* (Philadelphia, PA: University of Pennsylvania Press, reprint edn., 2002), p. 20. It has been well noted, that the men of MSHCA were not permitted to wear neckties, but if they did "it must be either plain white or black."

[24] Kelly Brown Douglas, *Sexuality and the Black Church: A Womanist Perspective* (Maryknoll, NY: Orbis Books, 1999), p. 6.

dark dresses with white lace cuffs and collars or long black skirts and white blouses with dark cotton stockings. Mandates regarding this particular style of dress often were ensconced in sanctimonious patriarchal hyperbole that stressed morality and modesty and thus functioned as an invaluable tool for those who wished not only to police women's bodies but also their sexuality.[25]

The supposed threat of the black female body and her sexuality has a dark and painful history that began with the first encounters between Europeans and Africans and persist to the present day.[26] The resultant dehumanizing images, myths, and stereotypes that labeled the black woman as depraved, lascivious, and seducing remained, and constituted many of the concerns surrounding black womanhood during the migration era. In fact, during the migration era, new fears and concerns emerged about the free, independent, and uncontrolled black female body, and along with this came new ways of policing and controlling their bodies.

It is not surprising that the Black Church was complicit in disparaging the black female body, vis-a-vis black womanhood. In fact, in her groundbreaking text, *Sexuality and The Black Church*, Kelly Brown Douglas reminds us that "[t]he manner in which black women are treated in many black churches reflects the western Christian tradition's notion of women as evil and its notions of black

---

[25] In her groundbreaking book, *Sexuality and the Black Church: A Womanist Perspective*, theologian Kelly Brown Douglas quotes Christian ethicist James Nelson and his extremely helpful definition of sexuality:

Sexuality is a sign, a symbol, and a means of our call to communication and communion. This is the most apparent in regard to other human beings, and other body-selves. The mystery of our sexuality is the mystery of our need to reach out to embrace others both physically and spiritually ... [Sexuality] is who we are as body-selves who experience the emotional, cognitive, physical, and spiritual need for intimate communion – human and divine (Douglas, p. 6).

[26] Douglas comments that "During these encounters ... Europeans were often struck by the stark differences in appearance between themselves and Africans." These differences, beyond culture, included complexion and sparse dress. Eventually, European travelers and subsequent colonizers concocted myths about Black sexuality that would furnish dehumanizing stereotypes and images surrounding the Black body in general and the Black female body in particular. Douglas, *Sexuality and the Black Church*, pp. 32-33.

women as Jezebels and seducers of men."[27] Thus, patriarchal efforts to protect black women from sexual predators, both black and white, while uplifting the race came to mean distinguishing black churchwomen from black non-churchwomen. Within Black Holiness-Pentecostalism the distinction between those who were black and holy (i.e. proper ladies who were chaste, and pious) and those who were not (i.e. "Jezebels" who were aggressive, cunning, and hyper-sexualized) often came down to the style of dress. The truly black and holy woman was to dress in modest clothing "that [did] not draw attention to the curves of her breasts, hips, or behind."[28] The goal was to publicly show that she was *sanctified* and therefore not available "for the sexual pleasures or bodily desires of either [herself] or others."[29] In other words, Black Holiness-Pentecostal churches like those affiliated with MSHCA attempted to hide the black female body by making it invisible through a form of respectability[30] that demanded sanctified women dress in "holy drag."

Nevertheless, there is another way in which to construe the holiness uniform, namely one that is still woman-centered and race-conscious but attempts to move us beyond respectability and towards a reclamation of power. In her text, *Saved and Sanctified: The Rise of the Storefront Church in Great Migration Philadelphia*, anthropologist Deidre Helen Crumbley reminds us that holiness codes surrounding dress were not just a way of policing, silencing, and making invisible the black female body. Instead, she claims that dress codes like those used by the women of MSHCA intentionally

---

[27] Douglas, *Sexuality and the Black Church*, p. 6

[28] Monique Moultrie, "After the Thrill is Gone: Married to the Holy Spirit but Still Sleeping Alone," *Pneuma* 33 (2011)), p. 243.

[29] Moultrie, "After the Thrill is Gone."

[30] Unquestionably, neither historical Black Protestant churches nor those affiliated with Black Holiness-Pentecostalism were the first to use style of dress in this way. Holy dress under the pretense of respectability was and has always been a tool for distinguishing one group/class from another and redefining the public image of Black women living in the United States. The National Association of Colored Women (NACW), founded in the late nineteenth century, is the recognized forerunner of this practice and since its founding Black women concerned with respectability politics, have busied themselves with *sanctifying* Black women's sexuality in an effort to counter stereotypes, downplay sexual expression, and combat sexual exploitation.

set out to degender and to desexualize women as a protective meas-ure against the widespread rape and lynch culture.[31] Attempts to make themselves invisible, even going so far as to wear black/dark colored clothing against their black/dark colored skin, was far from foolproof[32] and still problematic and reductionistic. Nevertheless, for the black and holy woman, her style of dress became an active yet coded means of articulating to the world around her, her unwill-ingness to be reviled or ravaged any longer;[33] therefore, the holiness uniform served as a practical way of returning to her a means of con-trol in sexual politics.[34]

The noble effort to be freed from objectifying and exploitative notions that misrepresented black women as highly sexualized, evil seductresses, and Jezebels, prompted black and holy women within the sanctified tradition, in general, and MSHCA, in particular, to employ "holy drag" as a culture of dissemblance. In studying the sex-ual vulnerability and powerlessness of black women "as victims of rape and domestic violence," Darlene Clark Hine notes that beyond being a woefully under-analyzed theme in black women's history – I would add American religious history – this dearth is in large part due to a long-standing impenetrable cult of secrecy among black women. She dubs this secrecy, "a culture of dissemblance" and de-fines it as the behaviors and attitudes of black women that created the *appearance* of openness and disclosure but actually shielded the truth of their inner lives and selves from their oppressors.[35]

---

[31] Crumbley, *Saved and Sanctified*, p. 146.

[32] The 1944 story of Recy Taylor is but one example of the limitations and the overall failure of this practice.

[33] A most troubling aspect of Black women's history in the United States is the fact that the Black female body has been the perpetual site of ridicule and abuse. Believed to be the antithesis of true womanhood, specifically that which constitutes the respect due to a "lady," the Black female body bore both the same violence and abuse that Black men suffered while ex-isting as "the unwilling [recipient] of the most depraved passions of White" men. Douglas, *Sexuality and the Black Church*, p. 39.

[34] Crumbley, *Saved and Sanctified*, p. 146. Also see, Arthur Huff Fauset, *Black Gods of the Metropolis: Negro Religious Cults of the Urban North* (Philadelphia, PA: University of Pennsylvania Press, reprint, 2002), p. 20.

[35] Darlene Clark Hine, "Rape and the Inner Lives of Black Women in the Middle West," *Signs* 14.4 (Summer 1989), p. 912.

The strict, and almost sacred, secrecy among black women is the effect of generations of having to endure "combined influences of rape (or the threat of rape), domestic violence, and economic oppression."[36] For black and holy women like Bishop Ida Bell Robinson, plain, non-disclosing, dress was not merely to deflect the unwanted gaze, although undoubtedly it included that, it also was a practical means of preserving their personal and sexual autonomy vis-a-vis "their productive and reproductive capacities, and their sexuality."[37] If we think of such sartorial choices as acts of active resistance, or even protests, we can see how black and holy women creatively took what was ready-at-hand, i.e. styles of dress, and validated it as sacred psychic space to harness power to partner with the work of the Spirit to (1) resist "tropes that castigated their sexuality,"[38] (2) attend to "the open wounds of the violence perpetuated in their bodies,"[39] and (3) dispose of cultural inscriptions that maligned their bodies as being anything other than the temple of the Holy Spirit.

So, if austere plain public personas and representations of their bodily selves did not re-inscribe socially oppressive and ill-fitted Victorian notions of womanhood and morality, what did it provide black and holy women in the sanctified tradition during the migration era? For one, I submit that much like the verbal cult of secrecy that Hine proposed, holy drag reclaimed their ability to thrive and not just survive. In other words, in holy drag black sanctified women collectively created alternative self-images:

> A secret, undisclosed persona [that] allowed [them as] individual wom[en] to function, to work effectively as ... domestic[s] in white households, to bear and rear children, to endure the frustration-born violence of frequently under-or unemployed mates, to support churches, to found institutions, to engage in social

---

[36] Hine, "Rape and the Inner Lives of Black Women in the Middle West," p. 913.

[37] Hine, "Rape and the Inner Lives of Black Women in the Middle West," p. 915.

[38] Monique Moultrie, *Passionate and Pious: Religious Media and Black Women's Sexuality* (Durham and London: Duke University Press, 2017), p. 7.

[39] Douglas, *Sexuality and the Black Church*, p. 73.

service activities, all while living within a clearly hostile white, patriarchal middle-class America.[40]

Secondly, black sanctified women dressing in holy drag was a subversive act of resistance and protest because they voluntarily participated in the very oppressive structures that existed to restrict their access to power, with the singular goal of reconfiguring notions of race, gender, and sexuality to fit their unique circumstances. Moreover, in the hands of black and holy women, specifically, those who constituted the poor and working classes, plain holy dress became a tool by which to take back two meaningful things: (1) how the world saw them and (2) how the world exerted power over them.

It is important to note that point number one is not just about representation and public image. Instead, it has more to do with a self-conscious effort to change interpersonal exchanges with those in positions of dominance and power. In other words, change in dress was supposed to signify a change in the way persons related to one another. Said differently, by choosing to wear a plain, austere style of dress black and holy woman were expressing a nonverbal command for mutual respect and human dignity.

Similarly, treating holy drag as a tool for taking back how the world exerts power over the Black female body, is also about social relations, but with particular attention to the body and how rules, regulations, and mores criminalize, objectify, or pejoratively label that which is "other." In choosing plain, austere styles of dress, black and holy women determined not only how their bodies were perceived, but also how their bodies would *live, move and have their being*. Here, the holiness uniform takes back from external forces the power that seeks to regulate the black female body. In so doing, holy drag signifies the black and holy woman as one who is both the bride of Christ and the temple of the Holy Spirit. This power move by black and holy women simultaneously shirks culturally inscribed denigrations of blackness while affirming blackness as the *Imago Dei*.

---

[40] Hine, "Rape and the Inner Lives of Black Women in the Middle West," p. 915.

Conclusion

By employing a prophetic social consciousness rooted in holiness and empowered by the supernatural, early Black Holiness Pentecostals embraced a progressive theology of salvation, albeit implicitly. Unquestionably, their sermons, songs, and doctrinal statements affirmed and maintained an unrelenting commitment to an evangelical understanding of the gospel, i.e. personal salvation. However, their practices indicate that they were also committed to a prophetic social gospel that defended the oppressed, pursued justice, and promulgated peace. By holding their concern for the eternal state of humanity's soul in tandem with their concern for the current state of their communities, neighborhoods, and race, Black Holiness-Pentecostals such as those who identified with the Mount Sinai Holy Church of America affirmed holiness as more than just "clean living." They also affirmed holiness as the work of the Spirit and a mechanism of economic, political, and social justice.

Unquestionably, the black sanctified tradition is, in fact the testimony of persons often on the margins who suffer or have suffered endless forms of physical, sexual, emotional, epistemic, and spiritual violence intended to bring about their full demise, yet have survived. In Black Holiness Pentecostalism adherents found communities that were equally attentive to their spiritual and material needs. For black and holy women in sanctified churches such as MSHCA, attention to their material needs often went beyond food, clothing, and shelter to include bodily concerns surrounding rape, the threat of rape, and domestic violence. So, while it is easy to look at holiness codes that pertain to dress as just another expression of black respectability politics, it behooves us to look closer. If we do, we will see how black southern migrant women like Bishop Ida Bell Robinson were able to survive, and in many cases, thrive, because they took what was ready-at-hand and used it to defend their human dignity as well as their prophetic voice. Although imperfect, and far from foolproof, style of dress was employed as a subversive tactic to reclaim their power *to live, move, and have their being* as black and holy. Thus, it is in the power of the Spirit – the Spirit of Justice and Truth – and in the face of the prevailing culture's anti-black racism and sexism, that these black and holy women uncompromisingly pursued and exhibited holiness, spiritual empowerment, and prophetic social consciousness.

Bibliography

Adams, Betty Livingston, *Black Women's Christian Activism: Seeking Social Justice in a Northern Suburb* (New York, NY: New York University Press, 2016).

Alexander, Estrelda Y., *Limited Liberty: The Legacy of Four Pentecostal Women Pioneers* (Cleveland, OH: The Pilgrim Press 2008).

—"Ida Robinson: Loosing Women to Lead," Henry H. Knight III (ed.), *From Aldersgate to Azusa Street: Wesleyan, Holiness, and Pentecostal Visions of the New Creation* (Eugene, OR: Pickwick Publications, 2010).

Baer, Hans A., and Merrill Singer, *African American Religion: Varieties of Protest and Accommodation* (Knoxville, TN: University of Tennessee Press, 2002).

Crumbley, Deidre Helen, "Raising Saints in Exile: Intergenerational Knowledge Transfer in a Storefront-Sanctified Church," in Cheryl Waites (ed.), *Social work practice with African-American families: An Intergenerational Perspective* (New York: Routledge, 2008).

—*Saved and Sanctified: The Rise of a Storefront Church in Great Migration Philadelphia* (Gainesville, FL: University Press of Florida, 2012).

Douglas, Kelly Brown, *Sexuality and the Black Church: A Womanist Perspective* (Maryknoll, NY: Orbis Books, 1999).

Fauset, Arthur Huff, *Black Gods of the Metropolis: Negro Religious Cults of the Urban North* (Philadelphia, PA: University of Pennsylvania Press, reprint, 2002).

Giggie, John Michael, *After Redemption: Jim Crow and the transformation of African American religion in the Delta, 1875-1915* (New York; Oxford: Oxford University Press, 2008).

Hine, Darlene Clark, "Rape and the Inner Lives of Black Women in the Middle West," *Signs* 14.4 (Summer 1989), pp. 912-20.

Moultrie, Monique, "After the Thrill is Gone: Married to the Holy Spirit but Still Sleeping Alone," *Pneuma* 33.2 (2011), pp. 237-53).

—*Passionate and Pious: Religious Media and Black Women's Sexuality* (Durham, NC: Duke University Press, 2017).

Mt. Sinai Holy Church of America, Inc., *Celebrating our Legacy – Mt. Sinai Holy Church of America, Inc* (Philadelphia, PA: Mt Sinai Holy Church of America, vol. 1, 1999).

—*Yearbook of First Annual Convocation of the Mt. Sinai Holy Church of America, Inc.* (Philadelphia, PA: Mt Sinai Holy Church of America, 1925).

—*Yearbook of Fourteenth Annual Convocation of the Mt. Sinai Holy Church of America, Inc.* (Philadelphia, PA: Mt Sinai Holy Church of America, 1938).

Pope-Levison, Priscilla, *Building the Old Time Religion: Women Evangelists in the Progressive Era* (New York: New York University Press, 2014).

Riley, Glenda, *Inventing the American Woman: A Perspective on Women's History* (Arlington Heights, IL: Harlan Davidson, 2014).

Robinson, Ida, "The Economic Persecution," *The Latter Day Messenger* 3 (May 23, 1935), p. 2.

Collier-Thomas, Bettye, *Daughters of Thunder: Black Women and Their Sermons: 1850-1979* (San Francisco, CA: Jossey-Bass, 1998).

Trotter, Joe William, and Eric Ledell Smith, *African Americans in Pennsylvania: Shifting Historical Perspectives* (University Park, PA: Pennsylvania Historical and Museum Commission and Pennsylvania State University Press, 1997).

Trulear, Harold Dean, "Ida B. Robinson: The Mother As Symbolic Presence," in J.R. Goff, Jr, and Grant Wacker (eds.), *Portraits of A Generation: Early Pentecostal Leaders* (Fayetteville, AR: The University of Arkansas Press, 2002).

Turner, William C., *The United Holy Church of America: A Study in Black Holiness-Pentecostalism* (Piscataway, NJ: Gorgias Press, 2006).

CHAPTER NINE

A CALL FOR THE AWAKENING OF THE PROPHETIC VOICE OF AFRICAN NEO –PENTECOSTALS

Babatunde Adedibu*

Scholars note that Azusa Street Revival was significant center of the outpouring of revivals and conversion. The Azusa Street revival became a meeting point of cultural diversity and the hub of missionary enterprise to the then known world as Europeans, Latinos, and people of diverse socio-economic backgrounds came to experience the outpouring of the Holy Spirit. While previous scholarship has noted that many indigenous people were responsible for evangelization across various cultures, it has not adequately acknowledged and even marginalized other centers of revivals of the Holy Spirit in the discourse on Pentecostalism.[1] For instance, in Pyongyang, which is

* Babatunde Adedibu (PhD, Northwest University, South Africa) is the Provost of the Redeemed Christian Bible College, Mowe, Ogun State, Nigeria. He also teaches in the Department of New Testament Studies, Faculty of Theology and Religion at the University of Pretoria, South Africa.
[1] The global religious landscape changed with the emergence of Pentecostal movement in the turn of the twentieth century. The nascent Pentecostal movement was accentuated by Azusa Street Revival Movement led by William J. Seymour, the Black Holiness preacher that started at the "Apostolic Faith Gospel Mission at 312 Azusa Street in Los Angeles." See, Noel Davies and Martin Conway, *World Christianity in the 20th Century* (London: SCM Press, 2008), p. 75. In many ways, the movement formed a new beginning in Christianity and multiplied across many cultural frontiers. However, the foundational principles of Pentecostalism originated in Jerusalem on the day of Pentecost in 33 CE (Acts 2.9-11). Some strands of Pentecostalism that share commonality with Classical Pentecostalism may trace

now the capital of North Korea, and in India there were Pentecostal outpourings. Some of them led to over 500 young men and women every day in prayer and deployment as "Holy Ghost missionaries" for global evangelization.[2] The multiplicities and diversities of pentecostalisms are quite pronounced in Africa and Diaspora due to its missionary ethos while it has been adjured to be polynucleated.[3]

It should be emphasized that African Pentecostalism is distinctively African and may be located theologically in the continuum of global Neo-Pentecostalism.[4] They tend to emphasize social ministries but not as prophetic in regard to social justice.

African Pentecostalism has gradually been redefined Africa, particularly in urban cities since the 1980s. While the West is becoming more secular, across Sub Saharan Africa, there have been continual changes; cinemas, school auditorium, shops and agrarian spaces have been transformed into Neo-Pentecostal sacred spaces.[5]

It is rather intriguing that despite multifaceted challenges of Sub Saharan Africa particularly dysfunctional economic clime, religious extremism, insecurity and poverty, the religious sector is arguably thriving. The changing Christian landscape in Sub-Saharan Africa is a reflection of the changing global Christian kaleidoscope

---

back to Agnes Ozman's experience of the Baptism of the Holy Spirit and speaking in tongues in in 1901 at Charles Parham's Bible College in Topekas, Kansas. Vinson Synan also notes that "as early as 1830, Scottish Presbyterian minister Edward Irving and a group of English evangelicals had predicted the restoration of tongues (as well as the other gifts of the Spirit) as signs of the end of the age." Synan suggests that perhaps Irving and his followers may have had a Pentecostal experience that prompted their prediction. See, Vinson Synan, "Pentecostal Millennialism: The Second Comers," Web:https://christianhistoryinstitute.org/magazine/article/pentecostal-millennialism-the-second-comers [Accessed 23July,2019]. Also, see Cecil Robeck, Jr, and Amos Yong, *The Cambridge Companion to Pentecostalism* (New York: Cambridge University Press, 2014), p. 15.

[2] Allan Anderson, *Spreading Fires: The Missionary Nature of Early Pentecostalism* (London: SCM Press, 2007), pp. 75-89.

[3] Anderson, *Spreading Fires,* p. 4.

[4] Ogbu Kalu, *African Pentecostalism: An Introduction* (New York: Oxford University Press, 2008), p. 14.

[5] Olufunke Adeboye, "'A Church in a Cinema Hall?' Pentecostal Appropriation of Public Space in Nigeria," *Journal of Religion in Africa* 42 (2012), pp. 145-71.

characterized by the "southernisation" of Christianity with the center of gravity of the faith now in the majority world.[6]

Some African Pentecostals affirm that the doctrines of wealth and health ideologies in which material goods are considered a measure of spirituality. This is a major theological dissonance with mainly white Classical Pentecostalism. Many label Neo-Pentecostal movement as "Prosperity gospel" – "name it, claim it" or "transactional faith." Prosperity ministers teach that God blesses people materially, spiritually and physically. One critic submits that:

> [Neo] Pentecostalism sings the praises of material success, a sign of sanctification and liberation from the feelings of jealousy that motivate witches. It emancipates the individual by hailing that his [or her] personal assets, blessings, capitalist accumulation and the relation to merchandise "armour–plates" believers against the menacing world of the invisible. In this respect, it inverts the "equation that linked wealth to evil doing and poverty to sanctity."[7]

Such perspective may be considered contentious among Neo-Pentecostals, particularly in the Africa. The above mentioned view disregards the African cosmological worldview of enchantment that resonates in Pentecostal's ideals of spiritual warfare. Interestingly, Neo-Pentecostal prosperity gospel elicits transactional orientation amongst religious hoppers and adherents leading to distinctive religious consumerism.[8] Benyah observes the nexus between consumer culture and Pentecostal/Charismatic Christianity:

> Material prosperity is enamored by a repertoire of success epitomized in the conspicuous consumption of modern products and

---

[6] Babatunde Adedibu, "Reverse Mission or Migrant Sanctuaries? Migration, Symbolic Mapping, and Missionary Challenges of Britain's Black Majority Churches," *Pneuma* 35 (2013), pp. 405-23; C. Währisch-Oblau, *The Missionary Self-Perceptions of Pentecostal/Charismatic Church Leaders from the Global South in Europe: Bringing Back the Gospel* (Leiden and Boston: Brill, 2009), pp. 35-36.

[7] E. Obadare, "'Raising Righteous Billionaires': The Prosperity Gospel Reconsidered," *HTS Teologiese Studies/Theological Studies* 72 (2016), p. 4.

[8] Kehinde Ayantayo, Adedibu Babatunde, and Igboin Benson (eds.), *African Pentecostalism: Probity and Accountability* (Akungba-Akoko, Ondo: Adekunle Ajasin University Press, 2019), pp. 52-65.

persistent grandiosity, especially in the media. The emphasis on prosperity gospel is to become more modern in outlook, sophisticated and powerful as a symbolizing feature of one's right standing with God in terms of payment of tithes and offerings.[9]

Not all Neo-Pentecostal churches in Africa and Diaspora are wealth or prosperity focused.[10] However, some of them have re-branded health and wealth ideologies into "success theology and a vision for growth"[11] which is centered on blessings due to claims that the church has answers to the existential challenges of people. Cartledge and Davies posit that:

> African observers like Asamoah-Gyadu argue that [Kingsway International Christian Centre is one of the several transnational churches founded in London by Nigerian Pastor Mathew Ashimolowo in 1988 but has registered its network of churches in Africa] KICC is less about prosperity per se and more about African empowerment. He suggests that KICC presents a challenge to the African population to rise above its historical importune circumstances and that this challenge is presented by Ashimolowo who seeks to advance the cause of African or Black people who "seem to belong to the bottom of the pile, or the bottom of the pyramid-economically, socially, physically [and] mentally." This means that motivational messages are used to encourage educational, business and social betterment in order to fulfill their destinies before God.[12]

Despite the "world accommodating" label sometimes ascribed to African Neo-Pentecostal churches on the bases of their "dominion

---

[9] Francis Benyah, "Commodification of the Gospel and the Socioeconomics of Neo Pentecostal/Charismatic Christianity in Ghana," in *Legon Journal of the Humanities* 29.2 (2018), pp. 116-45 (122).

[10] Gukurume Simbarashe, "Singing Positivity: Prosperity Gospel in the Musical Discourse of Popular Youth Hip-Hop Gospel in Zimbabwe," *Muziki* 14.2, pp. 36-54.

[11] Mark Cartledge *et al.* (eds.), *Mega Churches and Social Engagement*, p. 24.

[12] Mark J. Cartledge and Andrew Davies, "A Megachurch in a Megacity: A Study of Cyberspace Representation," *PentecoStudies* 13.1 (2014), p. 68, cited in Mark Cartledge *et al.* (eds.), *Mega Churches and Social Engagement* (Leiden; Brill, 2019), p. 25.

theology" or "prosperity gospel," the religious landscape of Africa and the African Diaspora has shifted because they believe the Holy Spirit has called the church to respond to the holistic needs of the people.

Holy Spirit in Neo-Pentecostal Discourse

Africans have an integrated worldview. For them, it only makes sense that personal transformation leads to societal transformation:

> This is why conversion and incorporation into the community of faith cannot be seen apart from the transformation of society. The person filled by the Spirit of God is impelled by that same Spirit to cooperate with God in the work of evangelism and social action in the anticipation of the new creation.[13]

This culminates in claims of empowerment of the adherents for Christian service as well as charismata (gifts of the Holy Spirit) characterized by glossolalia (speaking in tongues) historically and belief in premillennial eschatology. Anderson opines that the Pentecostal movement "is above all is a missionary movement."[14] It thus becomes pertinent to posit that the Holy Spirit equips the church as a missionary movement through the empowerment model through charismatic gifts of Jesus to his disciples in the Bible. The obvious implication of Pentecost with the outpouring of the Spirit is that it implies the transference of the missionary mandate of Jesus to the church.[15] This perspective as re-echoed was noted even as back as 1908 by Roswell Flower who noted that that "when the Holy Spirit comes into our hearts, the missionary spirit comes in with it; they are inseparable. ... Carrying the gospel to hungry souls in this and

---

[13] Evangelization, Proselytism and Common Witness: The Report from the Fourth Phase of the International Dialogue between the Roman Catholic Church and Some Classical Pentecostal Churches and Leaders, 1990-1997, p. 40.

[14] Allan Anderson, *To the Ends of the Earth: Pentecostalism and the Transformation of World Christianity* (Cambridge; Cambridge University Press, 2nd edn, 2013), p. 2.

[15] For further study, see Roger Stronstad, *The Charismatic Theology of St. Luke* (Peabody, MA: Hendrickson, 1984).

other lands is but a natural result."[16] Thus, arguably the outpouring of the Holy Spirit upon the church constitutes a community of authorization through Charisma for the sustenance of the missionary mandate of Jesus Christ through healing and reconciliation as well as social services. Moreover, Perkins argues that "evangelism is not fast talk aimed at gaining converts; it is a ministry in *word and deed* that leads people to the place where they can activate their faith in the person of Jesus for themselves, Jesus never put evangelism and social action at odds with one another, so neither should we"![17]

Acts is a missionary manual par excellence for Pentecostals:

Acts [of Apostles] is more than history for the Pentecostal; it is a missionary manual, an open-ended account of the missionary work of the Holy Spirit in the Church, concluding not with chapter 28 but with the ongoing Spirit empowered and Spirit directed preaching of today.[18]

Moreover, in the Early Church the apostles also maintained an integrated worldview – a nexus between doctrine and action. Perkins explains the role of Holy Spirit in teaching the word of God that brings people to Christ "who understands the way in which the poor suffer abuse and encourages us through the Holy Spirit. The Holy Spirit heals the gashes of our heart (Acts 10.38), comforts us (Acts 9.31) in (our) loss, and affirms our dignity in the face of dehumanization."[19]

Adewale points out three Greek words that Luke designate to the poor, which are πενιχρός, ἐνδεής, and πτωχός.[20] Adewale reasons

---

[16] Cited in Gary B. McGee, "Pentecostals and their Various Strategies for Global Mission: A Historical Assessment," in M.A. Dempster, B.D. Klaus, and D. Petersen (eds.), *Called and Empowered: Global Mission in Pentecostal Perspective* (Peabody: Hendrickson, 1991), p. 206.

[17] J. Perkins, *Beyond Charity: The Call to Christian Community Development* (Grand Rapids: Baker, 1993), p. 83.

[18] John Michael Penney, *The Missionary Emphasis of Lukan Pneumatology* (Sheffield: Sheffield Academic Press, 1997), p. 12.

[19] Perkins, *Beyond Charity*, p. 87.

[20] Olubiyi Adewale, "Developing a Social Action Agenda for the Poor: A Reading of the Lukan Poverty Parables for the Nigerian Context," *Spectrum: Journal of Contemporary Christianity and Society* 1.1 (April 2016), pp. 33-48 (34).

that in Luke's writings poverty is expressed thematically[21] and the "poor are not only the destitute but at the same time they are those who live in an outcast condition. These people represent the extremes of social and economic status."[22]

Nevertheless, most Neo-Pentecostal churches in Africa are energetically committed to witnessing God as the Redeemer but unconsciously not witnessing about God as the Creator. This view of God is myopic, thus problematic:

> God is Creator. He has made this world; He loves it. He still cares that men and women have enough to eat; decent houses to live in; worthy moral standards; noble literature and art; scientific research; everything. But men and women are estranged from Him. They are lost - in a state of rebellion and none of these things I've mentioned are salvation. So God the Creator became God the Redeemer ... Our job, as Christians, [is] to be His witnesses in both these capacities (as Creator and Redeemer). We witness to Him as Creator when we, too, care about men and women - food, housing, politics, laws, art, morality, every part of human life. When we stand for what is right and work for social justice. But we must also witness to Him as Redeemer. None of these things save. Individuals must come to Christ as [Savior] and Lord through personal evangelism. The better we witness to God as Creator, the more effective will be our witness to Him as Redeemer.[23]

From Anderson's observation above, it is implied that the same Spirit that empowers Africa Neo-Pentecostal for proselytization is a veritable source of motivation for active engagement in matters of social justice. Previous scholarship has highlighted the positive correlation between post resurrection global missionary mandate of Jesus to his disciples in Mt. 28.18-20 (Great Commission) and Jesus' Great Commandments: loving one another, as the seal of a true disciple (John 14),[24] seeking the kingdom of God and its righteousness

---

[21] Adewale, "Developing a Social Action Agenda for the Poor," p. 37.

[22] Adewale, "Developing a Social Action Agenda for the Poor," p. 37.

[23] J.N.D. Anderson, *Morality, Law and Grace* (London: Tyndale, 1972), p. 104.

[24] David McIlroy, "The Mission of Justice," *Transformation* 28.3 (July 2011), pp. 182-94.

(Mt. 6.33); while not negating the importance of justice in the fulfillment of God's law (Mt. 23.23). David McIlroy, citing D'Souza and Rogers, argues that:

> The Great Commission must always go hand in hand with the Great Commandment, and the Great Commandment is deeply linked with the need for involvement in the lives of those who are oppressed, persecuted, abused, and dehumanized. In the same way, Haugen argues that the commands to love God and to love our [neighbor] as ourselves are at the core of the Christian's calling. Accordingly, the call to remember the oppressed is couched in the logic of love: "Remember ... those who are mistreated as if you yourselves were suffering." The Scriptures are confident that if we imagine that we are the child prostitute, the torture victim, the child [laborer].[25]

Moreover, true justice is Christo-centric (Is 42.1; Col 1.28) which is enhanced by the proclamation of the good news as a function of the role of the Holy Spirit in convicting sinners as well as signs and wonders (Lk 4.18; Jn 14.12) and negating cessationists"[26] perspective. As part of the Holy Spirit's work in transformation of people through belief in the finished work of Christ, the believer has a role to play in pursuing righteousness or holiness (Matthew 5-7; Hab. 2.4).

Various views have been expressed by scholars with respect to the concept of Holiness. Within the purview of this work three types of holiness variants will be mentioned which are (a) Political holiness (b) Social Holiness and (c) Religious Holiness, the fourth Intellectual holiness will not be considered in view of the scope of this work.

Political holiness advocates included the likes of Sobrino, Thiede, Chiellebeck as well as Considine amongst others. Igboin's exploration of the subject matter copiously noted that political holiness from Considine's perspective entails "convergence of spirituality and social action oriented towards participating in God's ongoing work of salvation, albeit fragmentarily."[27] Thus, the church in

---

[25] McIlroy, "The Mission of Justice," p. 192.

[26] The school of thought that argues that the works of the Holy Spirit (speaking in tongues, prophecy, healing, and miracles) ceased at some point in history.

[27] Benson Igboin, "Unpacking the Holiness Spaces in Africa: A Radical Quest for Praxis of Holiness and Accountability in Africa," in Ayantayo

general is expected to reflect political holiness within her context against social, economic, and political structures that subjugate human dignity as well as power structures in such a society. Igboin further affirms Considine's position as he alludes to political holiness as a "salvific elixir in the here and now since salvation must first be conceived in the secular (terrestrial) space before its ultimate celestial realization."[28] In view of the social, economic and political discontinuities in many countries of the world particularly Africa, Igboin submits that the advocates of "political holiness realized early enough that human government as presently constituted is conceived in iniquity, born in sin, and sinning against the oppressed is its business."[29] The obvious implication is that there is the urgent need for the church to exercise its God given mandate through the empowerment of the Holy Spirit of being a Moses as of Old that delivered the Israelites to speak out (Prov. 31.8-9) on the unjust social, economic and political structures that dehumanize people caught in the web of poverty, marginalize, prostitution and underdevelopment in general.

Consequentially, Igboin agrees with Fung that "any act of salvation that does not take cognizance of the existential realities of the political and spiritual dynamics of the sinned-against is default, it is on the contrary to device to perpetuate the marginalization of the sinned against."[30]

One of the major proponents of social holiness was the founder of the Methodist Church, John Wesley who noted that it is inappropriate for sanctified Christians to disinvest itself from social concerns. This was a major feature of the evangelical movement in general in the 18th and 19th centuries as leading evangelicals were involved in social justices and social inequalities of their era. John Wesley is called both a preacher of the gospel and the prophet of social righteousness because he spoke on various social concerns of his days such as prostitution, gambling and corruption.[31] Wesley was

---

Kehinde, Adedibu Babatunde, and Igboin Benson (eds.), *African Pentecostalism: Probity and Accountability*, p. 243.

[28] Igboin, "Unpacking the Holiness Spaces in Africa," p. 243.

[29] Igboin, "Unpacking the Holiness Spaces in Africa," p. 244.

[30] Igboin, "Unpacking the Holiness Spaces in Africa," p. 245.

[31] Eddie Byun, *Justice awakening: How you and your church can help end Human trafficking* (Downers Grove: Inter Varsity Press Books, 2014), p. 96.

holistic as he posited that "the gospel of Christ knows no religion, but social; no holiness but social holiness."[32] Personal piety from Wesley's perspective must be reflective of social concern for one's neighbor based on love. Thus "you cannot be holy except you are engaged in making the world a better place. You do not become holy by keeping yourself pure and clean but by plunging into ministry on behalf of the world's hurting ones."[33] The contemporary implication of social holiness is that it offers the prism of re-reading the scriptures in the light of prevailing social, economic, racial and political dichotomies by addressing the inherent political structures which are responsible for human depravity and dignity.

Spiritual holiness cannot be exercised without a social context, for example, "spiritual holiness cannot be fully maintained without some dint of political involvement."[34] Holiness is expected to reflect in every facet of human endeavor. This stems from the understanding of the impact of the transformational work of the Holy Spirit in the life of people and which should reflect in their endeavors as well as incarnational lifestyle (2Cor. 5.17; Acts 12.26). Jesus endowed with the Holy Spirit was quite profound in addressing not only theological or spiritual matters alone but was committed to speaking against social and economic marginalization of people during his days (Acts 10.38).

In North America Evangelical churches have succeeded in demythologizing the Holy Spirit particularly since the advent of Civil Rights activism and Liberation Theology. Liberation theology "is a product of the influence of James Cone's fusion of Martin Luther King's and Malcolm X's 'theologies' of social equality and social injustice in relation to the egalitarian status of blacks in America and the repudiation of colonialism."[35] Liberation theology is under developed in the British space in comparison to the American space but markedly, the likes of Robert Beckford have largely been influenced by Cone's liberation theology praxis. Conversely, Africa's Neo-Pentecostal Churches are yet to rise to the challenge of appropriate

---

[32] Igboin, "Unpacking the Holiness Spaces in Africa," p. 247.

[33] Igboin, "Unpacking the Holiness Spaces in Africa," p. 247.

[34] Igboin, "Unpacking the Holiness Spaces in Africa, p. 247.

[35] Babatunde Adedibu, *Coat of Many Colours: Origin, Growth, Distinctiveness and Contributions of Black Majority Churches to British Christianity* (Gloucester: Wisdom Summit, 2012), p. 113.

contextual theological praxis to address social justice to a large extent within their context through biblical realism.

African Neo Pentecostals have a high view of the Scripture and the Holy Spirit/spirits and literal interpretation of the Bible. However, "this will only happen if and when the demands of the context impinge on our exegesis and do not flee from the Spirit-into either extreme supernaturalism."[36]

Neo-Pentecostal churches in the Global South are sometimes described as Progressive Pentecostals because of their commitment to social ministry.[37] Neo-Pentecostals are "Christians who claim to be inspired by the Holy Spirit and life of Jesus and seek to holistically address the spiritual, physical and social needs of the people of their community."[38]

Miller and Yamamori observed that "the emerging rhetoric in Progressive Pentecostal is that it is better to teach someone how to fish rather than simply give them a fish to eat."[39] Consequentially, development which is a buzz word across the globe resonates as a major feature of Neo-Pentecostalism in the Global South particularly due to the multiplicities of socio-economic and political discontinuities in many African states characterized by corruption, leadership ineptitude and the continued exploitation of the human and fiscal resources of these states through renewed contraption of the political class and foreign accomplices. Africa's Neo-Pentecostal churches are not only redefining the concept of development but are deeply embedded in the public spaces particularly in urban cities through their ritual, worship and missionizing ethos.

---

[36] Esther Acolatse, *Powers, Principalities and Spirits: Biblical Realism in Africa and the West* (Grand Rapids: Eerdmans, 2018), pp. 222.

[37] Donald E. Miller and Tetsunao Yamamori, *Global Pentecostalism, The New Face of Christian Social Engagement* (Berkeley: University of California Press, 2007), pp. 39-67; cf. Amos Yong, *In the Days of Caesar: Pentecostalism and Political Theology* (Grand Rapids: Eerdmans, 2010), pp. 34-35, who utilized the term "Pentecostal progressivism."

[38] Miller and Yamamori, *Global Pentecostalism*, p. 212. Smbarashe Hukurume, "Youth Empowerment and African Initiated Churches in Urban Zimbabwe," *Policy Brief* (Department of Theology: Humbolt University, Berlin, 2008), p. 1.

[39] Miller and Yamamori, *Global Pentecostalism*, p. 212.

African Neo-Pentecostal churches engagement in social action in the establishment of institutions, healthcare delivery, entrepreneurial development and empowerment in Africa and Diaspora. Various scholars have identified these churches as development actors within and outside Africa.[40] Neo Pentecostals in the Global South are rising from the ashes of Greek dualism of the eighteenth century that separated issues of spirit and matter that plagued the church. However, despite African Neo-Pentecostal churches' emphasis on social ministry, I argue that the prophetic voice and action as pertaining to social justice has been weak.

The Social Context of Africa and the call for the reawakening of the Prophetic Voice

Africa is the in the quagmire of social, economic, and political contraption conceived and articulated through royal ugliness and ruthless human caprice. The prevailing economic woes of Africa are a byproduct of long-standing centuries of oppressive structures by medieval feudal lords, neo-colonialists and fraud perpetuated through leadership ineptitude of Africans and foreign collaborators. Various statistics and report of international aid agencies give insight into the magnitude of the socio-economic malaise of Africa. For instance, Nigeria has been declared as the world poverty capital by the Brookings Institution, United States in July 2018, despite having the fastest developing economy in Africa with Gross Domestic Product of $400 billion.[41] Despite the attempts of the developed

---

[40] Afe Adogame, "African Christianities and the Politics of Development from Below," *HTS Teologiese Studies/Theological Studies* 72.4 (2016). Also, see, Babatunde Adedibu, "The Changing Faces of African Independent Churches as Development Actors Across Borders," *HTS Teologiese Studies/Theological Studies* 74.1 (2018); P. Öhlmann, M-L. Frost, and W. Gräb, "African Initiated Churches" Potential as Development Actors," *HTS Teologiese Studies/Theological Studies* 72.4 (2016); B. Offutt, L. Probasco, and B. Vaidyanathan, "Religion, Poverty and Development," *Journal for the Scientific Study of Religion* 55.2 (2016), pp. 207–15; Ignatius Swart and Elsabé Nell, "Religion and Development: The rise of a Bibliography," *HTS Teologiese Studies/Theological* Studies 72.4 (2016).

[41] Okonjo-Iweala Ngozi, *Fighting Corruption is Dangerous: The Story Behind the Headlines* (Cambridge: The MIT Press, 2018), p. 1.

countries to show their concern for eradicating poverty in Africa, it seems this is a mix bag of misfortune through various aids from these countries to Africa. This is aptly summarized in Christian Aid report that:

> For moves currently being made among members of the biggest and most influential "rich country clubs" betray a worrying shift in how they see aid commitments. Aid is viewed increasingly as a means of poor people and safeguarding the donor's interest, particularly their security, rather than addressing the real needs of poor people. Aid in other words is being co-opted to serve in the global "War on Terror."[42]

Almost five years after the Christian Aid Report of 2009, Damisa Moyo published a book entitled *Dead Aids: Why Aid is Not Working and How There is Another Way for Africa,* which is a critique of the ambiguous aids support to Africa and its misapplication. Nevertheless, the author has been criticized for sloppiness in the use of selective data, use of well-known regression analyses utilized by Dollar, Burnside, Boone, Collier Easterly, Svensson – all World Bank economists. Likewise, there were many reasons for the economic stagnation of Africa which was neglected in Dead Aids.[43] The import of Damisa Moyo's attempt is that despite the perceived inadequacies of the econometric analysis of *Dead Aids*, it unveiled the existence of smokescreen use by Aid donors to Africa which is fundamentally a vicious attempt of continued patronizing and fleecing the fiscal resources of Africa and Africans.

Despite global developmental initiatives such as the Millennium Development Goals; Sustainable Development Goals and so on, Africa is still plagued with a treatable disease like Malaria. According to World Health Organization (WHO) "in 2017, it was estimated that 435,000 deaths due to malaria had occurred globally, of which

---

[42] Christian Aid "The Politics of Poverty: Aid in the New Cold War." London: Christian Aid (2004) http://www.christianaid.org.uk/indepth/404caweek/.

[43] For further reading, see Paul Hoebink "Stagnation in Africa: Disentangling Facts, Figures and Fiction," in Monique Kremer, Peter van Lieshout, and Robert Went (eds.), *Doing Good, Doing Better: Development Policies in a Globalizing World* (Amsterdam: Amsterdam University Press, 2009), pp. 107-36.

403,000 deaths (approximately 93%) were in the WHO African Region. Almost 80% of all deaths in 2017 occurred in 17 countries in the WHO African Region and India."[44] Anecdotally, this might be linked to continued poverty of many African countries as "just $2 to $3 dollars per American and other citizens of the rich world would be needed each year to mount an effective fight against malaria,"[45] while it has been estimated that "approximately 377 million Africans will still be living on less than $1.90 a day, and very few African countries will have ended poverty."[46] However, the recent report of the World Data Lab of Brookings Institution, Washington DC indicates that "one in three Africans – 422 million people – live below the global poverty line. They represent more than 70 percent of the world's poorest people."[47] Sub-Saharan Africa is noted to be the region with the highest Prevalence of Undernourishment (POU), "affecting an alarming 22.7 percent of the population in 2016. The situation is especially urgent in Eastern Africa, where one-third of the population is estimated to be undernourished – the sub region's PoU increased from 31.1 percent in 2015 to 33.9 percent in 2016."[48] The degree of wretchedness and colossal waste of human resources blighted by the forces of poverty in many facets of several African countries is overwhelming as:

> the worst condition continues to be, largely in Africa. One out of three people in Sub–Saharan Africa is undernourished. High government debt burdens, inadequate funding for health and education, pervasive poverty, poor agricultural productivity, weak

---

[44] Global Health Observatory (GHO) data. https://www.who.int/gho/malaria/epidemic/deaths/en/ Accessed 17th August 2019.

[45] Jeffrey Sacs, "A Practical Plan to End Poverty," *Washington Post* (January 17th, 2005), p. A17.

[46] Kristofer Hamel, Baldwin Tong, and Martin Hofer, "Poverty in Africa is Now Falling but not Fast Enough," https://www.brookings.edu/blog/future-development/2019/03/28/poverty-in-africa-is-now-falling-but-not-fast enough/ Access-ed 17 August 2019.

[47] Hamel, Tong, and Hofer, "Poverty in Africa is Now Falling but not Fast Enough."

[48] FAO, IFAD, UNICEF, WFP and WHO. "The State of Food Security and Nutrition in the World 2017. Building resilience for peace and food security" (Rome: FAO, 2017), p. 6.

public institutions, and AIDS pandemic all are major causes. Sub-Saharan Africa 180 million or 33% of the total population of 539 million suffer from under-nourishment and the worst hit countries include Angola, Burundi, Serria Leone, Guinea, Somalia, Sudan, Ethiopia, and Eritrea.[49]

The above socio-economic challenges are dominant features in Africa excluding various political contraptions of ineptitude leaders who have transformed public service as an avenue for self-aggrandizement and fraud. This is the social context in which African Neo Pentecostal churches are proliferating with millions of adherents particularly in sub-Saharan Africa. In the light of the monstrous social, economic and political discontinuities in many African countries, some of the Neo–Pentecostal churches are trying to fill the void through their Corporate Social Responsibility.[50] In a previous research, I noted that African Initiated Churches inclusive of the Neo-Pentecostal strand are developmental actors across borders through sustained effort of harnessing social and religious capitals of their adherents to the socio-economic, health and educational discontinuities in their contexts a by-product of inability of many African countries to provide basic infrastructures for their citizen.[51]

Despite the social concerns of some African Neo Pentecostal churches like the Redeemed Christian Church of God led by Pastor E.A. Adeboye which is a transnational network of churches in 198 countries of the World which has been committed to the social concerns in Nigeria. According to the RCCG spokesperson, RCCG in Nigeria had spent not:

less than an approximate sum of N433.3 million [$ll8.7l million at the exchange of 360 naira to one dollar] between August last year [2012] to date [May 30, 2013] was expended on various activities

---

[49] Om Prakash Goyal, *Anti-social Patterns of Begging and Beggars* (New Delhi, India: Gyan Books, 2005), p. 30.

[50] B. Adedibu, "Pentecostal Approaches to Transformation and Development: The Case of the Redeemed Christian Church of God, Nigeria," in P. Öhlmann, W. Gräb, M-L. Frost (eds.), *African Initiated Christianity and the Decolonization of Development: Sustainable Development in Pentecostal and Independent Churches* (London: Routledge, 2019).

[51] Adedibu, "The Changing Faces of African Independent Churches as Development Actors Across Borders."

ranging from digging boreholes, education which include providing books for both primary and tertiary institutions across the country, procurement of drugs, gilt of glasses for those with eyes problems, care-giver for HIV positive and drugs, provision of toilets, libraries, classrooms among others.[52]

RCCG is one of several Neo-Pentecostal churches in Africa that tend to support the nexus between social action and evangelism. Marshall posits that:

[Evangelism] includes proclamation to the nations about obedience to God, to the prisoners about freedom, to the poor about release – in short, it includes many of the things now labeled as "social action." Repentance and conversion themselves involve turning from one life to another in every aspect of human existence.[53]

This development re-echoes the commitment of religious institutions in Nigeria; particularly the Pentecostal churches of late, to the social, economic and environmental concerns of the Nigerians. This is one of several Neo Pentecostal churches particularly in Sub-Saharan Africa that demonstrates their commitment to social concerns which is following the footsteps of Jesus Christ (Mt. 15.32-38; 25.35-36; Lk. 10.34; 11.42). As plausible this might look, it is imperative to note that most Neo-Pentecostal churches prophetic role in their various contexts is unnoticed despite mounting challenges of social injustices. The continued attitude of "state capture" amongst politicians and public office holders are more or less ignored by many leaders of African Neo-Pentecostal churches. Interestingly, African political actors – despite their continued intransigence and lack of commitment to rule of law, human abuses, ostentatious living, and disregard for human dignity – are welcomed as august guests at these churches. For instance, in Nigeria, Obadare describes the rising influence of the theocratic class in the political space in

---

[52] "The Christendom, Pastor Adeboye Commends RCCG's CSR, Insists On Improvement," Thursday, 30 May 2013. [Web] http://christendomnewspaper.blogspot.com/2013/05/pastor-adeboye-commends-rccg.html Accessed 27th March 2019.

[53] Peter Marshall, *Thine is the Kingdom* (Basingstoke: Marshall Morgan and Scot, 1984), pp. 36-37.

his book entitled *Pentecostal Republic* which vividly traces the theatrics of religious actors' quest for political power. Ironically, many African countries are witnessing the emergence of politicians who "attain some form of holiness status in the society through some of their works they do for the poor. Rather than call this kind of people a holy people, we refer to them as political entrepreneurs who use the religious space for their political entrepreneurs to trade."[54] The appropriation of the religious space as political space is any attempt of the political class to present a façade of spiritual holiness to the public. Many African Neo-Pentecostal church leaders uncritically condone this without prophetic polemic against the many social injustices they perpetuate.

Many church leaders have fallen to the trap of political entrepreneurs in Africa as many engage in well-orchestrated corruption of public politics as they astutely select "pastors or churches they forge alliance with. This is mainly done by weighing the influence of the pastor, the population and the spread of the church across geo-political zones."[55] Africa's Neo-Pentecostal space at times turned into a charade as some of the leaders of these churches, perhaps unintentionally, validate immoral, and corrupt leadership.

In Africa there are various forms of political intransigence and corrupt practices. Manipulative and political theatrics noted in the political space seems to impact on targeted Neo-Pentecostal churches by political entrepreneurs as many join these churches and within a short time are ordained as pastors thus parading the credentials of spiritual holiness and political gladiator thereby harnessing the religious and human capital of the members of these churches in enhancing their political aspirations.

Ironically, Old Testament prophets understood both the mind of God and what was happening in their context. They spoke out against sin and injustice in their society and fearlessly confronted religious, political and economic leaders. They saw both positive and negative patterns in the life of Israel–African Neo-Pentecostal church leaders should be doing the same in the contemporary setting because it is one of the roles of the Holy Spirit.

---

[54] Igboin, "Unpacking the Holiness Spaces in Africa," p. 249.
[55] Igboin, "Unpacking the Holiness Spaces in Africa," p. 250.

Conclusion

The role of the Holy Spirit in any facet of Christian service cannot be over emphasized. This chapter has demonstrated the nexus between the Holy Spirit in salvation and social justice within African Neo-Pentecostal praxis.

African Neo-Pentecostal churches, like other Christian churches in other parts of the Global South, are acutely involved is social actions in their contexts. Their actions seem more of a by-product of the failed state of the African context. So, they provide basic social, economic and educational infrastructures to their citizens. This chapter points out, however, that the African Neo-Pentecostal prophetic voice against corruption and unjust treatment of citizens is not pungent enough.

There is the urgent need for the spirit of Amos which is the Holy Spirit to be seen and heard from the pulpit of these churches addressing social injustices, marginalization, corruption and nepotism. The ability of these churches to speak to powers is a reflection of their commitment to the integrity of their sacred role as beacons of light and truth in any contexts. The Holy Spirit compels the African churches to "cry aloud against corruption and injustice"!

Bibliography

Adeboye, Olufunke, "'A Church in a Cinema Hall?' Pentecostal Appropriation of Public Space in Nigeria," *Journal of Religion in Africa* 42 (2012).

Acolatse, Esther, *Powers, Principalities and Spirits: Biblical Realism in Africa and the West* (Grand Rapids: Eerdmans, 2018).

Adedibu, Babatunde, "African and Caribbean Pentecostalism in Britain," Joe Aldred (ed.), *Pentecostals and Charismatics in Britain: An Anthology* (London; SCM Press, 2019).

—"Pentecostal Approaches to Transformation and Development: The Case of the Redeemed Christian Church of God, Nigeria," P. Öhlmann, W. Gräb, M-L. Frost (eds.), *African Initiated Christianity and the Decolonization of Development: Sustainable Development in Pentecostal and Independent Churches* (London: Routledge (2019).

—"The Changing Faces of African Independent Churches as Development Actors Across Borders," *HTS Teologiese Studies/Theological Studies* 74.1 (2018).

—"Reverse Mission or Migrant Sanctuaries? Migration, Symbolic Mapping, and Missionary Challenges of Britain's Black Majority Churches," *Pneuma* 35 (2013).

—*Coat of Many Colours: Origin, Growth, Distinctiveness and Contributions of Black Majority Churches to British Christianity* (Gloucester: Wisdom Summit, 2012).

Adewale, Olubiyi, "Developing a Social Action Agenda for the Poor: A Reading of the Lukan Poverty Parables for the Nigerian Context," *Spectrum: Journal of Contemporary Christianity and Society* 1.1 (April 2016).

Adogame, Afe, "African Christianities and the Politics of Development from Below," *HTS Teologiese Studies/Theological Studies* 72.4 (2016).

Allen Yeh and Tite Tienou (eds.), *Majority World Theologies* (Pasadena: William Carey Publishing, 2018).

Anderson, Allan, *To the ends of the Earth: Pentecostalism and the Transformation of World Christianity* (Cambridge: Cambridge University Press, 2nd edn, 2013).

—*Spreading Fires: The Missionary Nature of Early Pentecostalism* (London: SCM Press, 2007).

Anderson, J.N.D., *Morality, Law and Grace* (London: Tyndale, 1972).

Ayantayo, Kehinde, Adedibu Babatunde, and Igboin Benson (eds.), *African Pentecostalism: Probity and Accountability* (Akungba-Akoko, Ondo: Adekunle Ajasin University Press, 2019).

Byun, Eddie, *Justice Awakening: How You and Your Church Can Help End Human Trafficking* (Downers Grove: Inter Varsity Press Books, 2014).

Cartledge, Mark, *et al.* (eds.), *Mega Churches and Social Engagement* (Leiden: Brill, 2019).

Cox, Harvey, Fire *from Heaven: The Rise of Pentecostal Spirituality and the Reshaping of Religion in the Twenty-first Century* (Mowbray: Continuum International Publishing Group, 1995).

Davies, Noel, and Martin Conway, *World Christianity in the 20th Century* (London: SCM Press, 2008).

Dempster, M.A., B.D. Klaus, and D. Petersen (eds.), *Called and Empowered: Global Mission in Pentecostal Perspective* (Peabody: Hendrickson, 1991).

Hukurume Smbarashe, "Youth Empowerment and African Initiated Churches in Urban Zimbabwe," in *Policy Brief Department of Theology* (Humbolt University, Berlin, 2008).

Goyal, Om Prakash, *Anti-social Patterns of Begging and Beggars* (New Delhi, India: Gyan Books, 2005).

Kalu, Ogbu, *African Pentecostalism: An Introduction* (New York: Oxford University Press, 2008).

Miller, Donald E., and T. Yamamori, *Global Pentecostalism, The New Face of Christian Social Engagement* (Berkeley: University of California Press, 2007).

Obadare, E., "Raising Righteous Billionaires: The Prosperity Gospel Reconsidered," *HTS Teologiese Studies/Theological Studies* 72 (2016).

Offutt, B., L. Probasco, and B. Vaidyanathan, "Religion, poverty and development," *Journal for the Scientific Study of Religion,* 55.2 (2016), pp. 207-15.

Öhlmann, P., M-L. Frost, and W. Gräb, "African Initiated Churches' Potential as Development Actors," *HTS Teologiese Studies/Theological Studies* (72).

Okonjo-Iweala, Ngozi, *Fighting Corruption is Dangerous: The Story Behind the Headlines* (Cambridge: The MIT Press, 2018).

Penney, J.M., *The Missionary Emphasis of Lukan Pneumatology* (Sheffield: Sheffield Academic Press, 1997).

Perkins, J., *Beyond Charity: The Call to Christian Community Development* (Grand Rapids: Baker, 1993).

Robeck, Cecil M., Jr, and Yong Amos, *The Cambridge Companion to Pentecostalism* (New York: Cambridge University Press, 2014).

Stronstad, Roger, *The Charismatic Theology of St. Luke* (Peabody, MA: Hendrickson, 1984).

Währisch-Oblau, Claudia, *The Missionary Self-Perceptions of Pentecostal/Charismatic Church Leaders from the Global South in Europe: Bringing Back the Gospel* (Leiden and Boston: Brill, 2009).

Yong, Amos, *In the Days of Caesar: Pentecostalism and Political Theology* (Grand Rapids: Eerdmans, 2010).

CARING FOR PEOPLE
FIGHTING FOR JUSTICE

CHAPTER TEN

NOTRE DAME D'HAITI CATHOLIC CHURCH MISSION:
SPIRIT AND JUSTICE AT THIS "LIVING ROOM OF THE
HAITIAN COMMUNITY"

Adeline Jean*

Break a vase, and the love that reassembles the fragments is stronger than that love which took its symmetry for granted when it was whole.[1]

The Haitian-American community in South Florida is the largest settlement of its kind in the United States with approximately 46% of the nation's Haitian-American population[2]. It represents a diaspora that has found a home and has carved out a space for itself that

---

* Adeline Jean (PhD candidate, St. Thomas University) is engaging in a comparative study of the Catholic Mass as simultaneously a story and a narrative, a study of the Catholic Mass at a diasporic ethnic mission church as the site and source of political and social advocacy in the form of a hospitality theology and a study of *Conference on Theology in the Caribbean Today* as a ritual.

[1] Derek Walcott, "The Antilles: Fragments of Epic Memory," The Nobel Prize, Nobel lecture 7 December 1992, http://www.nobelprize.org/nobel_prizes/literature/laureates/ 1992/walcott-lecture.html. Haitian-Americans, united as clergy and congregants at Notre Dame D'Haiti Catholic Church Mission, typify this metaphor because out of a situation of hopelessness they have strengthened and transformed into advocates for each other.

[2] Steven A. Camaraota, "Fact Sheet on Haitian Immigrants in the United States," *Center for Immigration Studies* (January 25, 2010) https://cis.org/Fact-Sheet/Fact-Sheet-Haitian-Immigrants-United-States.

makes it possible for all Haitian-Americans, regardless of class, age, or gender to live, work, worship, and socialize together in ways that celebrate their otherwise common culture, history, and overall identity. Notre Dame D'Haiti Catholic Church mission (Notre Dame) in Miami-Dade County, Florida is the heart of "Little Haiti," where a large portion of this diaspora resides.

The pastoral and ecclesial motivation for this study at Notre Dame, which was to determine how the Mass creates a sense of belonging, led to an incidental discovery. Through the use of an ethnographic approach and liturgical qualitative research, it became evident that Notre Dame facilitates a home for its congregants and nurtures them toward a social justice-oriented faith, which originated in its founder's[3] vision. His vision was both to build a house of faith for Haitian migrants and to form them spiritually through and for social advocacy by using the Mass as a platform for social justice. I undertook this study with the intention of offering a summative evaluation of how the church mission of Notre Dame, through its Mass, has grown into a home, and in so doing, has become the catalyst of a social justice-oriented faith for its congregants.

My aim is to illustrate how Notre Dame is built on the foundation of social justice. The church mission was established to provide Haitian-Americans with a place to call *home*[4] due to their sheer numbers in South Florida. This in turn enabled Haitian-Americans to share a space where their common heritage could be celebrated. The Mass at Notre Dame soon became the site of unique social activism as it fostered hospitality in varying forms as an expression of Holy Spirit-inspired social justice.

In this study, the conception of social justice is that of clergy (Catholic priests) and congregants voluntarily giving of their *time*, *talent*, and *treasure*[5] for the good of others within their community.

---

[3] Father Thomas Wenski (the first priest appointed to lead the newly consecrated Notre Dame).

[4] In this study, *home* refers to the place where a people belong to as members of a family.

[5] This is a well-established concept in the US Catholic Church that signifies stewardship, usually at the parish level. Giving of one's *time*, *talent*, and *treasure* results from gratitude to God and is done with the intention of being generous to those in need. However, in this study, *time* refers to

This conception of social justice derives from Catholic Social Teaching and stresses the advancement of human dignity and the common good. As Elizabeth Phillips explains, "The central norms of Catholic Social Teaching include human dignity, solidarity, the common good, peace and justice."[6] *According to the United States Conference of Catholic Bishops, human dignity is the* "foundation of all the principles of [our] social teaching."[7] The Conference of Bishops affirms that "every person is precious" and "the measure of every institution is whether it threatens or enhances the life and dignity of the human person."[8] *Social advocacy at Notre Dame will be investigated generally by describing how Notre Dame has become like a family home, and specifically by describing and evaluating how the preaching style of the clergy and congregational participation during the Mass in this home environment promotes the human dignity and common good of Haitian-American congregants thereby enhancing life.*

Notre Dame is a mission church and religious site of hope for simultaneous human and cultural flourishing. It is accordingly a place of theological and sociological construct. At Notre Dame, Jesus' metaphor, "The Spirit blows where it wishes,"[9] couples with Paul's declaration, "The love of God has been poured out into our hearts through the holy Spirit that has been given us"[10], to offer new

---

time given, *talent* refers to the unique manner in which something is done, and *treasure* refers to something special that is done (which can include monetary giving).

[6] Elizabeth Phillips, *Political Theology: A Guide for the Perplexed* (New York: T & T Clark International, 2012), p. 39.

[7] United States Conference of Catholic Bishops, "Seven Themes of Catholic Social Teaching," United States Conference of Catholic Bishops, accessed January 2, 2019, http://www.usccb.org/beliefs-and-teachings/what-we-believe/catholic-social-teaching/seven-themes-of-catholic-social-teaching.cfm.

[8] United States Conference of Catholic Bishops, "Seven Themes of Catholic Social Teaching."

[9] John 3.8 (NASB). Here, in comparing the Holy Spirit to wind that is invisible and its work incomprehensible, Jesus is indicating that the work of the Holy Spirit as being beyond human understanding. Therefore, while people may see what they deem as evidence of the presence and work of the Holy Spirit, it is difficult to prove that presence and work.

[10] Romans 5.5 (NASB).

theological and sociological insight. The Spirit blows, fills, and empowers Christians to work towards achieving the common good. This work for the common good reflects the work of the Spirit during Pentecost: "All who believed were together and had all things in common."[11]

Method and Research Design

This study utilizes Holland and Henriot's pastoral circle/spiral, also known as the *circle of praxis*, to analyze, interpret, and understand the social justice particulars of the Mass at Notre Dame.[12] Social analysis that is clearly pastoral can be explained using this circle, which "emphasizes the on-going relationship between reflection and action."[13] This pastoral theological method allows for and has been widely used for studying and responding to social issues, especially social justice issues. This circle characterizes the relationships between four mediations or moments of experience: *insertion, social analysis, theological reflection*, and *pastoral planning*[14].

This study begins with *insertion* as the first "moment of contact."[15] This was accomplished through participant observation of five Sunday Masses, one weekday Mass,[16] and two focus group interviews. Each of the two focus groups comprised six congregants. Purposive sampling was used to create both groups. One group included leaders of various church ministries. The other group comprised a mixture of newly-arrived congregants, actively-involved congregants, long-serving congregants, and long-standing

---

[11] Acts 2.44 (NASB).

[12] Joe Holland and Peter Henriot, *Social Analysis: Linking Faith and Justice* (Washington, DC: Dove Communications and Orbis Books, 1983), pp. 7-8.

[13] Holland and Henriot, *Social Analysis: Linking Faith and Justice*, pp. 7-8.

[14] Holland and Henriot, *Social Analysis: Linking Faith and Justice*, p. 7.

[15] Peter Henriot, *The Pastoral Circle Revisited* (ed. Frans Wijsen, Peter Henriot, and Rodrigo Mejía; New York: Orbis Books, 2005), p. 17.

[16] The first Sunday Mass attended was informally observed from the perspective of a visitor. The five other Sunday Masses (including a Saturday Vigil Mass) and the one weekday Mass were attended for the purpose of participant observation.

congregants. Participant observation and interviews compiled a data of lived experience. The data of these lived experiences prompted the question: *What is happening to and among clergy and congregants at Notre Dame during the Mass?*

Social Analysis, the next moment of the pastoral circle, allows for a systematic and analytical review of the reality made evident in the data collected. Social analysis "examines causes, probes consequences, delineates linkages, and identifies actors."[17] As social analysis focuses on *systems*, this study's analysis will concentrate on one dimension of systems – *level*, which is that of the local church mission of Notre Dame. This analysis requires the complementarity of both historical and structural analysis. Therefore, this social analysis focuses on the question: *Why is this happening to and among clergy and congregants at Notre Dame during the Mass, and how does this depict social justice?*

To undertake this type of social analysis, this study first recounts a brief history of Notre Dame and then builds its analysis using metaphors. Using thick description narrative, a connection is established between *family,*[18] *meal,*[19] and the Notre Dame community. As the average heads of family advocate for its family members, so too does the clergy of Notre Dame for its congregants. This is most evident when they meet for *the meal of the Mass.*[20]

The third moment of the pastoral circle – *reflection* – provides an opportunity for more in-depth understanding of the analyzed experience "in the light of faith, scripture, church social teaching, and the resources of tradition."[21] Henriot's "faith reflection" and "theological reflection"[22] will allow for insights into the observed and recounted experiences derived through insertion and social analysis. The question that will be addressed is: *What do the actions and*

---

[17] Holland and Henriot, *Social Analysis: Linking Faith and Justice,* p. 8.

[18] In this study, the term *family* refers to a group of people who are related by birth, by marriage, or by other relationship, or by a shared place of habitation.

[19] In this study, *meal* refers to an occasion when food is prepared and eaten.

[20] In this study, *meal of the Mass* refers to the Liturgy of the Eucharistic, around which the entire Mass is centered.

[21] Holland and Henriot, *Social Analysis: Linking Faith and Justice,* p. 9.

[22] Henriot, *The Pastoral Circle Revisited,* p. 18.

experiences of the clergy and congregants during the Mass mean to Catholics in relation to social justice?

Pastoral planning, the fourth moment of the pastoral circle, necessitates responding, deciding, and acting in relation to the prior three moments. This is my point of departure with the pastoral circle. This study was not executed upon request nor undertaken as a parish initiative. This study was completed in order to personally evaluate the innovative particulars of social justice reflected in the Mass at Notre Dame. As such, no recommendations for action will be offered to Notre Dame. Consequently, the question that will be answered at this moment in the pastoral cycle is: *What is the significance of this study to the Catholic Church?*

The transformative characteristic of this study will be the pneumatological implications for Notre Dame and for the wider Catholic Church. This inferred impact discloses the pastoral circle's spiral nature: These pneumatological insights will lead to additional mediations of *insertion, social analysis, reflection, and pastoral planning* at other local and/or global levels. These additional mediations should break new ground rather than retrace the steps already taken in this study.

This study intends to prove that at Notre Dame belonging→community→home→social justice. This dynamic results from the infilling of the Holy Spirit[23] that is evident in the Spirit-led and Spirit-filled actions of Notre Dame's clergy and congregants. This study's focus on pneumatology is in relation to the presence and works of the Holy Spirit at the Mass at Notre Dame is the first of its kind at Notre Dame. This study has implications for the vision of local and global Catholicism, especially in terms of helping overlooked communities serving the less fortunate. It is possible that these research findings will contribute to new understandings on the importance and impact of the Holy Spirit-inspired Mass of Notre Dame, particularly as an instrument of social justice for its congregants. Moreover, this study is expected to prompt further qualitative social scientific research. This study contributes to the field of practical theological research as it relates to the ecclesial practices and

---

[23] "Be filled with the Spirit, addressing one another [in] psalms and hymns and spiritual songs, singing and playing to the Lord in your hearts" (Eph 5.18-19 NASB).

contributions of ethnic and minority religious communities. It will thereby help to extend the frontiers of ecclesial and qualitative research and of contextual practical theology.

The Distinctiveness of the Mass at Notre Dame

What is happening to and among clergy and congregants at Notre Dame during the Mass?

Based on my experience as a participant observer, the presence and work of the Holy Spirit is apparent during the Mass at Notre Dame. The Holy Spirit can be explained as present in the form of the gifts of the Spirit,[24] especially those of wisdom,[25] understanding,[26] knowledge,[27] and counsel.[28] The Holy Spirit is also present in the form of the fruits of the Spirit,[29] chiefly the fruit of kindness or giving. Through these gifts and fruits, the Spirit is evident and working within and through the priests at Notre Dame, which is exhibited in the choices they make as they celebrate the Mass. Christians acknowledge that the identity of the Holy Spirit was revealed through Christ's disclosure.[30] However, the Spirit was already present in the Old Testament. The "Catechism of the Catholic Church"

---

[24] The Seven Gifts of the Holy Spirit are wisdom, understanding, counsel, fortitude, knowledge, piety, and fear of the Lord (Isa. 11.2-3 NASB).

[25] "Wisdom (which helps a person to grasp the truths of religion)," A Redemptorist Pastoral Publication, *Handbook for Today's Catholics* (Missouri: Liguori Publications, 1994), p. 22.

[26] "Understanding (which enables the person to grasp the truth of religion)," A Redemptorist Pastoral Publication, *Handbook for Today's Catholics* (Missouri: Liguori Publications, 1994), p. 22.

[27] "Knowledge (which helps one to see the paths to follow)," A Redemptorist Pastoral Publication, *Handbook for Today's Catholics* (Missouri: Liguori Publications, 1994), p. 22.

[28] "Counsel (which helps one to see and correctly choose the best practical approach in serving God)," A Redemptorist Pastoral Publication, *Handbook for Today's Catholics* (Missouri: Liguori Publications, 1994), p. 22.

[29] "But the fruit of the Spirit is love, joy, peace, patience, kindness, goodness, faithfulness, gentleness, self-control" (Gal. 5.22-23 NASB).

[30] "But when he comes, the Spirit of truth, he will guide you to all truth. He will not speak on his own, but he will speak what he hears" (Jn 16.13 NASB).

states, "In him [John the Baptist], the Holy Spirit concludes his speaking through the prophets. John completes the cycle of prophets begun by Elijah."[31] In the New Testament, the Holy Spirit is similarly seen as active and working in the lives of John the Baptist and the Virgin Mary. With the completion of the Paschal Mystery, the Spirit of Truth was sent. Pope Francis notes, "Jesus says to his disciples: the Holy Spirit, 'he will guide you to all truth' (Jn 16.13), he himself being 'the Spirit of truth' (cf. Jn 14.17; 15.26; 16.13)."[32] Pope Francis further adds:

> The Holy Spirit, then, as Jesus promises, guides us "into all truth"[33]. He leads us not only to an encounter with Jesus, the fullness of Truth, but guides us "into" the Truth, that is, he helps us enter into a deeper communion with Jesus himself, gifting us knowledge of the things of God. We cannot achieve this on our own strengths. If God does not enlightens [sic] us interiorly, our being Christians will be superficial. The Tradition of the Church affirms that the Spirit of truth acts in our hearts, provoking that "sense of faith."[34]

The Holy Spirit is present in and works in the hearts of all, including the clergy and congregants at Notre Dame. They are inspired and guided by the Spirit of Truth to initiate and participate in worship in ways that are exclusive to their culture and spiritual needs.

Furthermore, the Church establishes that a priest acts *in persona Christi Capiti* – in the person of Christ the Head; that is, the priest represents Christ. In reflecting on the offices, that is, the duties of a priest, Pope Benedict XVI says, "The priest, who acts *in persona*

---

[31] United States Conference of Catholic Bishops, "Catechism of the Catholic Church," United States Conference of Catholic Bishops, accessed February 22, 2019, http://ccc.usccb.org/flipbooks/catechism/index.html#190/z.

[32] Carl E. Olson, "Pope Francis Reflects on the Work and Power of the Holy Spirit," *The Catholic World Report*, May 15, 2013. https://www.catholicworldreport.com/2013/05/15/pope-francis-reflects-on-the-work-and-power-of-the-holy-spirit.

[33] John 16.13 (NASB).

[34] Olson, "Pope Francis Reflects on the Work and Power of the Holy Spirit."

Christi Capitis[35] and representing the Lord, never acts in the name of someone who is absent but, rather, in the very Person of the Risen Christ, who makes himself present with his truly effective action."[36] Moreover, the Holy Spirit resides in the priesthood in a special way because Catholic tradition views the Holy Spirit as working in an extraordinary way in the Mass. The priest renews Christ's sacrifice of Calvary each time the Mass is celebrated, which culminates with the transforming of the bread and wine into the Body and Blood of Christ. If Catholics believe that the Holy Spirit resides in the priesthood and makes transubstantiation possible, one could assume that the Spirit is not lying dormant somewhere until the moment is right to appear. Rather, the Spirit is already present and working during the entire Mass. The Spirit is ever present, working through both priests and congregants. Within Catholicism, one Mass varies from the next because some priests and congregants may manifest outward and animated signs that suggest the Holy Spirit is present, thus making the Mass appear to be Charismatic-styled (as it is at Notre Dame). This charismatic style of Mass stands in contrast to a more traditional-styled Mass where the presence of the Holy Spirit is manifested by the priests and congregants in a less outward and animated manner.

According to Hitchcock and Bernarski, Catholic spirituality has traditionally taught that tangible and lively experiences are not essential to the reality of faith, and it has been reserved in accepting the genuineness of such experiences. To a great extent the nature of sacramental piety dictates this reserve.[37] Catholic Charismatics have often been criticized for their "personal style" of worship that is nurtured by "emotional consolations" that lead to "peak experiences" in prayer meeting settings [38]. However, the liturgical style at Notre Dame proves that such Spirit-led and Spirit-filled "emotional consolations" and "peak experiences" can serve as a vital part of the Mass experience and should not be critiqued as limited only to

---

[35] Emphasis original.

[36] Benedict XVI, "The Priest's Three Duties," *Eternal Word Network Television*, Apr 14, 2010. http://www.ewtn.com/library/papaldoc/b16prduties.htm.

[37] James Hitchcock and Glorianna Bednarski, *Catholic Perspectives: Charismatics* (Chicago: The Thomas More Press, 1980), p. 35.

[38] Hitchcock and Bednarski, *Catholic Perspectives*, pp. 32-33.

prayer meeting settings. Charismatic Catholics are further criticized for making prayer meetings and not the Mass the center of their lives. This criticism may stem from the fact that Catholic Charismatics tend to look for the same type of spiritual involvement and connection they experience in prayer meetings at the Mass. Still, this does not often occur if the priest is not open to outward manifestations of the Spirit either personally or among his congregants during the Mass. If congregants feel a deeper connection with the Spirit at Mass, it can be inferred that this will enable them to move away from merely executing repetitious conforming rituals that are often *performed* and not embodied.

It can be also be inferred that the clergy at Notre Dame has taken the right approach to the Mass; that is to say, they "got it right." If Catholic Charismatics rely on intense spiritual encounters within prayer meetings to *get high in the Spirit*,[39] every Catholic could have the same opportunity to have a similar experience during Mass as the congregants of Notre Dame. At Notre Dame, lively experiences and unreserved liturgical celebration are themselves acts of social justice in that the clergy give of their *time* (in preparing for and celebrating the Mass), their *talent* (providing an energetic liturgical celebration), and their *treasure* (their Spirit-led and Spirit-filled spirituality) for the advancement of human dignity and the common good of their Haitian-American congregants.

The pastoral circle was partly inspired by the Ignatian spirituality of Saint Ignatius of Loyola, who believed in "finding God in all things."[40] This means finding God in immediate surroundings and everywhere in the world. This can be likened to *reading the signs of the times*. Such a reading is "central to the [Catholic] church's social teaching," especially made explicit in Vatican II's *Gaudium et Spes*. *Gaudium et Spes* opens by announcing, "The People of God believes that it is led by the Lord's Spirit, Who fills the earth."[41] Reading the

---

[39] In this study, *getting high in the Spirit* refers to the feeling of spiritual euphoria.

[40] Ignatius Loyola, *Spiritual Exercises* (trans. George Ganss; Chicago: Loyola University Press, 1992), quoted in Peter Henriot, *The Pastoral Circle Revisited* (ed. Frans Wijsen, Peter Henriot, and Rodrigo Mejía; New York: Orbis Books, 2005), p. 15.

[41] Vatican Council II, *Gaudium et Spes* [Pastoral Constitution on the Church in the Modern World], in *The Basic Sixteen Documents of Vatican*

signs of the times requires the discernment of the Holy Spirit. This is similarly a "contextualization of experience,"[42] that is, "discernment done with a social foundation, a social purpose, and a social consequence,"[43] as is the case at Notre Dame. This *reading* is cognitive, affective, and effective. It is *cognitive* in that it is "an intellectual exercise leading to understanding."[44] It is *affective* in "touching the deepest of our values and strongly motivating our responses."[45] It is also *effective* "in the sense of organizing our responses with planning, execution, and evaluation."[46]

From a Catholic perspective, this understanding of reading the signs of the times makes it possible to explain how the clergy at Notre Dame are led by the Holy Spirit. As a Catholic Charismatic who uses a Spirit of discernment on a daily basis and more so in church ministry, it is possible for me to discern the experiences of worship during Mass at Notre Dame as Spirit-led and Spirit-filled. This is because I have developed personal insight on how the Spirit's presence and works are evident. It is also possible to affectively connect with the powerful presence of the Spirit at the Mass at Notre Dame because the Spirit's presence can be felt physically, emotionally, and spiritually. This encounter inspires a personal response – heightened prayer, tears, joy, and so on. The priests who celebrate the Mass can also *read the signs of the times* cognitively, affectively, and effectively through the power of the Spirit. In so doing, they know and understand what needs to be done in order to connect with their congregants. They rely on the Holy Spirit to make this connection possible. As they leave one Mass they physically and spiritually prepare all over again for the next Mass. Congregants, also led by the Spirit, *read the signs of the times* cognitively, affectively, and effectively. They know they are in a foreign country and that not all Catholic parishes will celebrate the Mass in a way that allows them to connect and to achieve spiritual fulfilment. Notre Dame provides such an opportunity. The priests at Notre Dame cater

---

II: A Completely Revised Translation in Inclusive Language (ed. Austin Flannery, OP.; Northport: Costello, 1996), p 13.

[42] Henriot, *The Pastoral Circle Revisited*, p. 16.
[43] Henriot, *The Pastoral Circle Revisited*, p. 16.
[44] Henriot, *The Pastoral Circle Revisited*, p. 16.
[45] Henriot, *The Pastoral Circle Revisited*, p. 16.
[46] Henriot, *The Pastoral Circle Revisited*, p. 16.

almost entirely to Haitian-Americans, which makes a big difference in their planning and decision-making, especially for the Mass. Congregants therefore choose to be at Notre Dame and to make the Mass personal, which is even more possible through their active participation.

Pope Benedict clarifies, "The priest does not teach his own ideas, a philosophy that he himself has invented, that he has discovered or likes ... What Christ said of himself applies to the priest: 'my teaching is not mine' (Jn 7.16)."[47] Kathleen A. Cahalan provides a similar contribution on this topic that offers further insight:

> The preacher's knowledge of Scripture, and capacity to exegete and interpret texts as well, is closely tied to the virtue of empathy and truth-telling. Empathy points to the gift of understanding and experiencing the feelings, thoughts, ideas, and circumstances of the hearer. The preacher does not speak about the biblical text as something from the past, but as the living word proclaimed in the present, in this time and place for this community ... as a witness on behalf of the community, preaching requires telling the truth, both about what the preacher witnesses in the text as well as in the community.[48]

It can therefore be said that the clergy at Notre Dame, allow themselves to be *taught* by the Holy Spirit and in turn *teach*. This means that they adopt a distinctive way of celebrating the Mass to accomplish the work they are called to. Their efforts are noticeable and notable and invite further discussion.

Notre Dame has Evolved into "The Living Room of the Haitian Community"

> Why is this happening to and among clergy and congregants at Notre Dame during the Mass, and how does this depict social justice?

Notre Dame came to fruition in a way that makes it possible to conclude that the Holy Spirit breathed life into this church mission

---

[47] Benedict XVI, "The Priest's Three Duties."
[48] Kathleen A. Cahalan, *Introducing the Practice of Ministry* (Collegeville, MN: Liturgical Press, 2010), p. 77.

calling it into existence.[49] Self-proclaimed as "The Living Room of the Haitian Community,"[50] Notre Dame's Holy Spirit-inspired social justice-oriented Mass is itself an act of social justice.

Two different meanings can be attributed to the term "living room" – one American and one British. While the American denotative and connotative definitions suggest that of a formal space, the British denotative and connotative definitions indicate the opposite, an informal space. Generally, in the Caribbean region, the term *living room* follows the British denotative and connotative meanings. Ideally, this is a place where family bonds are made because of the quality time spent together, so it can be considered as the heart or center of the home. Referring to Notre Dame as "The Living Room of the Haitian Community" suggests that this ethnic church is a place for Haitian-American families. It is a place where the Haitian-American congregation, that is, church community family, can meet, relax, and just be themselves because they have a common understanding of and a unique cultural relationship with each other as the members of an average family usually do. The living room is also a place for serious discussions and where typically all are welcomed and entertained.

In 1979, when Father Thomas Wenski became the director of the Haitian Apostolate for the Archdiocese of Miami, he lobbied for an ethnic parish for Haitians. Establishing this ethnic parish gave Haitians a sense of identity and a sense of belonging.[51] Father Wenski's vision was to establish not just a worship community but also a worship style that celebrated the uniqueness and vitality of that

---

[49] Before the physical building of the Notre Dame Church was built, the Haitian-American community came together for Mass at Corpus Christi Church, then at St. Mary's Cathedral, and later at the Archbishop Curley High School cafeteria. Without a permanent church location to call their own, Haitian-American congregants persevered, and despite the odds, built their own church mission.

[50] Revealed in casual conversation with Father Reginald Jean-Marie, the administrator of Notre Dame.

[51] Terry Rey and Alex Stepick, "Refugee Catholicism in Little Haiti: Miami's Notre Dame d'Haiti Catholic Church," in Alex Stepick, Terry Rey, and Sarah J. Mahler (eds.), *Churches and Charity in the Immigrant City: Religion, Immigration, and Civic Engagement in Miami* (New Brunswick: Rutgers University Press, 2009), p. 76.

community[52]. To accomplish this, "He [Father Wenski] learned the popular piety of the people"[53]. In so doing, Notre Dame became a special type of home. It became a place where people who share a common history and culture could come together in a comfortable family-like personal space. Notre Dame's history provided the soil for the notion of belonging→community→home→social justice to be sown.

Notre Dame has become "the living room of the Haitian community" because this is where Haitians achieved their initial sense of belonging just by the church's coming into existence. The term *belonging* in this study refers to *the sense of belonging* a Catholic person develops over time because he or she participates regularly in a specific Catholic parish or congregation and as a result develops ties there with the overall community[54]. A sense of belonging is closely linked with the notion of social justice where clergy and congregants worship together voluntarily giving of their *time, talent,* and *treasure* for the accomplishment of human dignity and the common good within their community. Like an ideal family whose members seek each other's interests and provide support for one another, at Notre Dame, *advocacy* has become a natural offshoot of the *family* who share a common *home,* their church *community,* the place where a *sense of belonging* is cultivated.

---

[52] Father Reginald Jean-Mary, in discussion with the author, May 2018, stated:

One thing I would say was and still constitutes the strength of Notre Dame, is that we have a good pioneer, Archbishop Wenski was very clever and brilliant in the way he started the mission by opening it up to the Archdiocese and make us feel that even though we have to open up, we are who we are. He did travel to Haiti and he must have learned a lot about how we celebrate and how we live our faith and how we participate in the mystery of the Eucharist. He learned about the popular piety of the Haitian people and community, which is very good.

[53] Father Reginald Jean-Mary in discussion with the author, May 2018.

[54] This is in contrast to the common understanding of *belonging,* which implies merely belonging as a member would to the Catholic religion or to a specific Catholic parish or congregation.

In casual conversation with Father Reginald Jean-Marie (Father Reggie), the current administrator[55] of Notre Dame, he explained that it took eight years from the launching of the project for the construction of Notre Dame for it to be completed and then dedicated in February 2014. Father Reggie stressed that it really took thirty-five years for the church to be built because the people, the living stones of the church, are the ones who really make it a church. What is more, this *home* was already established in the hearts of the Haitian-American congregants because it does not take foundations stones to build a home. Through solidarity and physical effort the congregants pooled their *time, talent, and treasure* over the first thirty-five years and continuing to build their own home, a home to promote the dignity and common good of the church community.

The Pneumatological Liturgical Celebration of Holy Mass

Why is this happening to and among clergy and congregants at Notre Dame during the Mass, and how does this depict social justice?

At the Mass at Notre Dame, Father Reggie sets the tone. Father Reggie, as mentioned previously, calls Notre Dame "The Living Room of the Haitian Community."[56] At the first focus group interview with leaders of Notre Dame's ministries, Meg, one of the interviewees, indirectly explained what Father Reggie means by this statement: "Notre Dame ... Father calls it, 'The living room of the Haitian community'. It's a center ... it's like we are the mother church."[57] Like a

---

[55] In casual conversation, Father Reggie explained that he is an administrator and not a pastor because Notre Dame is considered as a mission church, not a parish.

[56] It is ironic that at this first meeting with Father Reggie on January 31, 2018 to introduce this project, the meeting took place in an unlikely area of the parish office. It was a dimly lit room that contained a living room set, lamps, throw cushions, and drapes like a typical living room does. It felt like part of a *home*, like sitting comfortably in a family's living room. This was real-life irony – being welcomed in a living room by a priest who calls his mission church a *living room*. The mere fact that he uses a real living room to greet and entertain his guests as opposed to his office makes his description of his mission church all the more palpable.

[57] Meg added:

typical living room in the Caribbean context, the living room is the center of the home because this is where most of the family activities take place. Also, in relation to other South Florida churches with large congregations of Haitian-Americans, Notre Dame is the main church *center* to which Haitian-American Catholics in particular look up to. The Haitian culture is essential to this center. The repeated encounter with this culture at Notre Dame allows Haitian-Americans to develop a sense of belonging as they are able to recognize and maintain aspects of their identity that are decisively Haitian because they have "all things in common."

His captivating personality and innovative worship style makes Father Reggie a role model to Notre Dame's congregants of varying age groups.[58] He is also their *father* and *mother* combined.[59] With Father Wenski as his role model, Father Reggie learned what was necessary to maintain Notre Dame as a successful mission church and place of advocacy. This required a church that would not only attract and keep Haitian-Americans within a communal space, but one that would become a *home*, a home for transplanted people. Additionally, like Father Wenski who preceded him, Father Reggie – appointed as administrator in 2004 – sought to develop a liturgical style that takes into consideration and reflects Haitian culture[60].

If anything happens that took place in Haiti, you would not believe it. Within half an hour, the parking lot is filled up, and they rely on the church here ... Even though we have other Haitian communities, like we have Holy Family, we have St. James, St. Clement ... but this is the center, the mother. Like for the earthquake, within a few seconds, people were here asking, "What's going on?" "What are we doing?" "The time of the refugees, it's always the same thing" (Meg [ministry leader at Notre Dame D'Haiti Catholic Church] in discussion with the author, April 2018).

[58] Every interviewee alluded to this fact, each providing his or her own reasons and narrative proof.

[59] In this study, *father* and *mother* refer to parents who, in their role as heads of their family, take a personal interest in the well-being of their children.

[60] In an interview with Father Reginald Jean-Mary (administrator of Notre Dame D'Haiti Catholic Church), May 2018, he described the liturgical style at Notre Dame when he responded to my question on whether his congregants ever shared with him what they enjoyed the most about the Mass at Notre Dame and he responded by saying:

This liturgical style can be described as Charismatic Holy-Spirit inspired in that the priests and the people outwardly exhibit the fruits and gifts of the Spirit during the Mass.

The Mass at Notre Dame is the birthplace of social justice. Sharing the Eucharistic meal with each other creates a sense of belonging among Catholics because only fellow Catholics are invited to share in this meal. Such is the same for Haitian-American Catholics at Notre Dame. Sharing *the meal of the Mass* does not mean just partaking in Holy Communion, the actual *meal*. It means everything that goes into making the meal *a meal*. Having married into a Haitian-American family myself, I know that customarily in the average Haitian family meal, the members of the family are automatically invited, and they may somehow help to contribute to the meal. Throughout the meal family members are expected to engage in conversation. In the celebration of the Mass, this type of participatory family meal is replicated in these ways and more. Based on participant observation, *the meal of the Mass* is celebrated in a distinct way, which indicates the Mass is being used as an instrument of social justice for the benefit of the Haitian-American congregants. This is because the *time* invested in preparing and executing a Haitian-style Mass, the *talent* put forth by the clergy at the Mass in varying ways, and the *treasure* given by the clergy and encouraged of the congregants participating in the Mass are all acts of social justice because they have one aim – the promotion of human dignity and the common good of the congregants.

In the same way, Jesus advocated for his disciples on the night of the Last Supper. He gave of the *time* he spent with them, the *talent* of his divinity, and the *treasure* of his Body and Blood. He then said to them, "Do this in memory of me."[61] With these words he suggested that his disciples must do for others as he had done for them, his disciples. Father Reggie and the other clergy at Notre Dame

---

Yes [they have] – [they enjoy] the music and the homilies. The liturgies are very vibrant at Notre Dame, and when people come here, the one thing that attracts them is that they feel at home. They feel as if they are in Haiti. That's one thing you will hear from people who are travelling and visiting. They will come from Miramar, from Ft. Lauderdale, Homestead...because [they say] "Wow! This is like the Mass in Haiti – the great music, the great singing."

[61] Luke 22.19 (NASB).

engage in this type of social justice advocacy on behalf of their congregants. The clergy at Notre Dame manifests the influence of the Holy Spirit,[62] particularly in the way in which they choose to celebrate the Mass.

Welcome Holy Spirit! The Preaching Style at Notre Dame – Best Practices for the Catholic Mass

> What do the actions and experiences of the clergy and congregants during the Mass mean to Catholics in relation to social justice?

According to Vincent Walsh, "Charismatic Renewal, or Catholic Pentecostalism, has become a household word in the [Catholic] Church."[63] The term "Pentecostalism" suggests "an attempt to pattern Church life according to the Scriptural model of the Acts of the Apostles so that the power evident in the early Church would be manifest in our times."[64] During Pentecost, the early Church became filled with the Spirit and began to speak in tongues, yet they all heard and understood each other as if they spoke one language. Though the Church has moved further away from the Pentecostal outpouring of the Spirit, it is possible to renew the Spirit of Pentecost. Notre Dame does not claim to be a Charismatic church. Nonetheless, the way in which the priests celebrate the Mass allows for the consideration of the first experience of Pentecost to be extended to view the speaking in tongues in a common language in a new way. Fostering hospitality through the preaching style of the clergy at Mass can be interpreted as creating a common language among Haitian-American congregants at Notre Dame who individually speak their own linguistic version of Haiti's Creole or French language. However, at the Mass they are able to come together and speak one common *cultural* language that reflects the presence of the Holy Spirit so that all who believe are united and have "all things in common."

---

[62] 1 Corinthians 12.7 (NASB).

[63] Vincent Walsh, *A Key to Charismatic Renewal in the Catholic Church* (Holland, PA: Key of David Publications, 1974), p. 2.

[64] Vincent Walsh, *A Key to Charismatic Renewal*, p. 3.

In casual conversation, Father Reggie described his preaching style, which is a reflection of his *talent*. He states, "When I preach, I try to reach the people. I preach more in an encountering aspect to establish that bond, that connection, and establish a more participative method of preaching."[65] Personal observations of the Sunday Mass confirmed this, and this was also the same for the other clergy observed. These observations reveal the presence of the Holy Spirit working through the priests. This is demonstrated by their dynamic, animated, engaging preaching styles that reflect their "ability to allow the needed freedom of the Spirit," just one quality of a priest who is open to or involved in the Catholic Charismatic Renewal.[66] However, a priest may be just as open or docile to the Holy Spirit even if he is not involved in the Catholic Charismatic Renewal.

Throughout the homily during the first Mass observed, Father Reggie invited congregants to participate through question and answers and using story scenarios to which the congregants responded. Father Reggie, Father Simeon Jeannot (associate pastor), and two other priests who celebrated the Mass adopted a similar "communicative repertoire."[67] This can be described as follows: All the priests had similar preaching styles. They all asked the congregation questions or spoke in such a way that required a verbal response from the congregation. This back-and-forth communicative process mirrored a physical back-and-forth movement of the priest on the altar. The priests also moved freely about the altar, even stepping down from the altar into the area directly in front where they were level with the congregation. This stepping down is symbolic of Jesus' teaching and preaching style, which met people where they were. Jesus never tried to set himself apart from the crowd either physically or otherwise but instead tried to be at one with them. The Spirit came into the world for this same purpose – to maintain that oneness. One of the focus-group interviewees, Jessica, commented that this coming down to the level of the congregation was

---

[65] Father Reginald Jean-Mary (administrator of Notre Dame D'Haiti Catholic Church) in discussion with the author, May 2018.

[66] Walsh, *A Key to Charismatic Renewal in the Catholic Church*, p. 258.

[67] Mary McClintock-Fulkerson, *Places of Redemption* (New York: Oxford University Press, 2007), p. 116.

significant to her.[68] As a show of their *talent*, that is, their spiritual engagement with the Mass, some of the congregants responded with words like "Alleluia" and "Amen" or with specific answers to the questions asked. Regardless of the priests' preaching style, clearly the Gospel message was being delivered with the power of the Holy Spirit – a Spirit of truth.

This preaching style can be likened to that of call-and-response, "the ongoing conversational dynamic of the service"[69] The priest "*asks* and *solicits* and *invites*"[70] the congregation to respond.[71] This action creates a back-and-forth movement. Such a *conversation* demonstrates the control of the Holy Spirit, who guides its flow and direction. The Holy Spirit works in and through all present at the Mass, stirring up a call-and-response. This encourages a sort of social spirituality mirroring the social and cultural connectedness of the congregants at Notre Dame who have "all things in common." The practice of call-and-response finds resonance with a "call and response" theology of creation that describes, "God 'calls' ... and creation 'responds.'"[72] So too, Father Reggie can be likened to calling his congregation *into being* by facilitating them in finding a connection to the Gospel message within themselves and through a *face-to-face encounter* with their own cultural experiences and customs echoed in the homily. As these connections occur, guided by the Holy Spirit, the congregants respond aloud or spiritually in their hearts or in their minds. This is made visible by the lifting of hands as if in silent prayer, by closed eyes, by teary eyes, and by spontaneous verbal praises at times. More than twenty years of involvement in the Catholic Charismatic Renewal in the United States have made it possible for me to personally identify these as visible signs of the presence

---

[68] Jessica (congregant at Notre Dame D'Haiti Catholic Church) in discussion with the author, April 2018, asserts, "He [Father Reggie] gets engaged with the audience. He walks up and down the aisle. He asks questions. You're always alert because you don't know if you are going to be the next person to be asked a question. So, he gets you engaged in it, so that the message becomes clear versus the average Catholic Mass."

[69] McClintock-Fulkerson, *Places of Redemption*, p. 114.

[70] Emphases original.

[71] McClintock-Fulkerson, *Places of Redemption,* pp. 114-15.

[72] Marjorie Hewitt Suchocki, *Divinity and Diversity: A Christian Affirmation of Religious Pluralism* (Nashville: Abington Press, 2003), p. 29.

and working of the Holy Spirit. The lifting up of arms and expressing of audible prayers of praise are some external indicators of a Catholic Charismatic Mass, which suggests the Holy Spirit is present in the worship experience. In addition, personal experience validates that when the Spirit is present there is order and unity as was visible in the call-and-response observed.

The call-and-response liturgical practice allows for the "involvement of the community in the speech event," which is "a necessary element of the sermon itself" because "it signals the priority of the corporative identity of the congregation,"[73] who have "all things in common." Furthermore, "Liturgy is truly the work of the people. It is manifest that the priest is part of the community, and there are roles to be carried out."[74] Everyone is offered the chance to be a part of the liturgical experience in an active dynamic way bringing their *talents* (through active participation) and *treasures* (through spiritual participation that amass to create a spiritual atmosphere) into harmony for the benefit of all present.

Father Reggie and the other clergy's *talents* are beneficial in bringing the congregants together in added ways. Father Reggie's constant movement around the front of the altar as he preaches, his reaching out to his congregation for responses, his invitation to respond, and the use of the congregational response within the homily can be described as a tactic that helps to "shift [the] highly cognitive register to a dynamic of visual, intersubjective relationality"[75]. This is because his constant movement allows the congregants to move beyond what is being preached to seeing it being performed in "literal face-to-face recognition."[76] Congregants can transition from hearing the Gospel message (a mental process) to experiencing it (a subjective process) through Father Reggie's movements, gestures, personal stories, and connections. Father Reggie and the other clergy appeared to welcome the spontaneous responses of the congregants in whatever form they took – applause, loud shouts, quiet murmurs, nodding heads, other verbal responses. They in turn acknowledged the contributions made in various ways such as with

---

[73] McClintock-Fulkerson, *Places of Redemption*, p. 108.

[74] Mary E. McGann, *A Precious Fountain* (Collegeville, Minnesota: Liturgical Press, 2004), p. 154.

[75] McClintock-Fulkerson, *Places of Redemption*, p. 115.

[76] McClintock-Fulkerson, *Places of Redemption*, p. 115.

a smile, a nod, or a verbal affirmation. Again, years of experience in the Catholic Charismatic Renewal has taught me that such spontaneous congregant responses are also external indicators of the presence of the Holy Spirit. It can be inferred that the clergy have adopted this style to assist in making the liturgical experience more familiar and inclusive of the Haitian culture. This is done so that the liturgical experience can have a substantial effect on the congregants[77], all for the fulfilment of human dignity and the common good for they who have "all things in common."

It is clear that at Notre Dame the "liturgy is the work of the community."[78] This communal liturgical effort is an act of social justice because "preaching [is] – not only having a message and the power to communicate it, but knowing the lives of those who listen, keeping them engaged in the message, and touching soul to soul"[79]. Reflecting on the letters of Saint Paul in the New Testament, his teachings reveal not only knowledge and wisdom of the content he taught but also clear insight of the various communities to whom he addressed and personalized his messages. He attempted to make his preaching connect with the socio-cultural, economic, and political contexts of his listeners, as well as with their embodied practices. "*How*[80] the message is communicated is as important as what is proclaimed ... preaching is ... engaging in a Spirit-guided conversation. And always preaching moves toward action."[81] The overall preaching style at Notre Dame reflects a "Spirit-guided conversation."

At Notre Dame, the dessert comes before the entrée. The homily, like any dessert, leaves a sweet taste in the mouth of Haitian-Americans because this is where they receive the sweetest *taste* of Haiti before they receive the entrée of the Holy Eucharist. In an interview with Father Reggie, he described how this dessert is prepared: "I am preaching to them, but I am also engaging them into the homily,

---

[77] Patsy, one of the congregants interviewed in one of my focus groups said about the Mass, "I know other Masses [at other churches] are more like a meditation type, but here, everyone gets involved." Patsy (congregant at Notre Dame D'Haiti Catholic Church) in discussion with the author, June 2018.

[78] McGann, *A Precious Fountain*, p. 89.

[79] McGann, *A Precious Fountain*, p. 124.

[80] Emphasis was made in the original source.

[81] McGann, *A Precious Fountain*, p. 133.

telling them living stories of what I experienced in my pastoral jour-
neys, during my trips to Haiti, during my encounter with people in
the community, addressing issues that are relevant to them."[82]

During one celebration of the Mass, Father Reggie used the Mass
readings to reference different life experiences that the congregants
and he were familiar with in Haiti. He used those memories, their
mutual *treasure*, as points of intersection with the readings. Drawing on his own *talent* of sapiential wisdom,[83] Father Reggie brought
the Gospel message alive and made it contextual to the congregants.
Just as Jesus did, he tailored his message to suit his audience, using
stories about life in Haiti as Jesus used parables about fishing and
shepherding that were within His listeners' socio-cultural context.[84]

Personal experience with the Catholic Charismatic Renewal
makes it possible for me to also state that when people (including
clergy) speak from their personal experience of the Holy Spirit acting in their everyday lives, listeners will tend to look for a disguised
message given through the Spirit-led and Spirt-filled preaching that
speaks personally to them. As such, when the homily takes on a personal dimension, it becomes a powerful tool for connecting congregants with the Holy Spirit who is present within them and simultaneously in their midst.

Observations and interviews reveal that the homily serves as an
integral act of social justice because it takes the congregants emotionally *back* to Haiti through the use of stories and familiar images.
The homilies remind the congregants that they have something in
common and that they have a heritage that should not be forgotten
or denied. A distinct feature of the "communicative repertoire" of
the clergy at Notre Dame is not just the vibrancy of their homilies
but also their homilies' content. Observations indicate that all of the

---

[82] Father Reginald Jean-Mary (administrator of Notre Dame D'Haiti
Catholic Church) in discussion with the author, May 2018.

[83] Knowledge that is "engendered by grace and divine self-disclosure."
Edward Farley, *Theologia: The Fragmentation and Unity of Theological Education* (Eugene, OR: Wipf & Stock, 2001), p. 153.

[84] Father Reggie's homiletic approach can be described as providing
wisdom to congregants because "more particular than a whole way of life,"
they are "concrete *pieces of advice* about how to flourish." Miroslav Volf, A
Public Faith: How the Followers of Christ Should Serve the Common Good
(Grand Rapids, MI: Brazos Press, 2011), pp. 101-102.

homilies are so culture-specific that they could certainly enable congregants at *the meal of the Mass* to feel a sense of belonging in the sharing of familiar stories of their history and cultural heritage. Facilitating such experiences is an act of social justice as congregants are able to benefit from the *giving* of each clergy's *talents* and *treasures* that are meant to promote human dignity and the common good of Haitian-American immigrants who have "all things in common."

Mass observations reveal that the priests at Notre Dame, like Father Reggie, attempt to make the homily the place for Haitian-Americans to encounter their Haitian culture as it relates to the Gospel message. This is categorically a work of social justice – invoking and sharing the memories, the *treasure* of their common heritage. This can be described as a "cognitive participatory"[85] engagement technique. Through the ability to participate cognitively, aesthetically, and spiritually in the Mass, the community's action turns the church sanctuary "into a liberating space, a place of mutuality and interaction, of shared faith grounded in the One who is present."[86] This "One" who is present is really Father, Son, and Spirit, all co-equals of the same essence working in unison to make the worship space a spiritually liberating space. While the Mass readings center on the Word of God and the Liturgy of the Eucharistic on the Paschal Mystery,[87] the "Spirit-guided conversation" of the homily at Notre Dame reveal the presence and work of the Holy Spirit that allow for the Mass to be construed as a place of social justice *action*.

The Mass at Notre Dame is a Novel Catholic Charismatic Mass

What is the significance of this study to the Catholic Church?

The Mass at Notre Dame, which includes all of the following best practices, can inform all Catholic churches' liturgical celebrations: it is dynamic, participatory, conversational, and communal; it allows spontaneity and involves transparency through the clergy's sharing

---

[85] McClintock-Fulkerson, *Places of Redemption*, p. 112.

[86] McGann, *A Precious Fountain*, p. 100.

[87] The Paschal Mystery focuses on the suffering, death, and Resurrection of Jesus (the purpose of his Incarnation).

of personal stories; it is open to the presence and works of the Holy Spirit. These qualities describe an altered version of the characteristic Catholic Charismatic Mass. The typical Catholic Charismatic Mass usually begins with several praise and worship songs to prepare the congregants with a Spirit of thanksgiving for the liturgy. It also includes extended moments of spontaneous praise, especially after the "Gloria" is sung. These moments might include healing, and they also permit time for congregants to connect more deeply with the Lord. When the Preface[88] is prayed, the congregants can express spontaneous verbal exclamations of praise, thanksgiving, and worship. During the time of Consecration, as the Body and Blood of Christ are elevated, congregants are again encouraged to give verbal exclamations of praise, thanksgiving, and worship. At the Communion Rite when the "Our Father" is sung, a time of abandonment to the Lord, the congregants may be invited to pray or sing the "Our Father" with open often uplifted arms as a sign of such abandonment. After Communion, sufficient time is normally allowed for the Lord to speak and minister to the congregants through the indwelling of the Holy Spirit. At each time of these spontaneous prayers, congregants often pray in tongues. None of these usual aspects of the Catholic Charismatic Mass were observed at Notre Dame.

The Mass at Notre Dame is therefore unlike the customary Catholic Charismatic Mass and thus can be regarded as exemplifying a *novel* version of Charismatic. At such a Mass, hospitality is the key to social-justice advocacy. First, it helps to create a sense of belonging. Then, this leads to the establishment of a community. Next, a home environment (and atmosphere) is fashioned. As a result, belonging→community→home→social justice. The importance of hospitality, though sometimes underestimated, cannot and should not be taken for granted. "Hospitality is an important Christian practice that relates, in essence, to the Spirit-enabled ability to show kindness."[89]

---

[88] This is the prayer that precedes the Eucharistic Prayer, the main portion of the Liturgy of the Eucharist.

[89] John Swinton and Harriet Mowart, *Practical Theology and Qualitative Research* (London: SCM Press, 2nd edn, 2016), p. 86.

Conclusion

This study highlights the success story of an ethnic parish that caters predominantly to the needs of a particular cultural group. Catholic ecclesiology emphasizes the continued presence of Jesus Christ in the world as imbued by the life-giving presence of the Holy Spirit. The clergy at Notre Dame embody a spirituality in solidarity with immigrants. Also, in their witness of Christ using the gifts and fruits of the Spirit, they advocate for the spiritual needs of their Haitian-immigrant congregants. Social advocacy at Notre Dame is accomplished both from the top (clergy in leadership) and from the bottom (congregants of the grassroots), in a hospitable environment that leads to the formation of a home – all under the guidance of the Holy Spirit. These accomplishments at Notre Dame offer valuable insights for church ministry. Under the right leadership it is possible for a diasporic church community to not just survive but to flourish, thereby securing and celebrating its unparalleled identity. Also, while the Holy Spirit's presence and works are not always apparent, the eyes of faith can look beyond the spectacular to the familiar and find the Spirit present and working in the ordinary acts of social justice achieved through hospitality – the acts of preaching and participation. Social justice can likewise be viewed differently, beyond the spectacular, as simply a voluntary giving of *time*, *talent*, and *treasure* out of sheer brotherly and sisterly love. This giving promotes human dignity and the common good of all because they have "all things in common."

The findings of this study have revealed that Father Reggie and the clergy associated with Notre Dame engage in and promote a pneumatological ecclesial praxis. This has positively impacted their congregants and transformed their marginal positions as non-English-speaking immigrants living in a foreign English-speaking country to that of spiritually empowered Haitian-Americans. Their praxis of hospitality theology indicates the potential for a similar ecclesial mission that will cater to the pastoral needs (for love, acceptance, support, guidance, spiritual formation, and empowerment) of the Anglophone Caribbean-American Catholic diaspora of the Archdiocese of Miami. This is my personal vision for which I am encouraged by the following: "Ecclesial innovation and experimentation is not just a matter of thought, but is also one of action."[90]

Bibliography

Benedict XVI, "The Priest's Three Duties." *Eternal Word Network Television*. Apr 14, 2010. http://www.ewtn.com/library/papal-doc/b16prduties.htm.

Cahalan, Kathleen A., *Introducing the Practice of Ministry* (Collegeville, MN: Liturgical Press, 2010).

Camaraota, Steven A., "Fact Sheet on Haitian Immigrants in the United States." *Center for Immigration Studies*, January 25, 2010. https://cis.org/Fact-Sheet/Fact-Sheet-Haitian-Immigrants-United-States.

Henriot, Peter, *The Pastoral Circle Revisited* (ed. Frans Wijsen, Peter Henriot, and Rodrigo Mejía; New York: Orbis Books, 2005).

Hitchcock, James and Glorianna Bednarski, *Catholic Perspectives: Charismatics* (Chicago: The Thomas More Press, 1980).

Holland, Joe and Peter Henriot, *Social Analysis: Linking Faith and Justice* (Washington, DC: Dove Communications and Orbis Books, 1983).

Ignatius Loyola, *Spiritual Exercises* (Trans. George Ganss; Chicago: Loyola University Press, 1992). Quoted in Peter Henriot, *The Pastoral Circle Revisited* (Ed. Frans Wijsen, Peter Henriot, and Rodrigo Mejía; New York: Orbis Books, 2005).

"Knowledge (which helps one to see the paths to follow)." A Redemptorist Pastoral Publication, *Handbook for Today's Catholics* (Missouri: Liguori Publications, 1994).

McClintock-Fulkerson, Mary, *Places of Redemption* (New York: Oxford University Press, 2007).

McGann, Mary E., *A Precious Fountain* (Ed. Don. F. Saliers; Collegeville, MN: Liturgical Press, 2004).

Phillips, Elizabeth, *Political Theology: A Guide for the Perplexed* (New York: T & T Clark International, 2012).

Rey, Terry and Alex Stepick, "Refugee Catholicism in Little Haiti: Miami's Notre Dame d'Haiti Catholic Church," in Alex Stepick,

[90] Peter Ward, *Liquid Ecclesiology: The Gospel and the Church* (Boston: Brill, 2017), p. 2.

Terry Rey, and Sarah J. Mahler (eds.), *Churches and Charity in the Immigrant City: Religion, Immigration, and Civic Engagement in Miami* (New Brunswick: Rutgers University Press, 2009).

Suchocki, Marjorie Hewitt, *Divinity and Diversity: A Christian Affirmation of Religious Pluralism* (Nashville: Abington Press, 2003).

Swinton, John and Harriet Mowat, *Practical Theology and Qualitative Research* (London: SCM Press, 2nd edn, 2016).

"Understanding (which enables the person to grasp the truth of religion)," A Redemptorist Pastoral Publication, *Handbook for Today's Catholics* (Missouri: Liguori Publications, 1994).

United States Conference of Catholic Bishops, "Seven Themes of Catholic Social Teaching." United States Conference of Catholic Bishops. Accessed 2. January 2019. http://www.usccb.org/beliefs-and-teachings/what-we-believe/catholic-social-teaching/seven-themes-of-catholic-social-teaching.cfm.

United States Conference of Catholic Bishops, "Catechism of the Catholic Church." United States Conference of Catholic Bishops, Accessed February 22, 2019. http://ccc.usccb.org/flipbooks/catechism/index.html#190/z.

Vatican Council II, *Gaudium et Spes* [Pastoral Constitution on the Church in the Modern World], in Austin Flannery, OP (ed.), *The Basic Sixteen Documents of Vatican II: A Completely Revised Translation in Inclusive Language* (Northport: Costello, 1996).

Walsh, Vincent, *A Key to Charismatic Renewal in the Catholic Church* (Holland, PA: Key of David Publications, 1974).

Ward, Peter, *Liquid Ecclesiology: The Gospel and the Church* (Boston: Brill, 2017).

"Wisdom (which helps a person to grasp the truths of religion)," A Redemptorist Pastoral Publication. *Handbook for Today's Catholics* (Missouri: Liguori Publications, 1994).

Chapter Eleven

"When the Truth Does Not Set Free" False Accusations, Wrongful Convictions, and the Church

Michal Meulenberg*

> Do not make false accusations, and do not put an innocent person to death, for I will condemn anyone who does such an evil thing (Exod. 23.7 GNT).

> Dying on some court schedule or some prison schedule ain't right. People are supposed to die on God's schedule. Walter McMillian[1]

One hundred and sixty-six. That's the number of human beings that could have tragically lost their lives through the death penalty since

---

* Michal Meulenberg (PhD, Fuller Theological Seminary) is an Assistant Professor of Islamic Studies and Peace & Conflict Transformation Studies at Biola University. She additionally serves as Interim Director of Islamic Studies at Fuller Theological Seminary in Pasadena, California. Her research and activism are in the areas of Muslim-Christian relations, conflict transformation, and social justice advocacy.

[1] Walter McMillian was falsely accused of murder and put on death row. This story and this quote can be found in: Bryan Stevenson, *Just Mercy (Movie Tie-In Edition)* (New York: Random House Publishing Group, Kindle Edition, 2014), pp. 312-13.

its reinstatement in 1976, had it not been for those fighting to see justice happen and proving their innocence just in time.[2]

Sixteen. That's the minimum number of human beings in that same time period estimated to have been executed for crimes they did not commit and for whom justice did not come in time.[3] The actual number is likely higher.

Experts calculate that at least 4.1% of those on death row are, in fact, innocent.[4] Bryan Stevenson, founder and executive director of the Equal Justice Initiative and fighter of countless death row cases, puts the percentage higher at 11.1%.[5] In August 2019, the Innocence Project hoped to exonerate the one hundred and sixty-seventh person from death row, but their final efforts were denied by the court hours before the execution.[6] Instead, a statement was released that

---

[2] Death Penalty Information Center, *Innocence Database,* accessed 23 August 2019, <https://deathpenaltyinfo.org/policy-issues/innocence-database>.

[3] That's the number of human beings listed by the Death Penalty Information Center (U.S.) who were "executed but possibly innocent." The center clarifies, "There is no way to tell how many of the 1503 people executed since 1976 may also have been innocent. Courts do not generally entertain claims of innocence when the defendant is dead. Defense attorneys move on to other cases where clients' lives can still be saved." Death Penalty Information Center, *Executed but Possibly Innocent*, accessed 23 August 2019, <https://deathpenaltyinfo.org/policy-issues/innocence/executed-but-possibly-innocent>.

[4] S.R. Gross *et al.*, "Rate of False Conviction of Criminal Defendants Who Are Sentenced to Death," *Proceedings of the National Academy of Sciences of the United States of America* 111 (20) (2014), pp. 7230–35.

[5] Equal Justice Initiative, *Innocence,* accessed 23 August 2019, <https://eji.org/ death-penalty/innocence>. Also, there are not only innocent people on death row; plenty of innocent people are wrongfully convicted who do not end up on death row. The National Registry of Exonerations argues that by "any reasonable accounting, there are tens of thousands of false convictions each year across the country, and many more that have accumulated over the decades." The National Registry of Exonerations, *Exonerations in 2015,* accessed 23 August 2019, <https://www.law.umich.edu/special/exoneration/Documents/Exonerations_in_2015.pdf>.

[6] Innocence Staff 2019, *State of Texas executes Innocence Project client Larry Swearingen after U.S. Supreme Court denies stay,* accessed 23 August 2019,<https://www.innocenceproject.org/state-of-texas-executes-

the man they had come to love had uttered the following last words: "Lord forgive them. They don't know what they are doing."[7]

For followers of Jesus, these words echo the Messiah's when He also received the death penalty for a crime He did not commit. Jesus stood trial in the highest courts in the nation. He faced the betrayal of a close friend, false accusations, lying witnesses, no-one advocating for his innocence, and judges that cared more about public opinion than the truth. Reflections on the ways in which the teachers of the Scriptures perverted justice are often ignored due to the acknowledgement that Jesus' death was prophetic and foretold. Although of course true, that does not take away the fact that those in power seemed to think they were following Scripture by trying to produce witnesses and settling on a blasphemy claim when all other accusations proved to be contradictory and thus unusable. Attempts on Jesus' life had been made before, but this was the only one that involved a trial in both the Jewish and Roman courts and led to the death penalty.

Not only does Jesus' trial come to mind when thinking of wrongful convictions, Scripture is filled with mentions of injustice happening in courtrooms (Lev. 19.15, Deut. 16.19, Amos 5.10; 12), God's warning against oppressing the poor in court (Prov. 22.8-9, 31.8-9; Ps. 140.12), stories of unjust laws and judges (Isa. 10.1, Lk. 18.1-8, Acts 24.26-27), lamentations about dishonest accusers (Ps. 35.19-20; 43.1; 109.1-7; 26-31), a commandment and warnings against being a false witness (Exod. 20.16, Deut. 19.18-19, Prov. 14.5; 19.5), and God's hatred of injustice (Prov. 6.16-19; 17.15, 2 Chron. 19.7).

Jesus quoted from Isaiah that he had come to "proclaim freedom for the prisoners and recovery of sight for the blind, to set the oppressed free" (Lk. 4.18) and spoke out against oppressors throughout his ministry. He repeatedly chided the religious leaders that they had "condemned the innocent" (Mt. 12.7) and forgotten about the "weightier matters of the law" which includes justice (Mt. 23.23).

---

innocence-project-client-larry-swearingen-after-u-s-supreme-court-denies-stay/>.

[7] Innocence Staff 2019, *Innocence Project remembers Larry Swearingen's sense of humor, artistry, and optimism*, accessed 23 August 2019, <https://www.innocenceproject.org/innocence-project-remembers-larry-swearingens-sense-of-humor-artistry-and-optimism/>.

Christian ethicists Glen Stassen and David Gushee demonstrate in their book Kingdom Ethics: Following Jesus in Contemporary Context how Jesus did not only die "for our sins, including our injustice," but also "taught, embodied, and fulfilled the prophet Isaiah's four themes of justice."[8] These themes are:

> (1) deliverance of the poor and powerless from the injustice that they regularly experience; (2) lifting the foot of domineering power off the neck of the dominated and oppressed; (3) stopping violence and establishing peace; and (4) restoring (or welcoming) the outcasts, the excluded, the Gentiles, the exiles, and the refugees to community.[9]

After exploring each of the themes as seen in Jesus' life and ministry, Stassen and Gushee conclude that if Jesus "was that committed to justice in his context, we are required to be just as concerned about justice in our own."[10] Simply put: being a follower of Jesus requires caring seriously about justice. This includes, but is not limited to, the falsely accused, the wrongfully convicted, and all those incarcerated. Jesus taught that visiting those in prison is akin to visiting him (Mt. 25.39-40). This passage does not mention needing to know or find out why people find themselves in prison – we are simply to care and go. Furthermore, biblical writers Paul and Peter, themselves wrongfully incarcerated, mention themes that also apply to the criminal justice process such as stopping slander and lies (Eph. 4.25, 31, 1 Pet. 2.1), working for reconciliation (2 Cor. 5.18-21), and resolving disputes without resorting to lawsuits (1 Cor. 6.1-6).

What does all of this mean for us practically speaking today? How is a follower of Jesus to live out the teachings of Scripture when seeing mugshots of people accused of crimes, hearing claims of innocence even though a jury found someone guilty, reading about exonerations through DNA evidence,[11] and encountering the growing

---

[8] David P. Gushee, and G.H. Stassen, *Kingdom Ethics: Following Jesus in Contemporary Context* (Grand Rapids: Eerdmans, 2nd edn, 2016), p. 147.

[9] Gushee and Stassen, *Kingdom Ethics*, p. 131.

[10] Gushee and Stassen, *Kingdom Ethics*, p. 147.

[11] The National Registry of Exonerations keeps a database of information on those who have been exonerated due to DNA or in other ways. To date, 484 people have been exonerated due to the testing of DNA and a

number of movies, documentaries and podcasts proclaiming the justice system got it wrong?[12] This is where the guidance of God's Spirit is indispensable.

Leading lives empowered by God's Spirit means we allow the Spirit to guide every part of our lives, including how we look at what is happening in our society. When Jesus announced the outpouring of the Holy Spirit that was to come after his departure, he referred to the Spirit as "Spirit of truth" (Jn 16.13) and the "Comforter"[13] (Jn 14.26). It is these two aspects of the Holy Spirit that will be explored as it applies to understanding and responding to false accusations

---

total of 2481 people have been exonerated since 1989. The National Registry of Exonerations, *Exonerations by Year: DNA and Non-DNA,* accessed 23 August 2019, <(https://www.law.umich.edu/special/exoneration/Pages/about.aspx)>.

[12] Some examples of recent documentaries and podcasts that have gone viral are *Serial* (https://serialpodcast.org/season-one) and the HBO series on the same case (https://www.hbo.com/the-case-against-adnan-syed), *Making a Murderer* Season One and Two (Netflix.com), and *When They See Us* on the overturned conviction of the "The Central Park Five" now more accurately called "The Exonerated Five" (Netflix.com). Full list of recommended documentaries, films, and books on Actual Innocence: The Innocence Network, *Wrongful Conviction Media,* accessed 23 August 2019, <https://innocencenetwork.org/wp-content/uploads/Wrongful-Conviction-Media.pdf>.

[13] The Greek word *paraklētos* is translated in different ways: the Advocate (NIV, BSB, NET), the Counselor (CSB, HCSB, WEB), the Helper (ESV, BLB, NASB, NKJV, GNT, ISV), and the Comforter (AKJV, ASV, ERV) among others.

BlueLetterBible.org outlines its Biblical usage the following way: summoned, called to one's side, esp. called to one's aid: A. one who pleads another's cause before a judge, a pleader, counsel for defense, legal assistant, an advocate; B. one who pleads another's cause with one, an intercessor; i. of Christ in his exaltation at God's right hand, pleading with God the Father for the pardon of our sins; C. in the widest sense, a helper, succourer, aider, assistant; i. of the Holy Spirit destined to take the place of Christ with the apostles (after his ascension to the Father), to lead them to a deeper knowledge of the gospel truth, and give them divine strength needed to enable them to undergo trials and persecutions on behalf of the divine kingdom. Blue Letter Bible, paraklētos, accessed 23 August 2019, <https://www.blueletterbible.org/lang/lexicon/lexicon.cfm?Strongs=G3875&t=ESV>.

and wrongful convictions in the current criminal justice system in the United States.

The Spirit of Truth

> And the Spirit of the LORD will rest on him – the Spirit of wisdom and understanding, the Spirit of counsel and might, the Spirit of knowledge and the fear of the LORD. He will delight in obeying the LORD. He will not judge by appearance nor make a decision based on hearsay. He will give justice to the poor and make fair decisions for the exploited ... He will wear righteousness like a belt and truth like an undergarment (Isa. 11.2-5).

Jesus embodied the prophet Isaiah's words. He was guided by the Spirit of wisdom and understanding. He did not judge based on mere sight or hearsay but rather focused on justice, righteousness and truth. Each of these aspects is key when assessing the criminal justice system today. There is great need for wisdom and understanding, not judging based on appearance or making decisions on hearsay but instead focusing on truth and justice, especially for the poor and exploited.

During his trial proceedings, Jesus and his Roman judge Pilate discussed truth. Jesus mentioned he had come to "testify to the truth" (Jn 18.37). Pilate responded: "What is truth"?[14] What was

---

[14] NT wright in a sermon on this topic comments on this scene:
And John's point, in the middle of the massive irony, and the direct clash of the non-violent kingdom of God with the violent and ignorant armies of Caesar, is crystal clear: truth is what happens when heaven and earth come together as they were always meant to. Truth is therefore what you find in Jesus, who is the point where that happens. And truth is therefore what happens when the Spirit comes to fill, to guide, to commission, to empower the followers of Jesus... the followers of Jesus, may be truth-tellers, truth-tasters here at the Eucharist, truth-livers as we confront the lies in our own hearts and lives and communities, truth-doers in our public and political life... as humble hearts seeking after holiness and hope, and ready to find our minds and our manners remade by the truth, by the Truth Incarnate, by the Spirit of Truth whom he sends from the Father (NT Wright Page 2016, *Spirit of Truth*, accessed 23 August 2019, <http://ntwrightpage.com/2016/03/30/spirit-of-tru th/>).

going on in Pilate's mind to ask that question? Whatever it was, the conversation with Jesus impacted him so deeply that he concluded there was "no basis for a charge against him," a statement he asserted three times (Jn 17.38; 19.4; 19.6). Pilate furthermore sought out several ways to get Jesus released but ultimately gave in to sentence Jesus with the death penalty. This government official cared more about public pressure than the truth.

The pursuit of answering the question "What is truth"? is what many think lies at the heart of the criminal justice process in the United States. The prevailing belief is that the system can be trusted to almost always get it right and that the margin of error is so minimal it is inconsequential. In fact, the late Justice Scalia said as much by calling wrongful convictions an "insignificant minimum."[15] Citing research on this topic, Dan Simon, Professor of Law and Psychology at USC's Gould School of Law, remarks:

the denial of error is prevalent also among law enforcement officials who operate the system on a daily basis. A majority of surveyed police chiefs, prosecutors, and trial judges insist that mistaken verdicts are nonexistent or that they occur at an infinitesimal rate, at least within their own jurisdictions.[16]

It, therefore, comes as no surprise that prosecutors often resist reconsidering convictions even in the face of exculpating DNA.[17]

In general public there are varying levels of trust in how often the system gets to the truth. A Gallup Poll from 2018 found that 36% of respondents had "very little or no" confidence in the criminal justice system, 41% had "some," and 22% had a "great deal or quite a lot."[18] In that same year, the National Center for State Courts found that

---

[15] Justice Scalia's opinion can be found in *Kansas v. Marsh*, 548 U.S. 163, 193, 200 (2006).

[16] Dan Simon, and L.M. Bartles, *In Doubt: The Psychology of the Criminal Justice Process* (Cambridge: Harvard University Press, Kindle Edition 2012), p. 229.

[17] D.S. Medwed, "The Zeal Deal: Prosecutorial Resistance to Post-conviction Claims of Innocence," *Boston University Law Review* 84 (2004), pp. 125-83.

[18] L. Saad, 2018, *Military, Small Business, Police Still Stir Most Confidence*, Gallup, accessed 23 August 2019, <https://news.gallup.com /poll/236243/military-small-business-police-stir-confidence.aspx>.

22% of the thousand registered voters they surveyed had little or no confidence in the state courts and 52% thought judges are out of touch with their communities.[19]

When looking at racial bias, the Harvard Institute of Politics found in 2015 that among eighteen to twenty-nine-year-olds, 49% had little to no confidence "that the justice system can operate without bias."[20] This number was highest among African American youth of which two-thirds lack confidence in the judicial system. In 2019, Pew Forum Research found that "Black and white adults have widely different perceptions of how blacks are treated in America, but majorities of both groups say blacks are treated less fairly than whites by the criminal justice system (87% of blacks vs. 61% of whites)."[21]

In conclusion, on average about 22 to 36% of US persons have little to no trust in the system, and when specifically focusing on perceptions of racial bias in the system, that rate is even higher. These polls slightly differ in methodology of addressing perceptions of trust, confidence and fairness, but what is generally clear is that criminal justice officials (police, prosecutors, and judges) have a much higher trust that the system is functioning well than the public.

As a former prosecutor himself, Jim Petro similarly believed the justice system mostly got it right. This changed when he became the elected Attorney General of Ohio and was asked to help open the door for the Innocence Project to test DNA that resulted in the exoneration of an innocent man. Subsequently, he had over two hundred thousand DNA profiles created which led to many cold cases

---

[19] GBA Strategies 2018, *2018 State of the State Courts - Survey Analysis*, GBA Strategies, accessed 23 August 2019, <https://www.ncsc.org/~/media/Files/PDF/Topics/Public%20Trust%20and%20Confidence/SoSC_2018_ Survey_Analysis. ashx>.

[20] CBS/AP 2015, *Poll: Young Americans have "little confidence" in justice system*, CBS News, accessed 23 August 2019 <https://www.cbsnews.com/news/poll-young-people-have-little-confidence-in-justice-system/>.

[21] J.M. Horowitz, A. Brown, and K. Cox 2019, *Race in America 2019*, Pew Research Center, accessed 23 August 2019, <https://www.pewsocialtrends.org/ 2019/04/09/race-in-america-2019/#majorities-of-black-and-white-adults-say-blacks-are-treated-less-fairly-than-whites-in-dealing-with-police-and-by-the-criminal-justice-system>.

solved and revealed a staggering number of wrongful convictions. As a result of his experience, he changed his view on the death penalty: "with new awareness of the risk of conviction error and uneven application, I no longer support it."[22] It also opened his eyes to the fact that far more people are wrongfully convicted than he realized. Exactly how many, he writes, "only God knows," but he estimates that it impacts thousands.[23]

It was already seen that experts put the percentage of people wrongfully put on death row are between four and eleven percent. How many are wrongfully convicted of misdemeanors and felonies but do not face the death penalty is hard to know. James Acker, Distinguished Teaching Professor at the University at Albany School of Criminal Justice, notes what researchers and experts have said about this:

Owing to the formidable scope of "the dark figure of innocence" (Bedau & Radelet, 1987, p. 87; Garrett, 2011, p. 6), the information currently available about wrongful convictions has variously been described as "a drop in the bucket" (National Registry of Exonerations [NRE], 2016c, p. 2), "a tiny fraction" of the complete picture (Krajicek, 2015), and as the ever-popular "tip of the iceberg" (Findley & Scott, 2006, p. 291; Garrett, 2011, p. 11). We know with certainty, however, that systems of justice are prone to error. Documented cases of wrongful conviction are legion.[24]

He further states:

The Journal of Contemporary Criminal Justice 33(1) Survey respondents have speculated that anywhere between 0% and 20% of criminal convictions ensnare innocents, with criminal justice officials (police, prosecutors, defense attorneys, and judges) generally offering estimates that range, on average, between 0.5% and 3% (Ramsey & Frank, 2007; Smith, Zalman, & Kiger, 2011;

---

[22] Jim Petro, and N. Petro. *False Justice: Eight Myths that Convict the Innocent* (Fort Lauderdale: Kaplan Publishing, Kindle Edition 2011), p. 121.

[23] Petro, and Petro. *False Justice: Eight Myths that Convict the Innocent*, p. 68.

[24] J.R. Acker. "Taking Stock of Innocence: Movements, Mountains, and Wrongful Convictions," *Journal of Contemporary Criminal Justice* 33.1 (2017), p. 9.

Zalman, Smith, & Kiger, 2008). Even those relatively conservative estimates correspond to roughly 5,000 to 30,000 wrongful felony convictions and approximately 2,000 to 12,000 innocent people imprisoned annually (Zalman, 2012). They translate into many more thousands of erroneous misdemeanor convictions and jail sentences (Minton & Zeng, 2015; Natapoff, 2012; Roberts, 2013).[25]

Moreover, the unknowability of the exact number of people falsely accused and wrongfully convicted is due to the fact that some people plead guilty even though they did not commit a crime.[26] While possibly hard to understand if one has not been through this, a main reason for taking a "plea deal" is a fear of the risk of losing a trial and getting a far longer sentence.[27] For example, one might have thirty years hanging over their head for a crime they did not commit, but signing a plea deal for a lesser crime would result in only two years of prison time. With prosecutors often overcharging suspected crimes, the anguish over "the worst-case scenario" makes people feel pressure to "just get it over with" and sign for something less egregious. Especially for those who have children and do not want to run the risk of missing out on years of their lives, this difficult decision may sound like the better option. Others may even have the death penalty hanging over them and prefer to not risk losing a trial and being executed. Thus, they enter into a bargain that takes the death penalty off the table.[28] Others lack resources, as going to trial can be very costly. Still others may be pressured into the plea by their lawyer or public defender. The latter is especially more likely to happen to people with lower IQs, children, those who have mental challenges, or poor understanding of the English language and either no translation or poor translation is being offered. Each of these groups has

---

[25] Acker, "Taking Stock of Innocence," p. 10.

[26] Dervan Le and V.A. Edkins. "The Innocent Defendant's Dilemma: An Innovative Empirical Study of Plea Bargaining's Innocence Problem," *Journal of Criminal Law & Criminology* 103.1 (2013), pp. 1-48.

[27] A.D. Redlich *et al.*, "The Psychology of Defendant Plea Decision Making," *American Psychologist* 72.4 (2017), pp. 339-52.

[28] For an example of this, check out the story of Daniel Villegas: The National Registry of Exonerations, *Daniel Villegas*, accessed 23 August 2019,<https://www.law.umich.edu/special/exoneration/Pages/casedetail.aspx?caseid=5389>.

increased difficulty fully understanding the consequences of what they are signing.[29] Since 95% of criminal convictions (and 98% of federal cases[30]) never go to trial but are handled behind closed doors with plea bargains, there is no way of knowing how often an innocent person pleads guilty. The only thing that is known is that among those exonerated so far, about 15% had originally pled guilty.[31]

Of the 5% of criminal cases that are not "resolved" through plea bargains and do go to trial, all kinds of issues can occur that make it hard for someone to prove their innocence. Acker writes that "wrongful convictions often are plagued by problems of faulty eyewitness identification testimony, false confessions, overstated or flawed forensic testimony, police and prosecutorial errors or misconduct, substandard defense representation, and unreliable informants."[32] An increasing number of studies confirm how the legal process can knowingly or unknowingly go wrong in each of these areas. Multiple errors have the potential to create a "perfect storm" that all too easily paint the innocent as guilty.[33]

---

[29] Redlich *et al.*, "The Psychology of Defendant Plea Decision Making," pp. 339-52.

[30] J. Gramlich, Only 2% of federal criminal defendants go to trial, and most who do are found guilty. Pew Research Center, accessed 23 August 2019, <https://www.pewresearch.org/fact-tank/2019/06/11/only-2-of-federal-criminal-defendants-go-to-trial-and-most-who-do-are-found-guilty/>.

[31] The National Registry of Exonerations 2015, *Innocents Who Plead Guilty*, accessed 23 August 2019, <https://www.law.umich.edu/special/exoneration/Documents/NRE.Guilty.Plea.Article1.pdf>.

[32] Acker. "Taking Stock of Innocence," p. 12.

[33] Countless books and research articles have been written on all the things that can go wrong before and during trial that make it hard to come to the right verdict. Some that are recommended reading in order of publication: J. Dwyer, P. Neufeld, and B. Scheck, *Actual Innocence: Five Days to Execution and Other Dispatches from the Wrongly Convicted* (New York: Doubleday, 1st ed, 2000); J.B. Gould, *The Innocence Commission: Preventing Wrongful Convictions and Restoring the Criminal Justice System* (New York: New York University Press, 2009); B. Garrett, *Convicting the Innocent: Where Criminal Prosecutions Go Wrong* (Cambridge: Harvard University Press, 2011); D. Simon, *In Doubt: The Psychology of the Criminal*

The National Registry of Exonerations lists factors that impacted each wrongful conviction that led to exoneration since 1989. For example, of the 151 people exonerated in 2018, the two largest factors that led to their wrongful convictions were misconduct by police or prosecutors (107 cases) and perjury or false accusations (111 cases). Moreover, in 50 of the 151 cases, the alleged crime had actually never happened. Of the 107 cases that involved official misconduct, the most common type was police or prosecutors (or both) holding back exculpatory evidence. The other misconduct involved "police officers threatening witnesses, forensic analysts falsifying test results, and child welfare workers pressuring children to claim sexual abuse where none occurred."[34]

Simon's book *In Doubt: the Psychology of the Criminal Justice System* weaves together the growing body of research on these particular issues with extensive social science research, revealing how even well-intentioned people can create issues leading to wrongful conviction both in the investigatory and adjudicatory processes. He furthermore explains how issues with the adversarial model of the system, jury deliberation, and the limiting effect of the appellate courts can contribute to wrongful convictions. Common human error in perception, judgment and memory, as well as unconscious biases, can taint the process from beginning to end. He poses:

Justice Process (Cambridge: Harvard University Press, 2012); M. Godsey, *Blind Injustice: A Former Prosecutor Exposes the Psychology and Politics of Wrongful Convictions* (Oakland: University of California Press, 2019); J.R. Acker and A. Redlich, *Wrongful Conviction: Law, Science, and Policy* (Durham: Carolina Academic Press, 2019). Other recommended readings are the first-hand accounts of those who have been falsely accused and wrongfully convicted. For example: T. Craft and M. Dagostino, *Accused: My Fight for Truth, Justice, and the Strength to Forgive* (Dallas: BenBella Books, 2016); N. Berman *et al., Surviving Justice: America's Wrongfully Convicted and Exonerated (Voice of Witness)* (London: Verso, 2017); L. Caldwell *et al., Anatomy of Innocence: Testimonies of the Wrongfully Convicted* (New York: Liveright Publishing Corporation, 2017); and L. Bazelon, *Rectify: The Power of Restorative Justice After Wrongful Conviction* (Boston: Beacon Press, 2018).

[34] The National Registry of Exonerations 2018, *Exonerations in 2018*, accessed 23 August 2019, <https://www.law.umich.edu/special/exoneration/Documents/ Exonerations%20in%202018.pdf>.

[this analysis] leads to the conclusion that the investigative process produces evidence that is bound to contain unknown quantities of truth and error, and the adjudicative process is ill equipped to distinguish between the two. The limited accuracy of criminal investigations, compounded with the limited diagnosticity of criminal adjudication, lead to the conclusion that the criminal justice process falls short of delivering the precision that befits its solemn epistemic demands and the certitude it proclaims.[35]

He furthermore points out how these issues are by and large overlooked or denied by people who are part of the system, such as detectives, police, prosecutors, judges, and law makers. According to Petro this is where the general public can play a role. One of the barriers to getting exonerated, he mentions, is "the confidence that most Americans have in the justice system, making exoneration a low priority in the political environment that influences those who deliver justice."[36] He and his wife wrote a memoir that they hope "by the grace of God ... will help correct common misunderstandings with a critically important message: True justice is 'a search for truth', requiring constant vigilance, and is ultimately the responsibility of every citizen."[37] They identify eight myths every citizen should be aware of:

Myth 1: Everyone in prison claims innocence.
Myth 2: Our system almost never convicts an innocent person.
Myth 3: Only the guilty confess.
Myth 4: Wrongful convictions are the result of innocent
    human error.
Myth 5: An eyewitness is the best evidence.
Myth 6: Conviction errors get corrected on appeal.
Myth 7: It dishonors the victim to question a conviction.

---

[35] Simon, *In Doubt: The Psychology of the Criminal Justice Process*, p. 221.

[36] Petro and Petro, *False Justice: Eight Myths that Convict the Innocent*, p. 70.

[37] Petro and Petro, *False Justice: Eight Myths that Convict the Innocent*, p. 248.

Myth 8: If the justice system has problems, the pros will fix it.[38]

They dispel each myth using case studies, research, and data, concluding with suggestions for improving the justice system.

The truth that the criminal justice system does not always get it right, impacting thousands of people, is something everyone should care about. May believers in Jesus be guided by the Spirit of truth and awaken to this grave issue in our society. Christine Pohl, professor of Christian ethics at Asbury Theological Seminary, points out:

> Despite the importance of truth and truthfulness, we might be inclined to agree with the Old Testament prophet who cried that truth "stumbles in the public square." Isaiah's description of his day echoes into our own experience of contemporary public life: people rely on empty arguments and speak lies; "there is no justice in their paths." "Righteousness stands at a distance," honesty is excluded, and even the court system is corrupted by lies, empty pleas, and unjust suits (Isaiah 59).[39]

Lamenting these injustices follows the awakening to them. However, it should not be left there. Inaction and lack of involvement in addressing false accusations and wrongful convictions would ensure they continue to happen. Being part of the problem looks like buying into the myths about the US criminal justice system mentioned above. Being part of the solution looks like pursuing truth and asking others to do the same to seek change. Martin Luther King Jr states:

The church must be reminded that it is not the master or the servant of the state, but rather the conscience of the state. It must be the guide and the critic of the state, and never its tool. If the church does not recapture its prophetic zeal, it will become an irrelevant social club without moral or spiritual authority.[40]

---

[38] Petro and Petro, *False Justice: Eight Myths that Convict the Innocent*, pp. 243-48.

[39] Christine D. Pohl, *Living into Community: Cultivating Practices That Sustain Us* (Grand Rapids: Eerdmans, 2012), p. 113.

[40] Martin Luther King, Jr, *Strength to Love* (Minneapolis: Fortress, 2010), p. 59.

How this is done practically when it comes to the issue of wrongful convictions will be discussed in the conclusion. First, however, a second aspect of a spirit-empowered life must be considered: how do followers of Jesus comfort those impacted by false accusations, wrongful convictions, and incarceration?

The Comforter

> O God, whom I praise,
>   don't stand silent and aloof
> while the wicked slander me
>   and tell lies about me.
> They surround me with hateful words
>   and fight against me for no reason.
> I love them, but they try to destroy me with accusations
>   even as I am praying for them!
> They repay evil for good
> and hatred for my love. Ps. 109.1-5

The haunting stories of people who have been executed for crimes they did not commit as well as those who have made it out alive should give anyone pause. Impacted individuals have experienced deep pain and trauma. Even post-exoneration, the experience has long-term impact. Ronald Keith Williamson, for example, was falsely accused of raping and killing a young woman. Although he is one of the few lucky ones that got exonerated, he continues to live with intense trauma. He exclaims:

> No matter what happens to you, you are constantly put under this eye of distrust that you can never shake. I walked into a supermarket in town, and a lady picked up her child. The little girl said, "That's the man who was on the TV, Mommy." She rushed over and grabbed her child and said, "Don't go near him." I just left my stuff and walked out. It never, ever ends. It never ends. It never ends. It never will be ended.[41]

---

[41] Rimer, S. 2000, *Life After Death Row*, N.Y. Times, accessed 23 August 2019,<https://archive.nytimes.com/www.nytimes.com/library/magazine/home /20001210mag-deathrow.html>.

The pain of false accusations and wrongful convictions leads to a myriad of issues in the lives of the accused and their family and friends. Research on the aftermath of the exoneration experience is small but growing. There are legal,[42] social, financial, physical, and psychological repercussions.[43] Many of the issues faced are similar to anyone that has been through the criminal justice system: trouble getting jobs due to the fact that background checks will show that they have once been arrested and charged with crimes, social stigma and PTSD from the experience of being in jail and prison (sometimes leading to suicide), difficulty with the fact that society has changed in cases where there was an extended incarceration period, and relationships that have been hurt or become distant due to their absence. Other issues are unique to those falsely accused and wrongfully convicted. For example, Elmer Daniels was falsely accused of rape even though he had a strong alibi. Yet, when he was paroled in 2015, he was taken back to prison soon after "because he would not admit his guilt, which was required to complete his sex-offender therapy sessions."[44] It took three more years before he was finally exonerated.

Even those who may have won their trial and did not face conviction still have to deal with the fact that they have an arrest record and deep emotional scars. Tonya Craft, a woman falsely accused of aggravated child molestation by three girls, including her own daughter, writes about her harrowing experience in her memoir *Accused: My Fight for Truth, Justice, and the Strength to Forgive*. She recounts how she still runs into people every now and then who do

---

[42] One example is the fact that those who have been exonerated still have a record that can hinder them from obtaining jobs. An exoneration does not automatically lead to expungement. A. Shlosberg *et al.*, "The Expungement Myth," *Albany Law Review* 75.3 (2012), pp. 1229-41.

[43] Carolyn Hoyle *et al.*, *The Impact of Being Wrongly Accused of Abuse in Occupations of Trust: Victim's Voices* (University of Oxford Centre of Criminology 2016), Accessed 23 August 2019,
<https://www.law.ox.ac.uk/sites/files/oxlaw/the_impact_of_being_wrongly_accused_of_abuse_hoyle_et_al_ 2016_15_may.pdf>.

[44] The National Registry of Exonerations 2018, *Exonerations in 2018*, accessed 23 August 2019, <https://www.law.umich.edu/special/exoneration/Documents/Ex onerations%20in%202018.pdf>.

not believe in her innocence, how she was not allowed by the prison warden to come along with her church group to volunteer for "a prison program to help people cope with life behind bars," how she is hesitant to apply to be on her favorite TV show due to fact that they ask if you've ever been arrested, and how each time the doorbell rings she is triggered by the memory of the police coming to interrogate and threaten her.[45] The most painful part: she was separated from her two children for the years that it took to fight for her innocence. Rebuilding trust with them has been not been easy, but she reports that it's getting better. She reminds readers that her experience is something that can happen to anyone and highlights the importance for everyone to be involved to see change in the criminal justice system. Yet she also mentions that unless you've been through this, you can never know what it feels like.[46] This is a reminder for all to let the Holy Spirit work in and through us to be a comfort for those who have experienced grave injustice. Stassen and Gushee state:

> [those] who do not routinely suffer injustice frequently get lulled into a lack of concern for others who do suffer it. This is part of the moral blindness of the privileged. At the heart of Christian discipleship is entering into the pain and injustice of a suffering world – the way that God our Maker and Jesus our Savior did.[47]

Next, I will conclude with a discussion on how this is expressed in practice.

[45] Tonya Craft and M. Dagostino, *Accused: My Fight for Truth, Justice, and the Strength to Forgive* (Dallas: Benbella Books 2016), p. 401.

[46] Craft and Dagostino, *Accused: My Fight for Truth, Justice, and the Strength to Forgive*, p. 402.

[47] David P. Gushee and G.H. Stassen, *Kingdom Ethics: Following Jesus in Contemporary Context* (Grand Rapids: Eerdmans, 2nd edn, 2016), p. 147.

Conclusion

Only the Holy Spirit can give us the power and wisdom to incarnate the kingdom of God here on earth. Only the Holy Spirit can heal the wounds of racism and empower us to do justice. John Perkins[48]

Once the Holy Spirit has awakened us to the injustice of false accusations, wrongful convictions, and incarceration, this same Spirit will guide us into all truth to develop a compassionate heart for all those impacted. What follows are some practical action steps anyone can take to (1) seek truth and (2) comfort people:

Seek Truth

Address your bias and let God be the judge
It is not our place to cast judgment on people accused of a crime. Do not "throw the first stone."

When you see a mugshot and a press release from your local DA's office, realize that you don't have the full story and pray for the person.

When you read a news story of someone pleading guilty, realize that you don't have the full story and pray for the person.

When you hear of a jury convicting someone who continues to claim innocence, realize that you don't have the full story and pray for the person.

Educate yourself and others
Learn about the issues of false accusations and wrongful convictions. Several books, documentaries, and films are mentioned throughout this chapter to start with.

Learn about the issue of mass incarceration and its overlap with wrongful convictions. For a suggestion on where to start and how to get your church involved, see below.

When you see others condemning people who have been arrested and charged with a crime, step in and gently educate them.

---

[48] Brenda S. McNeil and R. Richardson, *The Heart of Racial Justice: How Soul Change Leads to Social Change* (Downers Grove: IVP Books, Expanded edn, 2009), p. 9.

Remind people of their right to be considered innocent until proven guilty and that even when "proven guilty," they may still be innocent.

Get Involved

Advocate for your local DA's office to have a proactive Conviction Integrity Unit (CIU) that works together with a local group affiliated with the Innocence Network[49] and gives account of their work to the public.[50]

Contact an Innocence clinic in your area and ask how you can help.

Advocate for the death penalty to be abolished once and for all.

Comfort People

Show up and be present

Be the opposite of Job's friends who were focused on finding out what Job must have done wrong to deserve his suffering. Job called them "miserable comforters" (Job 16.2). It is not our responsibility to find out if or what someone did or did not do. It is our responsibility to show up, be present, listen, and love on people.

Realize you will never know what it feels like to be falsely accused and wrongfully convicted unless you've been through it. Therefore, ask those accused what they need most and provide in their needs.

Show up for the family and friends of those falsely accused and wrongfully convicted. This will be one of the most, if not *the* most, traumatic thing they go through in their lives. They need to know people believe in the innocence of their loved one. They need people

---

[49] The Innocence Network is "an affiliation of organizations dedicated to providing pro bono legal and investigative services to individuals seeking to prove innocence of crimes for which they have bene convicted, working to redress the causes of wrongful convictions and supporting the exonerated after they are freed." To find a group local to where you live, visit https://innocencenetwork.org/.

[50] For more information on the recent development of CIUs and the role they can play to curb wrongful convictions if used appropriately, see: Exonerations in 2017, *III. Professional Exonerators*, accessed 23 August 2019, <https://www. law.umich. edu/special/exoneration/Documents/ProfessionalExonerators.pdf>.

to stick with them through all the ups and downs of helping him or her get exonerated.

Get your church involved
Encourage your pastor to look into the issue of the falsely accused and wrongfully convicted and preach a sermon on this.

Start a ministry group to care for those impacted by the criminal justice system. Invite community members that have been impacted to share their story and raise awareness.

The issue of wrongful convictions is closely tied with the issue of mass incarceration. Although the US contains only 5% of the world's population, it houses 25% of the world's incarcerated population. This complicated and dire issue needs the urgent attention of the church. An excellent book that will help you and your church care for those impacted by the criminal justice system and be part of the solution is Dominique DuBois Gilliard's *Rethinking Incarceration: Advocating for Justice that Restores.*[51]

Help with re-entry
Endless challenges and obstacles await those that return to society after having been convicted of a crime. Whether or not they were able to prove their innocence impacts what resources are available for them during the re-entry process. Offer help in any way you can.

Trauma impacts all incarcerated people in different ways. For the majority of people these scars will impact them for the rest of their lives. Be there for them both in the first few weeks *and* the years to come, especially if they show suicidal tendencies.

Speak up
Spread the stories of those who were falsely accused and wrongfully convicted so more people become aware. In time, a cultural shift may take place that could literally save lives.

I will end this chapter, and also the book in a rather unusual manner – with a quotation. Yet, what better way to end the book pointing to that which is inherent to the nature of the Holy Spirit, that is mercy, compassion, hope, and liberation. Recounting the funeral of

---

[51] Dominique D. Gilliard, *Rethinking Incarceration: Advocating for Justice That Restores* (Downers Grove: InterVarsity Press, 2018).

Walter McMillian whom he had helped get exonerated from death row, Bryan Stevenson states:

> Finally and most important, I told those gathered in the church that Walter had taught me that mercy is just when it is rooted in hopefulness and freely given. Mercy is most empowering, liberating, and transformative when it is directed at the undeserving. The people who haven't earned it, who haven't even sought it, are the most meaningful recipients of our compassion. Walter genuinely forgave the people who unfairly accused him, the people who convicted him, and the people who had judged him unworthy of mercy. And in the end, it was just mercy toward others that allowed him to recover a life worth celebrating, a life that rediscovered the love and freedom that all humans desire, a life that overcame death and condemnation until it was time to die on God's schedule.[52]

Bibliography

Acker, J.R., "Taking Stock of Innocence: Movements, Mountains, and Wrongful Convictions," *Journal of Contemporary Criminal Justice* 33.1 (2017).

Acker, J.R., and A. Redlich, *Wrongful Conviction: Law, Science, and Policy* (Durham: Carolina Academic Press, 2019).

Bazelon, L., *Rectify: The Power of Restorative Justice After Wrongful Conviction* (Boston: Beacon Press, 2018).

Berman, N., et al., *Surviving Justice: America's Wrongfully Convicted and Exonerated (Voice of Witness)* (London: Verso, 2017).

Blue Letter Bible, "paraklētos," accessed 23 August 2019, <https://www.blueletterbible.org/lang/lexicon/lexicon.cfm?Strongs=G3875&t=ESV>.

Caldwell, L., et al., *Anatomy of Innocence: Testimonies of the Wrongfully Convicted* (New York: Liveright Publishing Corporation, 2017).

CBS/AP 2015, Poll: Young Americans have "little confidence" in justice system, CBS News, accessed 23 August 2019

---

[52] Bryan Stevenson, *Just Mercy (Movie Tie-In Edition)* (New York: Random House Publishing Group, Kindle Edition, 2014), p. 314.

<https://www.cbsnews.com/news/ poll-young-people-have-little-confidence-in-justice-system/>.

Craft, T., and M. Dagostino, *Accused: My Fight for Truth, Justice, and the Strength to Forgive* (Dallas: BenBella Books, 2016).

Death Penalty Information Center, Innocence Database, viewed 23 August 2019, <https://deathpenaltyinfo.org/policy-issues/innocence-database>.

—Executed but Possibly Innocent, viewed 23 August 2019, <https://deathpenaltyinfo.org/policy-issues/innocence/executed-but-possibly-innocent>.

Dwyer, J., P. Neufeld, and B. Scheck, *Actual Innocence: Five Days to Execution and Other Dispatches from the Wrongly Convicted* (New York: Doubleday, 1st ed, 2000).

Equal Justice Initiative, Innocence, viewed 23 August 2019, <https://eji.org/ death-penalty/innocence>.

Exonerations in 2017, III. Professional Exonerators, viewed 23 August 2019, <https://www.law.umich.edu/special/ exoneration/Documents/ProfessionalExonerators.pdf>.

GBA Strategies 2018, 2018 State of the State Courts - Survey Analysis, GBA Strategies, viewed 23 August 2019, <https://www.ncsc.org/~/media/Files/PDF/ Topics/Public%20Trust%20and%20Confidence/SoSC_201 8_Survey_Analysis.ashx>.

Gilliard, D.D., *Rethinking Incarceration: Advocating for Justice That Restores* (Downers Grove: InterVarsity Press, 2018).

Gramlich, J., "Only 2% of federal criminal defendants go to trial, and most who do are found guilty." Pew Research Center, viewed 23 August 2019, <https://www.pewresearch.org/fact-tank/2019/06/11/only-2-of-federal-criminal-defendants-go-to-trial-and-most-who-do-are-found-guilty/>.

Gushee, D.P. and G.H. Stassen, *Kingdom Ethics: Following Jesus in Contemporary Context* (Grand Rapids: Eerdmans, 2nd edn, 2016).

Garrett, B., *Convicting the Innocent: Where Criminal Prosecutions Go Wrong* (Cambridge: Harvard University Press, 2011).

Godsey, M., *Blind Injustice: A Former Prosecutor Exposes the Psychology and Politics of Wrongful Convictions* (Oakland: University of California Press, 2019).

Gould, J.B., *The Innocence Commission: Preventing Wrongful Convictions and Restoring the Criminal Justice System* (New York: New York University Press, 2009).

Gross, S.R., B. O'Brien, C. Hu, and E. H. Kennedy, "Rate of False Conviction of Criminal Defendants Who Are Sentenced to Death," Proceedings of the National Academy of Sciences of the United States of America 111 (20) (2014).

Horowitz, J.M., A. Brown and K. Cox, "Race in America 2019," Pew Research Center, viewed 23 August 2019, <https://www.pewsocialtrends.org/2019/ 04/ 09/race-in-america-2019/#majorities-of-black-and-white-adults-say-blacks-are-treated-less-fairly-than-whites-in-dealing-with-police-and-by-the-criminal-justice-system>.

Hoyle, C., *et al.*, *The Impact of Being Wrongly Accused of Abuse in Occupations of Trust: Victim's Voices* (University of Oxford Centre of Criminology 2016), Viewed 23 August 2019, <https://www.law.ox.ac.uk/sites/files/oxlaw/the_impact_of_being_wrongly_accused_of_abuse_hoyle_et_al_201 6_15_may.pdf>.

Innocence Staff 2019, "State of Texas executes Innocence Project client Larry Swearingen after U.S. Supreme Court denies stay," viewed 23 August 2019, <https://www.innocenceproject.org/state-of-texas-executes-innocence-project-client-larry-swearingen-after-u-s-supreme-court-denies-stay/>.

—"Innocence Project remembers Larry Swearingen's sense of humor, artistry, and optimism," viewed 23 August 2019, <https://www.innocenceproject.org/innocence-project-remembers-larry-swearingens-sense-of-humor-artistry-and-optimism/>.

King, M.L., Jr, *Strength to Love* (Minneapolis: Fortress, 2010).

Le, Dervan, and V.A. Edkins, "The Innocent Defendant's Dilemma: An Innovative Empirical Study of Plea Bargaining's Innocence Problem." Journal *of Criminal Law & Criminology* 103.1 (2013).

McNeil, B.S. and R. Richardson, *The Heart of Racial Justice: How Soul Change Leads to Social Change* (Downers Grove: IVP Books, Expanded edn, 2009).

Medwed, D.S., "The zeal deal: Prosecutorial resistance to post-conviction claims of innocence," *Boston University Law Review* 84 (2004).

Wright, N.T., "Spirit of Truth," viewed 23 August 2019, <http://ntwrightpage. com /2016/03/30/spirit-of-truth/>.

Petro, J. and N. Petro, *False Justice: Eight Myths that Convict the Innocent* (Fort Lauderdale: Kaplan Publishing, Kindle Edition 2011).

Pohl, C.D., *Living into Community: Cultivating Practices That Sustain Us* (Grand Rapids: Eerdmans, 2012).

Redlich, A.D., *et al.*, "The psychology of defendant plea decision making," *American Psychologist* 72.4 (2017).

Rimer, S., "Life After Death Row," *New York Times*, viewed 23 August 2019, <https: //archive.nytimes.com/www.nytimes.com/library/magazine/home/ 200012 10mag-deathrow.html>.

Shlosberg, A., *et al.*, "The Expungement Myth." *Albany Law Review* 75.3 (2012).

Saad, L., "Military, Small Business, Police Still Stir Most Confidence," Gallup, viewed 23 August 2019, <https://news.gallup.com/poll/236243/military-small-business-police-stir-confidence.aspx>.

Simon, D., *In Doubt: The Psychology of the Criminal Justice Process* (Cambridge: Harvard University Press, Kindle Edition 2012).

Stevenson, B., *Just Mercy (Movie Tie-In Edition)* (New York: Random House Publishing Group, Kindle Edition, 2014).

The Innocence Network, Wrongful Conviction Media, viewed 23 August 2019, <https://innocencenetwork.org/wp-content/uploads/Wrongful-Conviction-Media.pdf>.

The National Registry of Exonerations, Exonerations in 2015, viewed 23 August 2019, <https://www.law.umich.edu/special/exoneration/Documents/E xonerations_in_2015.pdf>.

—Exonerations by Year: DNA and Non-DNA, viewed 23. August 2019,<(https://www.law.umich.edu/special/exoneration/Pages/about.aspx)>.

—Daniel Villegas, viewed 23 August 2019, <https://www.law.umich.edu/special/exoneration/Pages/casedetail.aspx?caseid=5389>.

—Innocents Who Plead Guilty, viewed 23 August 2019,

<https://www.law.umich.edu/special/exoneration/Docu-
ments/NRE.Guilty.Plea.Article1.pdf>.
—Exonerations in 2018, viewed 23. August 2019,
<https://www.law.umich.edu/special/exoneration/Docu-
ments/Exonerations%20in%202018.pdf>.